LOUISIANA STAT
NATIONAL FOOTBALL CHAMPIONS
1958

UNDEFEATED - UNTIED - SUGAR BOWL CHAMPS

PRESIDENT TROY MIDDLETON - A.D. JIM CORBETT
FOOTBALL COACH PAUL DIETZEL

GO TEAM - WHITE TEAM - CHINESE BANDITS

PAUL DIETZEL ©

# Call Me Coach

# Call Me Coach
## A LIFE IN COLLEGE FOOTBALL

### Paul F. Dietzel

LOUISIANA STATE UNIVERSITY PRESS    BATON ROUGE

Published by Louisiana State University Press
Copyright © 2008 by Louisiana State University Press
All rights reserved
Manufactured in China
First printing

Designer: Laura Roubique Gleason
Typefaces: Trump Mediaval text; Bodoni display
Printer and binder: Everbest Printing Co. through Four Colour Imports, Ltd., Louiville
                              Kentucky

Library of Congress Cataloging-in-Publication Data
Dietzel, Paul F.
   Call me coach : a life in college football / Paul F. Dietzel.
      p.  cm.
   ISBN 978-0-8071-3374-3 (cloth : alk. paper)  1. Dietzel, Paul F.  2. Football caoches—
United States—Biography.  3. Football—Coaching.  I. Title.
   GV939.D54  2008
   796.332092—dc22
[B]
                                                                         2008008713

This book is a personal recollection. All names, dates, and events herein are accurate to
the best of the author's knowledge and all opinions expressed are his. The photographs
and the rights to reproduce them in this book have been provided by the author, except for
those photographs for which the author obtained a license or permission for reproduction
as noted. Any inquiries for permission to reprint or reproduce his images should be addressed to the author.

# Contents

# Acknowledgments

When I decided to write my autobiography, it soon became obvious that I needed help. I was extremely fortunate to enlist the aid of two unbelievably talented people. My former secretary Pat Dale volunteered to type the manuscript after I dictated it. Tom Continé, an extremely gifted author and scholar, corrected and edited the manuscript. With delightful good humor and dogged persistence, those two labored through innumerable hours of corrections, revisions, and rewrites.

From the very outset, I had hoped that LSU Press would publish my book. They are LSU, and I am LSU. The Press has a reputation for excellence in the publishing field. One of the major reasons for the book's smooth flow through the production process is the Press's director, MaryKatherine Callaway, an extremely pleasant and understanding person to work with, and a great "head coach" who has molded an excellent team at the Press. Trade book editor Margaret Hart introduced me to the publishing business. It would be impossible to find a more thorough or helpful copyeditor than George Roupe. And it has been a real pleasure to work with multitalented production and design manager Laura Gleason, a real jewel.

I must also thank some generous financial supporters of this publication. Jimmy Field, the fine quarterback of the 1961 Tiger team, along with Gus Kinchen, Mickey Mangham, Bo Campbell, Buddy Soefker, Merl Schexnaildre, Durel Matherne, Jake Netterville, Dr. Jack Andonie, Dexter Gary, James Fleet Howell, and H. F. Anderson organized and sponsored a fund that helped bring this book out with its many wonderful photographs. It is hard to find words adequate to express my gratitude to these generous friends. They have continued to bless my life.

Please remember as you read this book that many of the events described took place many, many years ago. In most instances, my recollections seem very clear. (Then again, sometimes I'm not so clear about what I did yesterday!) Some details may not be quite as precise as others, but I've tried to make the text as accurate as memory will allow.

Many of my former players are mentioned or appear in photographs throughout this book. If it were possible, I would like to mention every one of the fine young men I coached. All the lettermen players I coached at LSU, Army, and South Carolina are listed in the back of the book, and we hope to establish a Web site where they will be listed as well.

Some players have remained in close touch through the years: Rollie Stichweh, John Johnson, and Cadet manager Reesa Barksdale from West Point; John Gregory and team captain David DeCamilla from South Carolina; and Jimmy Field, Scooter Purvis, Gus Kinchen, Durel Matherne, and Johnny Robinson from LSU. But all the players I have coached are vital members of my football family, and I cherish the times we have spent together. How very fortunate I am to have been their coach and to have had Anne and my family at my side, sharing these memories through the years. I have been blessed indeed.

# Call Me Coach

# I
# Early Years

When I came to LSU as head coach in 1955, the football program had been in the doldrums for quite some time. In our first three rebuilding seasons, the Tigers won only eleven games, lost seventeen, and were tied twice. Although our players gave their best, opponents just outmanned us and wore us down week after week. I was uncertain that I could weather the howls of disgruntled fans and alumni, but with the unwavering support of LSU's president, General Troy H. Middleton, I survived. As we prepared for the 1958 season, though, with a cadre of fine returning players and an outstanding freshmen class moving up, things had changed, and the prospects of a winning season seemed brighter. As it turned out, the Tigers had indeed come of age.

Because of the lack of team depth, which had plagued us since 1955, the staff and I developed a novel plan that would allow us to play a greater number of athletes. The result was the creation of LSU's revolutionary three-team system. Although half a century has since passed, the names of those squads are as familiar to Tiger football enthusiasts today as they were then—the White Team, the Go Team, and the never to be forgotten Chinese Bandits. LSU finished the 1958 regular season undefeated and untied and then beat Clemson in the Sugar Bowl. The Tigers were collegiate football's undisputed national champions.

The very next year on Halloween night, Billy Cannon's famous run—arguably one of the greatest efforts in the annals of college football—and the Tigers' ensuing goal-line stand resulted in a 7–3 win over archrival Ole Miss. After a heart-wrenching 13–14 loss to Tennessee, LSU finished the season ranked fourth nationally. Once again, it was time to rebuild.

In 1961, my final season as LSU's head coach, the Tigers won the Southeastern Conference title and handed Ole Miss a 10–7 loss, after which I was quoted as saying, "I hope the '58 and '59 teams will forgive me, but this has to be one of the greatest victories I've ever experienced."

These peaks and valleys of my coaching tenure at LSU are, in some ways, parallel to the events of my life overall. Looking back through the years, I find myself ever grateful for the exciting and wonderful twists and turns my path has taken. My playbook has been abundantly rich and full. My life has truly been better than I deserve!

# First Recollections

I was born on September 5, 1924, in Fremont, Ohio. Within a few years, the country found itself in the throes of the Great Depression, and times were hard. We moved around a lot from town to town in Ohio where my father was able to find employment. Dad worked at a Ford agency as an automobile mechanic. He could take anything apart and put it back together. He could listen to your car engine run and tell you what was wrong with it. My dad was always inventing things. He thought that a spotlight on the driver's side of a car could be adjusted from inside the car; as it was, spotlights were fixed in one direction. One day, a salesman from the Ford factory came by and my dad showed him his invention. The fellow said that it would leak and wouldn't work. That salesman never came by again but a year later, out came this spotlight which could be adjusted from inside and guess whose name was on it: the name of that salesman.

My father, Clarence Dietzel

My parents were dedicated churchgoers who kept the Sabbath and kept it holy. On Sundays when we bought a newspaper, we had to hide it under wraps in the backseat of the car so that no one would see that we were reading it and violating the Sabbath. After church, family activities were strictly limited; we stayed at home, read the newspaper, and napped in the living room. That was about it.

The first time I remember moving was to Tiffin, Ohio. I attended first grade in Tiffin and was an active rascal, climbing trees and doing all the kinds of things kids did then. By the time I was in second grade, we had moved to Findlay, and it was there that I was introduced to the great game of football, which has fascinated me ever since. Of course, at the time, I couldn't have realized that football would one day become the focal point of my professional life. My mother happened to be an avid football fan. Since there was no money to spare for tickets, we would stand outside the fence and watch the Findlay High School football team play. From our vantage point, we saw very little of the action on the field, but we could hear the noise of the crowd and feel the excitement generated by the teams on the field. That was good enough for us.

We lived on East Lima Street, very close to the city dump. There were a lot of wood shavings at the dump, and one day as I was playing with matches, which greatly intrigued me, I accidentally set fire to the city dump. It was very exciting because all the fire trucks came racing down the street to the dump, but what happened to me afterwards was not exciting at all.

Toys were scarce at our house. That winter, I tried my best to be a very good young man because I wanted an electric train. I saw a train advertised in the newspaper that sold for $3.33. Although I knew we probably could not afford it, I wanted that train really bad. You have never seen a better behaved or more mannerly young man than I was that year. I wanted to be sure that Santa Claus would bring me that train. And he did!

We were extremely poor. We couldn't afford staples like milk. Our main dish at most meals was bread and butter, with sugar and coffee poured over the top. Since that was what we ate most of the time, I don't know how I ever managed to grow. After one year in Findlay, we moved once again, this time to Green Springs.

Green Springs is a farming community of about four hundred people, but on Saturday nights the population swelled to six hundred or more. There was one main street where all the activities took place and where all of the stores were located. The road into Green Springs from the south crossed a railroad track that ran by a big sauerkraut factory. At that end of town, you could smell sauerkraut; at the other end of town was the town's namesake, Green Springs, a sulfur mineral springs that gushed seven million gallons of sulfur water a day. Of course it smelled very sulfurous. So at the south end of town was the aroma of sauerkraut and at the north end the smell of sulfur. In between was where people lived.

Since we were quite poor, we moved in with my father's parents, John and

My sister, Gevy, and I

Ida Dietzel, who lived on County Line Road. On one side of the road was Sandusky County and on the other side was Seneca County. At that time I was three years old, and my sister, Genevieve, was eight. My grandpa had a small barn, some cows, and some chickens. He milked his cows, poured the milk into Ball jars, and delivered the milk to customers around town. It was lots of fun when I got to ride with him on his deliveries.

On Sundays, chicken was on the menu. I would cringe when my grandfather took out his big ax and chopped off the chicken's head. The headless chicken kept flying around. I didn't like that at all.

One of the very good things about living with Grandma and Grandpa was that my uncle Elmer Parker, who owned and ran the local grain and feed store, lived right next door. He was very nice, but the real wonder was that his two sons, Allen and Paul, were missionaries to India. They would spend very little time in Green Springs, but they would bring their children along on their occasional visits. Imagine the appeal to a little hick kid like me whose longest trip was to Tiffin or Fremont, about fifteen miles away. One of Paul Parker's children was a teenage girl named

My grandparents, Ida and John Dietzel, in Green Springs, Ohio

Kittu, a name I thought was exotic. She would regale me with tales of their exciting boat trips to India and their many adventures there. She even taught me a beautiful Indian lullaby (which I learned phonetically of course). It went

> Niny baba niny
> muckan rhody chinny
> muckan rhody hobcy ah
> soba baba sobia.

That little lullaby stuck with me and would have another important significance later in my life.

We didn't live with my grandparents for very long; eventually we moved closer to town, still on County Line Road, and into a very small house. Our new home had no indoor plumbing, so I had to go two doors down to our preacher's house and carry back pails of water for the family. Our outdoor plumbing was a "Roosevelt Monument," and although inconvenient, it was kind of thrilling to go out in the cold and snow of winter to the outhouse. An old Montgomery Ward catalog was always on hand from which you could tear as many pages as you might need to complete your business.

We lived two miles from Green Springs School, which served all twelve grades and was at the other end of town. Since there were no buses for town kids, I walked to and from school each day. The older boys liked to take the younger ones, like me, to the sulfur springs at lunch and dunk them in the ice cold sulfur water. It was very embarrassing to return to school with my shirt wet and grass-stained, because all the other kids laughed at me. When I got home after a dunking, my mother always let me know that she was not at all pleased with me or the condition of my clothes.

In the fields outside town, farmers raised watermelons and cantaloupes. Some of my friends and I loved to raid the watermelon patches, break one open and scoop out and eat the heart of the melon. We ate quite a lot of melons that summer. Once I managed to gorge myself until I got sick. It was a lot of fun until the farmer caught us, and then the fun ceased.

My dad was always tinkering with things. At that time, we had an old Essex with spoke wheels and would drive to the farm of my uncle Glen and aunt Jenny Dietzel for a visit. Since there was always lots of good cream at Uncle Glen's farm, we generally made ice cream. It was really rich and creamy. My dad thought it would be a great idea if someone sat on the freezer while he put the freezer's crank handle into the spokes of one of the back wheels of the Essex. Dad would jack up the car and run the motor very slowly. The ice cream froze in no time at all and got so hard that the handle snapped off the freezer, ending that operation once and for all.

After a while we moved downtown into an apartment above the Pennzoil gas station that my dad ran. We sold gas for about twelve cents a gallon. I washed cars for twenty-five cents a car, and for every one I washed, I got to keep a nickel.

Since the county was building a new school in Green Springs, classes were temporarily moved into the tin-roofed town hall, located above the fire station. The hall was sectioned off into rooms to provide space for classes, an office, and a study hall, which teachers took turns supervising. Some of the other boys and I were always cutting up in study hall. One of our favorite tricks was to use a big rubber band to shoot staples at the tin roof. The result was a resounding bang. Miss Schwartz, one of the teachers who monitored study hall, would spot the guilty boy and slap his face, but she wasn't very strong, and the slap didn't sting very much. One day I got caught. I didn't realize it, but in addition to Miss Schwartz, Miss Doyle was on duty, too. She was a lot stronger than Miss Schwartz and slapped me so hard that she knocked me right out of my seat. My, that made an impression. In the future, I looked around more carefully.

Every year, the school held a poster contest that I always entered. I never won, but year after year I kept trying. It never occurred to me at the time that that poster contest might have been the beginning of a lifelong hobby and passion that would eventually bring me much joy and a very special kind of fulfillment.

When I was in grade school, roller-skating was a big craze. There were lots of sidewalks in Green Springs, but to avoid a painful fall, you had to know where the sidewalks were cracked and broken. There was a young lady by the name of Nancy Finn that I wanted to roller-skate with, but I was far too shy to ask her. Once, a heartless older student wrote me a note that read, "Dear Paul, I would love to go roller skating with you," and signed it "Nancy." I was thrilled to learn that she had agreed to go skating with me, but then I learned the note wasn't from Nancy at all. I found it very hard to forgive that boy.

There was a wooded area near the high school. To my playmates and me, it was a huge forest. We were afraid to go into those woods because we thought wild Indians lived there. Worse yet, we were sure that if we ever ventured in, we'd never find our way out. In spite of our fears, we liked to play there and tried to be very careful so that we would not disappear and never be found. Years later, I returned to Green Springs and visited those same woods. I was surprised to find that the once dark and forbidding place was only a little lot with a few trees growing on it. Your perspective certainly does change with time.

I still had my $3.33 train set, and one day I was invited, along with a couple of other boys, to Bruce Schuster's home to play. The Schusters had a big house near our Pennzoil station. Several of us took our train sets. We made one large track out of our smaller ones and used books to elevate the tracks, creating imaginary hills for the trains to climb. It was great fun. One day, Bruce's mother asked me, "Paul, do you have a girlfriend?" I answered, "Well, I like Nancy, but she likes John McConnell and your son, Bruce. She doesn't like me." Mrs. Schuster replied, "Oh, she likes the nice boys, huh?" Well, the meaning of her comment never occurred to me until I thought about it later. She was letting me know, perhaps unintentionally, that we were considered to be from the "wrong side of the tracks."

There were some other fun things in my life. I really love fudge, and anytime my parents left the house, as soon as they drove away, I went into action. I'd get out the pan and the sugar and make myself a batch of fudge. I would pour the hot fudge over waxed paper and, as soon as it cooled, would eat the whole batch, wash the pans, and carefully put them away. I don't think it ever occurred to my mother and father that I had made fudge while they were gone. If they knew, they didn't say anything. That was the beginning of my love affair with fudge, which has endured to this day.

Wednesday nights in Green Springs were very exciting. The townspeople would set up a platform in the middle of the one and only downtown street, which was closed at both ends so that no cars drove through. Everyone in the area who played an instrument would congregate on the platform and serenade onlookers with a concert. These concerts were especially fun for my pals and me. We would circle round and round, shoulder to shoulder in time with the music, all the while drinking soda pop. I often drank so much soda pop that I would get sick. Sometimes we'd fill paper sacks with water, climb up on the top of the little buildings that lined the street, and drop the sacks on the unsuspecting folks below.

One of our favorite tricks at Halloween was to take an empty thread spool, cut notches in the ridges around both ends, put a big spike through it, and wrap string around the spool. Then we would go to someone's house, hold the spool by the spike to a window, and pull the string really hard. The roar it made on the window was unbelievable; it seemed to rattle the whole house. As you might expect, we'd run like the dickens to escape. There was one man we especially enjoyed annoying. We called him "Hunky Estep," although I had no idea how he got that name or what it meant. Hunky took great offense at our pranks and would get really mad. He'd chase us, but of course he couldn't catch us. We had another trick for Hunky. We would take a brick and tie a two-foot cord to it with a nail on the end of the cord. Then we would go to the window of his home, stick the nail in the slot of the window, and hang the brick down so it would lie against the side of Hunky's house. We'd tie another, very long string to the brick, which would reach all the way over to the other side of the street, where we'd hide and wait. When the string was pulled, the brick banged against the house and made a booming sound. Out would come Hunky yelling at the top of his voice, "I'm going to catch you! I'm going to get you!" But that just made our prank funnier still. There were a few other tricks that were fun for us, but I'm not sure how much fun they were for other folks!

It was in Green Springs that I first ventured into the world of business. I had a magazine route, and every week I delivered the *Saturday Evening Post* and *Collier's,* which I sold for five cents a copy to my subscribers. I sold these magazines to a few people in town, but my main customers were patients in the TB sanitarium, which was at the edge of town by the sulfur springs. I never thought about it at the time, but now I wonder how lucky I was that I didn't get TB. I felt that it was quite a feat to sell all my magazines. I think I made a cent and a half on each magazine I sold.

But these fun days were about to end. My parents' marriage started unraveling, and they decided to part and go their separate ways. Their breakup was tough to take because I loved both of them dearly. My mother left with another man and moved far away, first to Minnesota and then to Shedd, Oregon. Her new husband was a hairdresser, and she became a hairdresser too. I remember my mother as being very talented and very smart. In the ensuing years, I received letters from her, perhaps once or twice a year. The only time I actually saw her again was in the late 1950s. During my coaching tenure at LSU, I conducted a football clinic at Sun Valley, Idaho. She and her husband came to the clinic, and we saw each other for the first time in many years. That was the last time I saw my mother. Both she and her husband passed away several years later. Although I respected her as my mother, we just didn't have a normal mother-son relationship.

Shortly after my mother left, a stepmother arrived. She had been a former neighbor of ours in Tiffin and had three children, a daughter who

My mother, Catherine, and my stepfather, Don Courtier

My sister, Gevy, and her husband, Bob Perin, Green Springs, Ohio

was my sister Genevieve's age and two sons younger than me. Things deteriorated very quickly. To escape the problems at home, when Genevieve was seventeen she married Bob Perin, the boy next door. I'd gotten to know Bob because he would take me on his truck with him to Toledo. Bob and his brother had a produce operation. They would drive to Toledo, pick up an order, then drive around to all the little independent stores in the area to make deliveries. Bob knew that I liked bananas, so he'd always break off a bunch for me. I would eat them all day long. I don't know why I didn't get tired of bananas, but I never did. Bob drove that big old truck like a wild man, and I enjoyed that nearly as much as I did the bananas.

Times were tough, really tough. My father was not doing very well running the gas station, so he took a job in Mansfield with the Charles Hoffman Company. Mansfield, a much larger town than Green Springs, was about sixty miles away, and my father commuted to and from work daily. Since he was such a fine mechanic, he began installing furnaces for the heating department of the company, and it wasn't very long before he became the manager of the department. It was then that we moved from Green Springs to Mansfield.

## Off to Mansfield

In Mansfield, we lived in a company house on Walnut Street across from the Hoffman Company. My sister, Gevy, had married and moved away, and the situation at home had steadily deteriorated since my stepmother and her three children had moved in with us. My stepmother and I couldn't seem to get along no matter how hard I tried. Finally, I realized that I really needed to get out of the house and to stay away from her as much as possible. A part-time job would do just fine.

It didn't take very long to find one. I took a job setting up bowling pins at the local bowling alley after school. Although I had to work late at night, it was a good job for me. I was able to keep some distance from my stepmother and earned enough money to buy some sorely needed clothes for school. In those days, pins were set up by hand—you were it! If you were lucky, you worked two adjoining lanes simultaneously, and of course, for this double duty, you got double pay. I recall sitting on the narrow rail above the pins and holding my breath as the bowling balls came roaring down the alleys. I figured that it was a pretty good idea to remain perched securely on that rail because, when the ball struck the pins, they flew with great force in every direction. Although I was never seriously hurt, I managed to get my fair share of bruises, which to us pin boys, were badges of honor.

On weekend afternoons, before reporting for work at the bowling alley, I went to the movies, which I greatly enjoyed. There was always a double or triple feature at the Majestic Theater, and to avoid going home, I'd sit through the features twice. To this day, I still enjoy movies, although I no longer want or need to see them twice.

I was big for a boy my age and fibbed about my birth date in order to obtain a Social Security card, which would enable me to get a "real" part-time job. With card in hand, I applied for a job at Bazley's Meat Market and was hired as an apprentice. I really liked this job and learned a lot about the science of meat cutting. Years later, the experience at Bazley's would come in handy, but as it turned out, in settings I could not have predicted or even imagined at the time.

Although I had never participated in organized basketball, I neverthe-less tried out for the team at John Simpson Junior High School. It seems that adolescence was playing havoc with my developing motor skills, and at the time, I was much too clumsy to make the team. Luckily for me, there was another sport I really liked. On summer weekends, my pals and I played sandlot football at a place called Black's Meadows. Our oppo-nents were other kids from town, one of whom was a guy by the name of Bill Doolittle. After graduating from Mansfield High, Bill attended Ohio State University and played football for the Buckeyes. He eventually en-tered the coaching profession and enjoyed much success as head coach of the Mansfield Tygers. Decades later, when I was appointed head football coach at the United States Military Academy at West Point, I hired Bill as my backfield coach, and a boyhood friendship was transformed into a professional relationship by a series of twists of fate. I believe that play-ing sandlot football all those years ago sparked my lifetime affair with the game.

Massillon, one of Mansfield's rivals, beat us badly year after year. For some time, Coach Paul Brown of Massillon had organized and developed junior high school football teams as feeders for his program. By the time those boys reached Massillon High, they had "already been saucered and blowed," to borrow one of Coach Paul "Bear" Bryant's favorite sayings. Mansfield's coach, J. Russell Murphy, recognized the connection between the Massillon feeder program and its perennial superiority over all com-ers on the gridiron. Coach Murphy leveled this playing field when he or-ganized the first junior high football team in Mansfield's history at John Simpson Junior High School. The team practiced at the high school and was coached by Murphy and his assistants. Since no one else wanted to play center, I became center on the single wing and continued in that position throughout my high school and college football careers. Success came quickly. Not only were we the first junior high school football team in Mansfield's history, we were also the first to go undefeated. As it turned out, this was the first of four undefeated football squads of which I was a part.

In my high school years, I worked at Bazley's Meat Market every free minute I could find. Work began on Saturdays early in the morning and continued until 11:00 P.M., for which I earned $3.25, or, about twenty cents an hour. For me, this was a princely sum. By my sophomore year, I had developed sufficient muscular control to finally make the basketball team. Whenever there was a football or basketball game, I'd leave work at Bazley's in time to dress out and play. Work at Bazley's and practice at school kept me busy and away from home most of the time.

Coach Murphy's efforts to create a junior high feeder program for his high school team began to pay off. By my sophomore year, there was a marked improvement in the quality of our team's play, but as might be expected, the teams we played against were also getting better. Mansfield's big rival was Massillon, coached by Paul Brown, of future fame and renown. Coach Brown, a superb organizer, was innovative and brilliant—years ahead of his time in his approach to the game.

Many factors contribute to the success of a football program. For Massillon, one was the organization of its school district. By design or by accident, as the town grew in population, rather than construct more high schools as other school districts did, the Massillon school board opted to simply add on to the existing facility. The result was the creation of a reservoir of talented athletes much larger than that of competing schools. Massillon had two or three junior high school teams that were coached by Paul Brown's assistants and played regular schedules with teams from Ohio, West Virginia, and Kentucky. It was common knowledge that if a Massillon coach identified a promising prospect at an opposing school, by the next school year, that player's father happened to find employment at the Timken Roller Bearing Works in Massillon. What coincidence! What recruiting!

Massillon's teams wore fancy uniforms with gold britches and white shoes. They would dress out about a hundred players, and when Massillon took the field, an endless stream of athletes kept coming out, coming out, coming out. Their stadium seated over twenty thousand fans and was packed to capacity, game after game. The Massillon band was huge and about as good as most college bands in the country. All of this combined, very powerfully, to intimidate opposing teams well before a game even started.

In my sophomore year, Massillon beat us unmercifully by a score of 73–0, which was not at all unusual because they defeated their other opponents just as badly. But change was in the air. Mansfield's team had begun to steadily improve, and in the next school year, Massillon beat us only 38–0, in what turned out to be their lowest-scoring game of the sea-

The undefeated Mansfield High School Tygers, 1941

son. Then came my senior year, which coincided with the long-awaited turning point in the Mansfield-Massillon rivalry. Like the boys from Massillon, my pals and I had learned the game's fundamentals on an organized, well-coached junior high team. We had grown up, and the playing field had at last been leveled. That year, we played at Massillon and tied them, 6–6. Mansfield went on to win the remainder of its games, and we became Ohio's state champions. This was the second undefeated football team of which I was a part.

For most of my time in high school, my focus was centered squarely on football, basketball, track, and work at Bazley's. During my half-hour lunch break at Bazley's, I'd race over to Cooney Miller's pool hall and squeeze in a few games while wolfing down my hot dog before returning to work. My academic interests took a backseat to sports, but I did discover three courses that I really liked—mechanical drawing, biology, and speech. Except for those courses, my grades were average and I was content to get by with as little work and study as possible.

I had a speech teacher by the name of Walter Mickey, whose influence changed the whole course of my life. One day when I was cutting up in

At 6 feet 2 inches and 181 pounds, I played center for the Mansfield Tygers.

his class, he suddenly announced, "Paul Dietzel, in five minutes you're going to give the class a two-minute impromptu speech, the subject of which will be 'What Gold Cannot Buy.'" Well, shocked though I was, I managed to give that speech. At the end of class, Mr. Mickey asked me to remain. I was sure I was in trouble. To my surprise, Mr. Mickey escorted me to the principal's office and asked the secretary for my transcript. After briefly browsing over the document, he said, "Paul, you and I both know that you're not going anywhere; the general course of study you're taking leads nowhere. I think you should aim higher. Why not change to the college preparatory track with emphasis on pre-engineering? Because of your athletic ability, you'll likely be offered a college scholarship, but wouldn't it be a terrible thing if you aren't able to meet college admission requirements because of your choices of high school courses and less than stellar grades, even in those?" Without any prompting, I immediately agreed. Mr. Mickey then enrolled me in college preparatory courses, such as algebra, geometry, chemistry, and physics.

The notion that college was a real possibility for me had never entered my mind. For the first time in my life, I began to study and take the academic side of school seriously. The effort slowly began to pay off; my grades improved from C's in the general-study courses to A's and B's in the college prep courses. I learned that, with work and effort, I could succeed academically as well as athletically. Mr. Mickey changed my life for

Basketball days with the Mansfield Tygers

the better. At the time, I couldn't gauge the full impact his care and advice would have on my life, but I know now that it was one of the best things that could ever have happened to me.

Another of my life's truly great blessings came quite unexpectedly one summer when I worked as a helper to a man named Noble Gardner. Noble installed furnaces for the Charles Hoffman Company, where my father was head of the heating department. All in all, Noble was one of the homeliest men I've ever met. He was a small man with glasses, a bald head, and buckteeth. He stuttered and spit when he talked. But there was one grand thing about this man: he had a love affair with the Lord, and

High school days: senior pictures of me and gorgeous Anne

he faithfully witnessed to all he met. When he spoke of Jesus, his stuttering stopped and his face seemed to glow. I recall my dad once telling him, "Noble, I think that's fine, but stop trying to save the woman of the house and install the furnace!" When I worked with Noble, we were usually in a dark, dusty basement of a house. My job was papering the pipes, which involved cutting asbestos paper into strips, plastering the strips with glue so they would stick to the pipes, and then wrapping the pipes with the strips. I took great pride in my work, but why I didn't get asbestos poisoning, I'll never know.

Since I had grown tall and was fairly strong, I could help Noble lift the big radiators that had to be set on the tops of the forced-air furnaces. These radiators were quite heavy and it took the two of us to lift them. One day, while installing a furnace, Noble Gardner introduced me to the Lord Jesus Christ. It was then that I decided to give myself to the Lord, and my life was changed forever. I owe much to Noble for his faithful witnessing, and I will never forget him.

Although I couldn't possibly have realized it at the time, I was about to meet the one true love of my life. Late one afternoon after track practice, as I walked through a mostly deserted school building, I heard this clickety, click, click. Curious, I stepped into the typing classroom, and there, sitting by herself, was this girl that I recognized but barely knew.

I thought that she was quite cute and decided this was a good time to get better acquainted. Her name was Anne Wilson. After a short conversation, I said, "Come on, I'll walk you home." Along the way, I got up enough courage to ask if I might come by one day with my records for us to listen to. Anne's response was not at all encouraging. She simply replied, "I don't think so." But I persisted and finally persuaded her to go on a date, which turned out to be a short walk to the local drug store for a Coke.

A second and bigger date soon followed; we went to a movie and then had ice cream at the drug store, which happened to be across the street from Anne's house. We dated five or six times before I was allowed to kiss her goodnight, and that really got my attention. This girl was special.

After a while, Anne and I started going steady, and naturally I became well acquainted with her parents, Katherine and Luther Wilson. These two wonderful people became almost like parents to me. They were wonderful and filled a void in my life. I was frequently invited over for meals, and Mrs. Wilson even started mending my clothes. They showed me real love.

Graduation finally rolled around. Since Anne was half a class ahead of me, she graduated in January. Even though we were going steady, she was escorted to her senior prom by one of her classmates, as school policy required. I was not at all happy with this turn of events, but that was the way it had to be.

On the night of the dance, I sat on her front porch with "Dad" Wilson, waiting for Anne to come home. Suddenly, a hotshot from school came

The Mansfield Tygers basketball team, 1942

roaring down the alley on one side of the Wilson's house in his bright and shiny convertible. He slammed on his brakes, and, when he did, cinders flew everywhere. Startled, Mr. Wilson stood up to better see who was causing such a commotion. The kid then rudely gave him the finger and sped off across the street to the drug store. By the time he came out, I was there to greet him, and was right in his face with a few choice comments. He recognized me from school and apologized for what he had done. He got back into his car and drove off very slowly. When I returned to the porch, Mr. Wilson just beamed. He was proud that I had taken up for him and had put that boy in his place. From that time on, we were buddies.

Except for Anne and work at Bazley's, athletics dominated the rest of my high school life. I managed to win the district discus championship, although I would be embarrassed to say what the winning distance was. In my senior year, I was selected to the state basketball tournament's all-tournament team. To this day, I feel pride in having accomplished these things. From my early years to the present, athletics have been the great passion of my life.

A confrontation between Coach Paul Brown of Washington High School of Massillon and the school's football booster club president taught me an abiding truth about athletics: you've got to win! In Massillon, the booster club ran the football program. In an earlier year, before Washington High's final game, the booster club president informed Coach Brown that if he didn't win the Canton McKinley game, he would be fired. Washington won that game, and Paul Brown continued as head coach. He produced a nine-year stretch of Ohio state football championships for Massillon and went on to coach at Ohio State University, where his team won a national championship. During World War II, he successfully coached at the Great Lakes Training School. After the war, he coached the Cleveland Browns to an unprecedented record before leaving to take the helm of the Cincinnati Bengals. Coach Brown was to become a football coaching legend and one of the true giants of the sport.

As a direct result of our outstanding senior year, most of the graduating players on the Mansfield High football team were offered college scholarships. After all, we were the undefeated state champions of Ohio! I was invited to visit Ohio State, Lehigh, and Case Institute of Technology. I thought Ohio State was fine except that it was by far too big and I would surely get lost in the shuffle. On visits to the fine engineering schools of Lehigh and Case Institute, I met fellows who seemed to be constantly at work on their slide rules, even at breakfast. I decided that perhaps this was a bit deeper into academics than I wanted to get. Coach Paul Snyder and his wife took me and a fellow Mansfield athlete to the University of Tennessee and then to Duke University. I immediately fell in love with Duke, which had a gorgeous campus and a good football team, which had played in the Rose Bowl the previous year. That particular Rose Bowl had been moved to Duke's home in Durham, North Carolina, because of the war, which we were then immersed in. As it turned out, I was offered scholarships in football and basketball. I accepted the football scholarship, and I was soon bound for Duke.

## Scholarship Time at Duke

I enrolled at Duke University in September of 1942. Simultaneously, Anne enrolled in Miami University of Ohio, where she became a cheerleader for the football team. The separation was quite a change for both of us, and although we were still an "item," we agreed to date other people.

At Mansfield High School, I had been Honorable Mention All-State Center on the state championship football team. Big deal! I soon learned that Duke had also recruited a first team all-state center from Altoona, Pennsylvania, who happened to be a bit bigger than me. But for some reason unknown to me, he dropped out of school.

Duke had recruited a very strong freshman team, with a fine running back by the name of Howard Hartley and some excellent linemen such as Garland Wolfe and Big Frank Irwin. Since my chief competitor had left school, I became the starting freshman center. At that time, freshmen were not eligible for varsity play.

We were coached by a fine gentleman, Herschel Caldwell. The Mansfield High School Tygers had employed the single-wing formation, in which the center passed the ball directly to the tailback or the fullback. Having large hands, I snapped the ball with my right hand. Coach Caldwell immediately noticed this and instructed me to put both hands on the ball. I replied, "I've always centered the ball with one hand, Coach."

Duke University's varsity squad, 1942. I'm number 52.

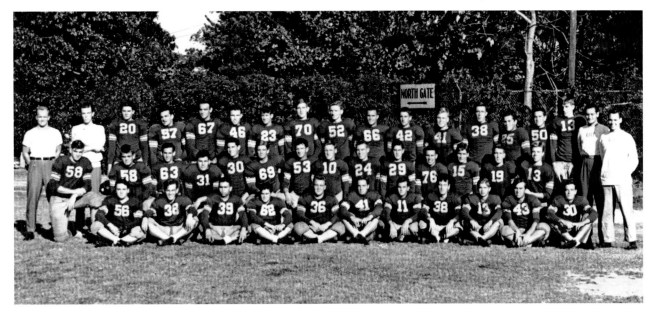

Coach Caldwell retorted, "Here at Duke we center the ball with two hands!"

My response was quick and polite: "Yes, Sir, Coach! Thank you!"

One of the true pleasures of spring practice came on the day we freshmen got to scrimmage the varsity, which had some excellent athletes like wingback Buddy Luper, tailback Tom Davis, and fullback Leo Long, from "Sout" Orange, New Jersey—not "South" but "Sout"! The varsity ran a sweep, and as linebacker, I chased the tailback and tackled him on the sideline, both of us crashing out of bounds. As we jumped up, he handed me the ball and said in his slow southern drawl, "I might have known—a damn Yankee!" Welcome to the South. The freshmen team held its own against the varsity that day.

Another day at practice later that spring, the usual hubbub of crashing bodies, groans, and shouts suddenly became strangely quiet. I couldn't imagine what was going on until a teammate pointed to an army officer standing on the sidelines. He was the former Duke football coach, Wallace Wade. Coach Wade commanded such great respect. It was an awesome moment.

The Duke freshmen team played a regular schedule against other Southern Conference schools. One opponent was the freshmen team from the University of North Carolina at Chapel Hill. They were reported to be a good team with a big, strong, and unusually talented fullback. Some of my teammates referred to him as "Doc," which seemed strange to me. This guy just happened to be none other than Doc Blanchard of future West Point fame. He eventually became known nationally as West Point's "Mr. Inside," with his counterpart, Glen Davis, as "Mr. Outside." Both players were to become Heisman Trophy winners. Doc indeed had great size and speed—he had the biggest legs I had ever seen. However, in spite of the talented Doc Blanchard, our Duke freshmen team was better all around and won the game handily.

The nation's armed services were drafting young men from college campuses at a very rapid pace. During spring practice, I received notice that I would soon be drafted. Since Duke had the naval and the naval air force reserves on campus, I wanted to sign up with the naval air force. My dad advised me against it, though, because in World War I, these reserve units were called up almost immediately. So I went back home to Ohio and enlisted in the army air corps instead. As fate would have it, my Duke teammates who signed up for the reserves remained at Duke and eventually graduated while I was piloting a B-29 Superfortress out in the Pacific theater.

Of course, there was much more to Duke University than football. I had scored fairly high on the math and science placement tests that all freshman were required to take. I enrolled in engineering, which was located, for the most part, on the women's side of campus. Since I was housed on the men's campus, I rode a bus to and from class every day.

The first math class I was assigned was an advanced course with a professor who had helped interpret Einstein's theories—obviously a very bright fellow. I recall that he walked to the board, scribbled a problem, then erased it almost immediately with little explanation, and asked, "Everyone got that, I presume?" I had no clue what he was talking about and suddenly realized that I was in the wrong class. I dropped that one and luckily found one that was a bit more on my level.

Freshmen engineers were required to wear "dinks," funny blue hats similar to those worn by sailors. We wore our dinks turned down and walked everywhere on campus in single file. There were a couple of upperclassmen who took it upon themselves to see that freshmen strictly followed the rules laid down for them. However, two of my freshman football teammates, namely Frank Irwin and Garland Wolfe, were also engineering majors. Frank was a tremendously built fellow; in fact, I always thought of him as the original Lil' Abner. He had made up his mind that he was not going to wear his dink turned down or walk in single file. So I made sure that I walked to classes with Frank and Garland to avoid being accosted by the enforcers. Later, when the fraternities issued rush invitations, I ventured into the Phi Delta Theta party, and greeting the rushees were—guess who: those same couple of fellows who loved to make sure we followed the rules! I decided not to join that fraternity.

At that time, Duke had established a system of delayed fraternity rushing, which meant no rushing except at the official parties. But since most of the men were being drafted, the rules seemed to be relaxed a bit. In spite of the delayed rushing rules, SAE "dirty rushed" me; I shook hands with the SAEs and accepted their bid. I was now a fraternity man! To celebrate, my SAE contact, Cos Korowicki, escorted me to a local college hangout for the first beer I had ever had. I thought it was awful.

Duke also taught me a valuable lesson in politics. The university is designed in quadrangles, with residence halls designated alphabetically. I was in House N. Eventually, I ran for house president and won. Then my buddies encouraged me to run for class president. Voters could designate candidates as their first, second, or third choice, etc. An opposing candidate decided to fix the election and visited the other houses, telling each, "You give our candidate a second choice and we'll give yours the same, but be sure to mark House N's candidate, Paul Dietzel, as your sixth or seventh choice." When the vote was tallied, I carried a clear majority until all of the sixths and sevenths came in. Welcome to the world of politics.

As fate would have it, Anne had become acquainted with Sid Gillman, Miami University's outstanding new football coach. One day Anne told Sid that she was from Mansfield and that her boyfriend, in school at Duke at the time, was Paul Dietzel. Anne recounts that Sid's eyes perked up—he had recruited me for Dennison College, where he had previously coached. Sid began writing to me, and I'm happy to say his letters continued all through my army air corps career. Of course, there was a constant stream of letters from Anne telling me, among other things, how nice it was at Miami.

Since I was leaving to join the army air corps, it was not possible to pay even a brief visit to Miami, in Oxford, Ohio, to serenade my SAE sweetheart. In my absence and in my place, my fraternity brothers at Miami, whom I had never met, serenaded her for me. That was a splendid thing for those boys to do.

# II
# You're in the Air Corps Now

My first stop in the army air corps was Keesler Field in Biloxi, Mississippi, which, I can assure you, was no garden spot. As we marched in, we were greeted with that infamous army warning, "You'll be sorry." Stationed at Keesler were about ten thousand new aviation cadets and another ten thousand who had "washed out" of the flight training program due to its many difficulties and physical requirements and were headed for the infantry or other assignments. We lived in tents, and it was very hot and humid. Our daily routine was mostly physical training and drill.

After basic training at Keesler, which, thankfully, didn't last too long, I was assigned to the college training detachment at Syracuse University in New York. My buddies and I spent several days on a train traveling to Syracuse. Unbelievably, that troop train rolled right through my hometown of Mansfield. Since Mansfield was not a planned stop, I wrote a quick note and yelled to someone as we slowly moved through town, "Would you please mail this for me? It's to my girlfriend." That kind person mailed the letter, in which I told Anne that I was sorry I couldn't get off the train and I was on my way to Syracuse.

Aviation Cadet Paul F. Dietzel

Compared to Keesler, Syracuse was a paradise. Three other cadets and I lived in the kitchen of the Sigma Chi house, which was directly across from a large dormitory called Simms Hall. We ate in the Simms Hall cafeteria and, by comparison with the food at Keesler, we were eating high on the hog.

At Syracuse, there was quite a large detachment of well over two thousand aviation cadets, who were matriculating with four thousand other engineering students. There were also about eight thousand coeds on campus; however, orders stipulated that cadets couldn't leave the dormitories at night. Being very gung ho and determined to do my best to follow the rules, I remained in the dorm at night. I was in the college training detachment to drill, to attend classes, and to study, which, unfortunately, did not include studying the girls. Most of the guys stepped out every night and always had plenty of dates because there were so many college girls available. But following the rules was not really that hard for me because I was very much in love and very naïve.

The assignment at Syracuse lasted for three months. At one point,

The honor squadron on parade. I'm in the front row.

Corps Adjutant "Brown Noser"

someone posted a picture of a cadet with a big, long nose on the Simms Hall bulletin board. The cadet's nose had been colored brown and the picture was labeled "Brown Noser." For fun, I wrote "Corps Adjutant" on it. When the assignments for the final month were announced, a cadet named Paul Dent was chosen as corps commander. Surprisingly, I was selected as corps adjutant and got plenty of ribbing about that, since I was the one who had scribbled "Corps Adjutant" on the cartoon of the "Brown Nose" cadet.

About this time, Anne came up for a brief visit and was able to enjoy one of the cadet parades. The corps adjutant is the fellow who stands off to the side, observing the cadets entering the area for the parade. When everyone is in place, he marches across the parade grounds in short, quick steps, almost like running, and then stops abruptly in front of the corps commander and shouts, "Sir! All present and accounted for!" Anne thought that was a riot and couldn't believe that I was the cadet racing across the parade grounds in such a hilarious a fashion.

After Syracuse, my next stop was Maxwell Field, Alabama, for pre-flight training. There were thousands of aviation cadets stationed there. I have no idea precisely how many, but I had never seen so many troops before. We marched everywhere—to physical training, to drill, to the mess hall.

Our recreation was basketball, and each squadron had its own team. Near the end of my stay at Maxwell, it was announced that the "permanent party personnel" team from the base would play an all-star team of cadets. Well, the permanent party team had a number of pros, since many professional players were in the army, too. Obviously, this was a very fine basketball team. I was excited to learn that I had been chosen to play for the cadet all-stars and really looked forward to the competition. But as fortune would have it, on the day before the big game, I came down with a case of the mumps!

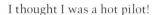

Anne and I in Syracuse

## Flight Training

After Maxwell Field, I began actual pilot training. My first assignment was in Decatur, Alabama, where I was stationed from January through March 1944. I learned to fly a PT-17, a Stearman biplane. I learned to love that Stearman. I could fly it, and more importantly, I could even land it. The Stearman was called a "ground-looping son of a gun" because it had a narrow landing gear, and if you were a bit care-less when landing, it would ground-loop, spin-ning around in a circle, or even worse. Although it wasn't really dangerous, it was very embarrass-ing if it happened to you. The plane was a two-winged beauty, with an open cockpit, and seemed to have been made for stunt flying—spins, rolls, loops, and such. I managed to master "lazy eights," "pylon eights," and "eights along the road," which were required maneuvers. When I took my flight check, I did those pretty well. Then my instruc-tor said, "Give me a snap roll," and I did. Then he asked for a slow roll, and I gave him an eight-point slow roll, which happened to be my specialty. Ap-parently he was satisfied, as he remarked, "I can see what you've been practicing."

I thought I was a hot pilot!

The town of Decatur sponsored a weekly rec-ord hop at the local VFW. Young ladies from the area came to dance with the cadets. I met one I re-ally enjoyed dancing with, but I enjoyed the fact that her mother invited me to dinner even more. That very kind lady fried the best chicken and baked the most wonderful biscuits, to which I did more than justice. But there was never any doubt

The Stearman biplane we flew in primary training

in my mind that I belonged to Anne.

In the three months at Decatur, our motor skills, athletic ability, and stamina were constantly being tested. These attributes were crucial, as both valuable military equipment and other soldiers' lives would be in our hands as pilots. I was honored to be named the "Outstanding Athlete in the Corps of Cadets." I still have that award.

Courtland, Alabama, near Decatur, is actually where we aviation cadets were immersed in instrument flying and engine maintenance. I was introduced to the VT-13A, better known as a Vultee Vibrator, and completed seventy-seven hours of flight training in that aircraft.

My flight instructor was a Lieutenant Blassingame, who told me that a major from wing headquarters was coming to test some cadets on instrument flying and that I was one of the cadets to be tested. Since so many cadets had washed out, I was very worried. After my flight test, the major said nothing to me. Now I was really worried. I asked Lieutenant Blassingame how I had done. He told me I had done fine. When I mentioned how worried I had been to have been selected, he said, "I picked you because you are my best student." I wish he had told me that before the test!

I was then transferred to advanced two-engine training on the AT-10 at Freeman Field in Seymour, Indiana. I had always enjoyed instrument flying, but at Seymour I had a funny experience. I had an instructor who got lost each time we came in to land. The traffic pattern called for us to enter on a forty-five-degree angle to the downwind leg. He could never figure out that procedure, so he always had me enter the traffic pattern and land the plane. One night, I was flying with only another cadet. I was to practice night landings at an auxiliary field. As soon as we took off, all of our lights went out. We were flying on instruments with nothing but a flashlight. We flew completely around the traffic pattern at the field and then buzzed the tower to alert them that we had a blacked-out plane (we could receive from the tower but could not transmit). The tower advised all traffic to ascend to two thousand feet and watch out for a blacked-out plane. We were finally cleared to land, which we did. An MP car with a big "Follow Me" sign taxied us to the officer of the day. He asked us, "Didn't you check out your voltage regulator before take-off?" I said, "Yes, Sir, we certainly did, and it checked out fine." I found out later that base officials thought we had dealt with the situation pretty well. This was in April and May of 1944.

I constantly told my southern roommates in Alabama that it surely would be fine if we were sent up north where it's cool. Well, that summer in Seymour, Indiana, had to be one of the hottest on record. My friends constantly reminded me, "Boy, it sure will be nice to be up north where it's cool!" But it was far from cool in Seymour. My luck!

After eighty-one hours in the AT-10, I graduated and won my silver wings. Anne and my father and stepmother came for the ceremony. Anne pinned my wings on at graduation. It was a wonderful moment. Having my father at my army air corps graduation was very special to me, as I had seen him only sporadically since I had been at Duke and in the air corps. His health was deteriorating, and we were separated by many miles.

One of the last times I saw Dad was at the Columbus (Ohio) Quarter-back Club, where I was one of the honorees. To have my dad at such an occasion was very gratifying to both of us. Years later, my dad died of heart complications at the age of sixty-two. On his deathbed he said, "Don't be sad, I'm just going to be with the Lord." After Dad's death, I went to Mansfield, Ohio, to arrange his funeral and settle his financial affairs. One of the saddest days of my life was going through his car and his papers, the things he touched last. I really missed him.

Anne and I with Cadet D. L. Davis (left) of the Syracuse College Training Detachment

After graduation, I was immediately transferred to Smyrna Army Air Base in Tennessee for training in the four-engine B-24 Liberator bomber in the fall of 1944. It was while I was there that Anne and I decided to get married. Anne's mother didn't like it and felt we ought to wait until after the war, but we were not interested in waiting. I had ordered a little wedding ring for Anne at the PX. It was not very fancy, but it was all I could afford. We were married on September 25, 1944, in the Smyrna Army Air Base chapel. Two of our favorite people from my cadet days, Jimmy and Glo Davis, stood up with us. For our honeymoon, we took a bus into Nashville to spend the night. As I had to fly the next morning, it was a very short honeymoon.

From that time on, we moved from one place to another. We were told, "Don't even think about trying to bring your dependents, because there is no place for them to live." We didn't pay any attention to that, naturally. Outside of Nashville, in Murfreesboro, we found a wonderful lady, Mrs. Ryan, who had a big antebellum home. She rented us a room with kitchen privileges. Another couple taking one of her rooms was Captain Steve Stevens and his wife, Mary. Thanksgiving came around, and Mrs. Ryan insisted that we use her lovely china and silver. Anne found one small chicken for our Thanksgiving dinner. We were having Steve and Mary as our guests, and then I called and asked Anne if I couldn't bring a buddy named John Dougy, who had no place to go. And then another. It was a task to divide that little chicken up among six people. Anne did a fantastic job with the potatoes and dressing, along with a fine pump-

Our wedding day in Smyrna,
Tennessee, September 25, 1944

kin pie, and the table setting was outstanding. It was a wonderful Thanksgiving.

After completing B-24 training in November, I was posted to Lincoln Army Air Base in Nebraska for reassignment. This was in the middle of winter, and it was very cold. The temperature never rose above ten degrees Fahrenheit. I was required to check in at the base each morning to find out if my orders had been issued, but then I was free for the rest of the day. At Christmastime Anne got a job at Gold's Department Store in the candy department. Gold's gave a fine Christmas dinner to all its employees, so we rode downtown on the bus and enjoyed a Christmas feast. On New Year's Eve, Anne and I went to the Cornhusker Hotel for a holiday dance. We left the dance at about 12:30 A.M. but hadn't realized that buses stopped running at 11:00 P.M. We finally managed to stop a cab and avoided a long, frosty hike home. When we returned to our small apartment, it was so cold that we went to bed with our clothes on and piled every bit of clothing that we owned on top of the bed cover. It was a cold Nebraska New Year's Eve.

New orders finally came, and we were transferred to Clovis Army Air Base in New Mexico. As we were preparing to leave Lincoln, we bought a 1936 Ford two-door sedan for two hundred dollars, a small fortune at the time. We named the car "Old Betsy." She was black with yellow spoke wheels and red plaid seat covers. That Ford got us safely all the way to Clovis, but it did use quite a bit of oil. If I could hold the speed to thirty-five miles per hour, I had to put in just two quarts of oil each time I filled up with gas. If I got a bit reckless and drove at fifty-five miles per hour, then I had to put in five quarts of oil each time I put in gas. But all in all, Old Betsy was a great little car, and we were glad to have her.

When we arrived in Clovis, there was no place to stay—the town was packed with military people. But in Portales, a small town about twenty miles away, we were able to find a room with a fine couple, Shorty and Artie Greenhaw. They were really great people. Shorty, as his name implied, was short, and so was Artie. Artie baked pies for the downtown café, which wasn't very fancy. Shorty was a cowboy. He wore cowboy boots and a cowboy hat. Every Saturday, the people from around Portales came to town to "swap." They might swap a truck for a couple of horses, for example. It was really something. And Portales was the only town I've ever been in that had a wooden boardwalk around its little town square. But Shorty and Artie were such wonderful people. They gave us kitchen privileges. It didn't take much to haul everything we had to their place, because it was in one footlocker, which sat at the end of our bed. The Greenhaws didn't have a washing machine, so Anne washed our clothes in the bathtub and hung them outside. That was fine as long as a sandstorm didn't blow up, which occurred on a regular basis. The clothes would then be covered with sand and would have to be washed again. Sometimes when we parked the car, even with the windows up really tight, there would be as much as a half inch of sand throughout the car when we returned.

Anne and I with "Old Betsy." In the lower left photo, she's parked in front of Shorty and Artie Greenhaw's house, where we rented a room in Portales, New Mexico.

There were two other officers living in Portales, and both of them had cars. We decided to carpool, so each of us had to drive only once every three days. On one of my days to drive, after I picked up the other two officers, they immediately fell sound asleep. There is one straight road going across the desert from Portales to Clovis, and along the way I must have dozed off, too. All of a sudden, I looked up and there were headlights right in my face. I swerved the car, and the guy in the other car must have been asleep, too, because we sideswiped each other really hard. By the time I got out of the car my two buddies were wide awake. I could just barely detect a scratch on the side of Old Betsy. If you did that in one of today's cars, you'd tear the whole side off.

While in Clovis, I learned to fly the B-29 Superfortress, the largest airplane anyone at the base had ever seen. Each time it landed, enlisted men would come running over to see this new marvel. My fellow airmen and I flew quite a few cross-country trips to prepare for service in the vast Pacific, where all our flights would be very long indeed. Once, we took off from Clovis, flew to Los Angeles, then to Chicago, and finally back to Clovis. This was unheard of for any other aircraft. The B-29 was pressurized, which made it feel like driving a Cadillac after riding in a jeep. It was such a fantastic airplane.

The B-29s were needed so badly that they had been taken right off the assembly line and sent into combat without proper testing. The B-29s had engine problems that did not surface at Clovis but eventually cropped up out in the Pacific. The engines would overheat on the ground while just taxiing on the runway. The problem was finally solved by installing baffle plates around the engine's cylinders to cool them.

Once, flying over Los Angeles as our flight instructions required, we checked into ground control. I called in and said that we were over the L.A. station at thirty-three thousand feet at such and such time and that we were flying from Clovis, New Mexico. The fellow on the ground control said, "Would you please repeat your altitude?"

"We're at thirty-three thousand."

"Are you sure?"

I said, "Yes, Sir, we're up here. We're trying to get over the top of these clouds, but we can't." He was amazed to hear that an airplane was at that altitude over his station.

After we completed our training at Clovis, we were given leave before we were to return there for reassignment. Naturally we wanted to go to Ohio to visit family and friends. Because of the way "Old Betsy" burned oil, we had decided we needed a better, later-model automobile, and we had gone to Lubbock and traded our Ford for a 1941 Dodge—a big mistake. The bright red car had nice-looking tires, which turned out to be painted black. We had two blowouts on the way back from Lubbock to Portales. We decided the car must have been a taxi before we bought it.

After a difficult trip to Mansfield, our tires were worn out. Since we had to report back to Clovis on time, I went to the head of the Ration Board and showed him my orders and begged him for new tire rations. He agreed, and we purchased four new Firestone tires. We were home free, or so we thought. Even though we had just had the oil changed, as we were driving through East St. Louis, our engine started clanking really loud. A mechanic we found said we had thrown a rod and ruined the engine. It was the weekend that President Roosevelt died. We told the mechanic about my orders and that I had to be on time at Clovis. He said, "We have a rebuilt De Soto engine that will fit your car. If we work all night, we can install it for three hundred dollars." We had to wire Anne's dad for a loan. We spent the night in our clothes in a room over a noisy bar. By the next morning, those mechanics had our car ready. We will be forever grateful to those kind and understanding East St. Louis mechanics.

Back at Clovis, I soon received my new orders. I was transferred to Mather Field in Sacramento, California, which was the takeoff point for duty in the Pacific. Anne and I walked the streets of Sacramento until we found a house with a room for rent. Each day was like sitting on pins and needles. It was frustrating because we didn't know when orders would come. When they finally did arrive, I asked Anne not to come to the airport to watch us take off, but of course, she did anyhow. As I was flying to a place called Tinian in the Marianas, Anne and a friend named Cuppy began their drive back home to Ohio. Anne later told me that they would drive awhile, then stop and cry awhile. When she returned to Mansfield, she lived with her parents and found a job at Reed's department store as manager of the jewelry department.

We knew our mail might be censored, so before we parted, Anne and I had worked out a plan for me to let her know my general whereabouts. We took a map of the South Pacific and centered a dot on Honolulu and used a compass to draw ever-widening circles all the way out. Then we divided the circles into sections like slices of pie, so we had the circles to tell how far out it was and the pie wedges to tell the direction. We numbered the sections of the pie and labeled the circles A through E. When I got to Tinian, I wrote to Anne that she needed to check the car's engine for D-12 fluid. Anne would know that I was on Tinian, and no one else would be the wiser.

## My Time in Combat

We took off from Hawaii for Tinian, and on the way refueled at Kwajelein Atoll, a tiny speck of an island out in the Pacific. I was twenty years old. Only one man in our crew was older, and not by much. There we were flying over this huge expanse of water, searching for an island in the middle of the Pacific with a navigator who had never navigated across an ocean. And if you don't think the Pacific Ocean is huge, you just haven't flown over it in an airplane making only two hundred twenty-five miles per hour. After an eternity, we sighted Tinian and landed safely, although there was no radio beam to home in on, since the Japanese could also use the same signal.

The brand new airplane, which had been issued to our crew in Sacramento, was taken from us and replaced with one that had been in service a lot longer. Herb Kent, our airplane commander, was moved from our crew to another. His spot was filled by an excellent pilot who had al-

*The Banana Boat*, which brought us safely home twelve times

ready flown about half of his missions. His name was LeRoy Arants, and he was from Georgia.

Our B-29 was named *The Banana Boat*, and about the time it was assigned to us, we began bombing missions. We had a tough, cigar-chewing commander by the name of General Curtis LeMay, who had just recently taken command. General LeMay studied the strike reports and decided that our bombing was tremendously inaccurate because of our high-altitude approach and the prevailing wind currents. Although we were using the newly developed Norden bombsight, the extremely strong winds over the Japanese Empire would blow most of our bombs far off target. General LeMay issued orders for the B-29s to go in at five thousand to nine thousand feet, a much lower altitude than before. This diminished the effect of the winds on our bombs, and our accuracy improved dramatically.

My first mission over Tokyo, a city of bamboo houses, took place on May 25, 1945. More than three hundred B-29s dropped napalm gasoline gel bombs on the city. The bombs were designed to explode in the air and scatter miniature bomblets everywhere. These were so hot that they would burn through steel girders. Tokyo was transformed into an inferno; it was terrible and unbelievable. Half of the city was burned out, and more people were killed in that raid than lost their lives in both of the atomic attacks on Hiroshima and Nagasaki. In many ways, the Tokyo fire raid changed the course of the war in the Pacific, as the Japanese finally realized that their home islands could not be protected from the American Superfortresses.

The Marianas comprised the islands of Saipan, Tinian, and Guam. There were two B-29 wings on Tinian, and one each on Guam and Saipan. For takeoffs and landings, B-29s required runways with a minimum length of 8,500 feet. Army engineers had determined that runways sufficient for use by B-29s could not be built on Tinian, as the atoll was composed of coral. However, Navy Seabees proved them dead wrong and in a short period of time, constructed not one but four 8,500-foot parallel runways on the island. The Seabees had used bulldozers to scrape up tons and tons of coral and piled it in layers until the runways were strong enough to support the tremendous weight of fast-moving Superfortresses. Those runways are still there today.

Tinian was our takeoff point for raids over the Japanese home islands. En route, our squadron had to pass near Iwo Jima, approximately half-way between the Marianas and Japan and still held by the Japanese at that time. Our big bombers were constantly attacked by fighter planes based on the island as we flew our missions to and from the Japanese homeland. And as you would expect, the enemy on Iwo would warn the Japanese fighter command on the home islands of our approach. Consequently, we were always warmly welcomed by swarms of enemy aircraft, as well as by nests of ground-based antiaircraft batteries. Our losses in planes and men were great; it became obvious that Iwo Jima had to be neutralized. Our high command made the decision to invade and secure the island. Prior to the initial landings, the atoll was shelled night and day by naval units. Battleships, cruisers, and destroyers, supported by an armada of smaller ships, took part in the assault. Simultaneously, army and naval air forces bombed Mount Suribachi, which was strongly held by enemy troops. The island was so heavily shelled and bombed that it seemed impossible that any of the enemy could have survived. Dead wrong! The Japanese had tunneled in deeply, very far below the surface of the ground. Their subterranean hospitals, dormitories, mess halls, and command centers remained safe and secure in spite of the rain of fire from high above.

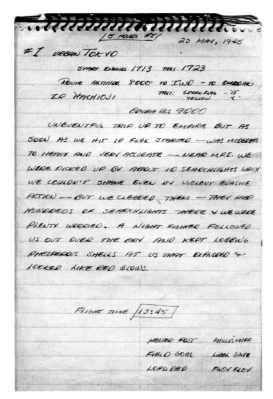

Above: Personal log of my first mission over the Japanese Empire. Right: Cover of the *Pirate's Log*, a historical record of the Sixth Bombardment Group, with which I flew my first mission over Tokyo, the first devastating firebomb raid of May 1945.

When wave after wave of our invasion troops landed, they were met with withering fire from the dug-in and camouflaged Japanese. Marine tanks and half-tracks sank into the coral ash as they came ashore on the beaches. The fighting was fierce and brutal with no quarter given; thousands of our fine young men were killed and wounded. The sacrifice in human lives was terrible. In time and at great cost we prevailed, and Iwo Jima was taken. It was a battle that will never be forgotten.

Prior to our victory at Iwo Jima, the B-29s flew their missions over Japan without the protection of fighter air cover. Without covering fighters, the B-29s were relatively easy targets for enemy Zeros. Things changed after the fall of Iwo. The army air corps immediately brought in squadrons of P-51s, one of the great fighter planes of all time. These P-51 Mustangs were equipped with auxiliary fuel tanks, which greatly extended their range and allowed them to escort the bombers all the way to Japan. The protection they provided significantly reduced our bomber losses. One of the saddest things I remember was the ditching at sea of one of these Mustangs, which had run out of fuel while fending off a Japanese Zero. To rescue downed pilots, the navy stationed ships, called Dumbos, all along the route that the bombers and fighters flew. When one of our aircraft was forced to ditch, a call was made to give the location of the downed plane to the nearest Dumbo. Many pilots were saved, but many were also lost. These men were heroes to all of us.

I flew missions to Yokohama, Kobe, Akashi, Yokkaichi, Fukuoka, Kashagin, Moji, Ube, and Imiji in late May and June of 1945. In early July, my group was selected to drop contact mines in the major Japanese harbors to disrupt enemy shipping. For this mission, the bombers were required to make the drops at an altitude not exceeding nine thousand feet, and at an airspeed of approximately two hundred miles per hour. If either of these guidelines was exceeded, the mines would usually explode upon contact with the water.

One such mission required my squadron to fly over the Japanese mainland to Fusan harbor off the coast of Korea and return home to our base on Tinian the same way. This meant that we would spend at least four hours in the air over Japan without air cover. Not good! As a last line of defense, the Japanese had begun to use kamikaze suicide pilots to ram the B-29s. Kamikaze aircraft were truly like rockets with bombs attached. The intense flame created by the rocket engine looked like a ball of fire, so naturally, we nicknamed them "Balls of Fire."

As we were leaving Japanese air space on the return trip from Fusan, almost everyone on board was asleep; "George," the autopilot, was flying the aircraft. Suddenly, the center turret gunner, Joe Roos, shouted over the intercom, "Ball of Fire at nine o'clock." Immediately, the crew came to life. A kamikaze was heading directly for us—and fast, too! I've never been so scared; I could almost hear my knees shaking. Anyone in a situation like that who says he is not scared is either crazy or a liar, or both. I very carefully held my breath, pressed the mike to my throat and said, "Don't shoot until he gets close." I hoped the crew couldn't hear the quavering in my voice. We were all transfixed on that Ball of Fire homing in on us at nine o'clock, but strangely, it didn't seem to be getting any closer. Suddenly, the clouds parted and the rising sun brightly shone through. The Ball of Fire turned out to be our beacon home. After the scare, we had a good laugh at the expense of Joe Roos. But the entire crew remained wide awake until we landed on Tinian. Later, Joe said to me, "Lieutenant, I want you to know one thing. If you hadn't been so calm when I spotted that Ball of Fire, I think I would have jumped right out of the plane."

My reply was nothing more than the plain truth and exactly the way I felt at the time. I said, "Joe, you've gotta be kidding. I was as scared as anybody in that airplane. I just caught my breath long enough to tell you not to shoot until he got close. We were all scared, and if you say you weren't, then something's wrong with you. I want you to know that everyone was scared."

Yawata, a major Japanese naval base, was located in the Shimonoseki

Straits, between the islands of Kyushu and Honshu. The base was heavily fortified and deemed a death trap by the American airmen who attempted to bomb it. One of my best friends, former teammate Ken Smith, had been stationed at a B-29 base in southern China. The base was established as a staging point for air raids on Yawata. The high mountains in that part of China were nicknamed "the Hump" by our aviators, who flew over it at great risk. Ken was one of the unlucky fellows who never made it—he was lost somewhere over the Hump. Of the ninety-nine B-29s assigned to fly the Hump, only about a third ever hit their targets, and only about a third returned safely to their bases in China. Everyone dreaded receiving orders to attack Yawata.

In the early morning of July 9, 1945, my crew, along with many others, attended a briefing to receive mission instructions. After a brief review of some basic ground rules, a large map was uncovered and clearly marked our target—the dreaded Yawata on the Shimonoseki Straits. A hush fell over the group.

We took off for Yawata and flew down the straits between Kyushu and Honshu at an altitude of nine thousand feet, the prescribed ceiling for dropping mines. Ahead we could see searchlights crossing from both sides of the straits and directly above the base. Antiaircraft flak began to burst everywhere—so thick it seemed you could almost walk on it. Luckily, we were able to skirt a bit to the right of it. Our radar bombardier, Tony Pantelas, called out, "Correct five degrees to the left." I followed his instructions and piloted the plane right down the middle of "Hell's Alley." It was just like what we all imagined Hell to be. There had been other B-29s ahead of us and more were behind us, but as far as we could see, we were all alone. We had arrived over the target at a lull in the battle. I realized that the planes that had flown in first had stirred up the Japanese, and now we were headed directly into the inferno of searchlights and exploding flak. I wanted to get us out of there. I descended slowly, picking up airspeed all through the bombing run. At three hundred miles per hour, our radar man released ten 2,000-pound mines attached to parachutes. The B-29 jerked and jumped up, bouncing almost uncontrollably. We watched the drop to see if the wind turbulence had ripped the parachutes off the mines. It had not.

To get out of there as fast as I could, I turned south and flew right over Kyushu at an altitude of only five thousand feet. Fortunately for us, no Japanese night fighters scrambled to attack us. We headed out to sea and back to Tinian.

Finally, I called up our navigator, Roy Person, to make sure the bomb bay doors were closed. He said, "Yes, they're fine."

Then I asked him, "How high are the mountains on that island of Kyushu we just went over?"

He said, "Well, they're between seven and eight thousand feet."

I said, "You've got to be kidding! We must have gone down a valley between those mountains, because we flew over at five thousand feet." We felt we had a charmed life that night.

Running low on fuel, we landed on Iwo Jima, even though the battle for the island was still raging. A fellow in the tower ordered, "Clear the first intersection because they're still fighting at the end of the runway." We quickly refueled and took off for Tinian. Many years after the war had ended, I learned that our group had been awarded the Presidential Unit Citation for having flown the longest mission of the war. Seventeen hours is a long time to be sitting in a B-29, but we were all thankful that we were lucky enough to finally get back on the ground. Many others were not so fortunate.

On one of our earlier missions, we had been instructed to fly in formation at a high altitude. A formation is composed of four elements, with four B-29s in each—sixteen airplanes in all. We were to fly lead plane in the second element, with one element in front of us and two others behind and below. Soon after taking off, our plane developed a minor engine problem which made us a bit late, so the other B-29s formed up without us. By the time we arrived, another plane had taken our assigned place as lead aircraft in the second element, and we found a spot in one of the rear elements. As we were flying toward our target, a Japanese reconnaissance plane was spotted ahead of us flying at the same altitude as we were, undoubtedly charting our course, airspeed, and altitude. We knew that this information would be communicated by radio to the "welcoming committee" on the ground and that the enemy antiaircraft batteries would be ready to greet us. Unexpectedly, the Japanese reconnaissance plane turned directly into our formation and made a head-on pass straight through. He managed to shoot out three of the engines on the B-29 that had taken our place in the second element. The plane stalled out and dropped into the sea, with no parachutes appearing. That entire crew was lost. Had it not been for a minor engine problem that caused our plane to lose its place in formation, it might well have been us who crashed into the sea. Somehow, I felt then that I would survive the war and return safely to my beloved Anne.

## Lead Crew School in the USA

After the twelfth mission, our crew was selected to return to the States for "lead crew" training, where we would learn to be squadron leaders. On the way, we stopped briefly in Hawaii. I was a sorry-looking mess. My hair was long, and I had gotten badly sunburned and blistered sunbathing on Tinian. I was not a pretty sight.

We then landed in California, and I hitched a ride on an army air corps standby flight into Columbus, Ohio. From there, I bummed a ride to Mansfield and arrived there very early in the morning. I went immediately to Mr. and Mrs. Wilson's home, where I knew Anne was staying. Anne had no idea that I was coming home and could not believe that I was there. For a few minutes, she seemed to be in a state of shock. Needless to say, we were so happy to be together again!

My new assignment was in California's Mojave Desert at the Muroc Army Air Corps Base, which had no accommodations for servicemen's dependents. But that didn't bother us. Anne and I made the long drive without incident. My orders had authorized new tires, and the car's engine had been replaced. No problems. Upon our arrival, we found a small cabin in the middle of the desert. I'm not sure how we found it, but we did. As it turned out, we were there only a little more than two weeks. Lead crew flight training was intense but not especially memorable.

Each night, we went to a movie and then to the officer's club for steaks and Cokes. The prices were incredible—a quarter for a steak with all the trimmings and a nickel for a soft drink. In our desert cabin, there was a bale of straw near the back window with a contraption rigged up to slowly drip water on to the straw. A fan was placed behind the bale to blow air across the wet straw. Amazingly, this primitive air-conditioning unit worked very well and cooled the cabin very effectively.

It was during our brief stay in the Mojave that the war came to an end. To everyone's great surprise, it was announced that an atomic bomb had been dropped on Japan by a B-29 based on Tinian. Not many days later a second nuclear bomb was dropped, and soon after that the war ended. I recall that one of the runways on Tinian was surrounded with a high chain-link fence. It was constantly guarded by MPs, and no unauthorized personnel were ever admitted. It had always puzzled me that there were no gun turrets on the B-29s that were parked within the fenced area. One of these planes was the *Enola Gay*.

We were given a few days leave and decided to drive to the mountains near Lake Arrowhead with another couple, Paul and Jeanie Isenberg. We stopped at a little country store and asked the owner where we might find a place to stay. This kind man said, "Well, I'll tell you. I've got a cabin up in the mountains not far from here, and you're welcome to stay there. I'll give you some bacon and eggs and butter, too." I said we'd be very grateful and asked how much it would cost. "It won't cost you a penny. You've already paid your bill," he told us. That's the way people were during and right after the war—the country was completely unified.

Back at base, we were given the option of returning to Tinian with a rank increase of two levels, or we could choose to be discharged. It didn't take long to sign the discharge papers! So Anne and I took off for home.

Shortly thereafter I was sent to Kelly Field in Texas to complete four hours of flying time so that I could collect my flight pay. The pilot instructor took me up in an AT-6, a plane I had never before flown. It was one of those ground-looping sons of guns with very narrow landing gear. As we touched down, it began to loop and I slammed on the opposite rudder pedal. Wrong pedal! After we sashayed back and forth a ways down the runway, the instructor took over the controls and taxied in. Since I still had three hours of flying time to complete, I took off again and flew around until my three hours were up. In attempting to land, I made the mistake of overcontrolling the plane, and it bounced from side to side all the way down the runway. I finally came to a stop, a bit embarrassed but none the worse for wear.

# III
# I Become a Coach

## The War Is Over—Back to College

Back in Mansfield, Anne and I had to wait a few months to enroll for classes in Miami University's summer session. Since I had some time on my hands, I took a job at the Mathis Clothing Store. Anne's parents let us stay at their house until school started. One weekend, we drove down to Oxford to look for a place to live, but all available rentals had already been taken by the great number of veterans and their families who were also coming back to school. Finally, we found a place where a trailer could be parked, but we didn't have a trailer. Luckily for us, my sister, Genevieve, and her husband, Bob Perin, came to our rescue. They just happened to have a very small trailer, so small in fact that I could only stand erect in one place, and that was at the ventilator shaft in the middle of the trailer. A Mr. Bair lived on a corner lot in a large house with a garage in the rear. He let us park our trailer there beside several others, but none of them was as tiny as ours.

Bob and Gevy drove that trailer all the way from Green Springs to Oxford and refused any payment for their generosity. But Gevy and Bob had always been extremely kind to Anne and me. In earlier years, Gevy

Our first home in Miami, Ohio, 1946

Anne and I in the door of our ten-foot by twenty-foot trailer, 21A

was valedictorian of her Green Springs High School class. She was smart enough to teach me a few lessons. After she and Bob had two sons, Jimmy and Johnny, I would visit them and had a great time playing with those boys. Once I was demonstrating a front flip to them and I heard my ankle snap. This was before the start of that year's football practice for the Miami Redskins. Fortunately, my injury was not serious, but I toned down my showing off to my nephews.

I learned one other lesson from Gevy, at the dinner table. Gevy was a fine cook, especially an excellent baker. Jimmy and Johnny had not eaten their meal, but Gevy served them a nice slice of chocolate cake anyway. I immediately asked, "You're not going to let them have cake since they wouldn't eat their meal, are you?"

Gevy replied, kindly but firmly, "Paul, after you get married and have children, you raise them as you wish. These are my boys and I will raise them the way I see fit." That was the end of that conversation.

Bob was a fine husband to Gevy and a good father. Gevy and Bob got into the travel trailer culture and took many fine trips with friends who also loved to travel. They finally settled into a large double trailer home in Florida. Unfortunately, Bob suffered an unexpected illness and passed away much too early. Gevy moved back to Green Springs to be close to her sons and their families. Then, tragically, Johnny also passed away, leaving his fine wife, Ann, and their children. Jimmy and his family are still living in Cleveland. Gevy was living in an assisted living facility when she passed away in 2002. I've really missed her. Our daughter-in-law, Judy, is amazed that Anne and I have hardly any living relatives of our generation, but it is true. When Judy and her family, from Livingston, Louisiana, get together for Sunday dinner, there are more than thirty family members present.

As soon as we were settled in, I began practicing football, because with Sid Gillman, Miami's coach, you always practiced football. There were very many veterans coming back to school, almost too many to count, and it seemed that most of them were football players. At opening practice, seven centers lined up, including one who had been an All-American at Miami.

Anne got a job at the Phi Delta headquarters, and I worked part-time at Kroger's meat market. To alleviate the housing crunch, the university invested in two hundred trailers. Each unit provided two 10- by 20-foot efficiency apartments with living room, bedroom, kitchen, and bath all competing for space in one room. I built us a breakfast nook with padded seats and a nifty radio cabinet. We could hear almost everything that went on next door in the adjoining efficiency; when our neighbor turned on the water, we knew it. One of the fellows living several spaces down from us said he was having a great time enjoying the view until his neighbor discovered his peephole. Welcome to Veterans Village.

My dad, who was still living in Mansfield, gave us an old heating unit and told me how I could convert it into a crude air-conditioning unit. I followed his advice, and sure enough, we had the only air-conditioning unit in Veterans Village.

Anne and I lived in 21A, and Art and June Goldner, who became as close to us as family, were in 21B. Art had been a navy pilot, and I could not have had a dearer brother. June was like a sister to Anne. Over the years, we've spent great vacations and holidays with them. They became godparents of our children, and we were godparents for their son, Tim.

Anne and I went to a record dance at the SAE fraternity house and found a bunch of young students necking and carrying on; being older and married, we felt out of place. Another time, Art and June invited us to the Sigma Chi house, where most of the members were married veterans. We felt more at home there and visited so often that people thought I was a Sigma Chi.

Anne with my coach and great friend, Sid Gillman

I began an accelerated premed course because I had decided I wanted to become a surgeon. Compared to my poor academic record at Duke before the war, my grades at Miami were quite good. My undergraduate minors were in math and physical education. One of the requirements in the physical education minor was the successful completion of a class in dance. Although I thought I had done well, the instructor gave me a C. Boy, was I mad! That turned out to be the only grade below B that I made at Miami University, and I couldn't do a thing about it. I tried talking to the dance teacher, but I couldn't persuade her. She really liked the girls, and they all got good grades. She definitely did not like football players, especially me, since I happened to be the captain of the team.

Sid Gillman was an outstanding coach and developed a very fine football team at Miami. We were invited to play Texas Tech in the Sun Bowl in El Paso. The Sun Bowl officials informed Coach Gillman that Miami could not bring a black player to the game. At the time, there was only one black athlete on our team; he was a substitute but a fine guy, by the name of Bill Harris. Coach spoke with Bill and told him that he didn't know what to do. Bill insisted that Miami should commit, and so we did. We won the game by one point and brought the ball back and presented it to Bill Harris.

Sid Gillman was a remarkable person and probably the smartest football coach I've ever known. He worked very hard and taught us the value of effort and persistence. Bill Walsh of San Francisco 49ers fame once wrote, "People give me credit for inventing the West Coast offense, but I didn't. I learned it from Sid Gillman."

Each week, a theater in Oxford would feature the RKO news, which always included a segment of college football highlights from around the country. Sid would borrow the film, and since the athletic department did not own a 35-mm projector, he would adapt it to a 35-mm slide projector. Each frame of the film had to be pulled through the projector by hand, and there were often twenty or more frames for each play. Although the task was tedious, we were able to diagram plays that schools like Michigan, Army, and Notre Dame were using. Whenever Coach Gillman found a play that worked especially well, you could bet that it would eventually show up in our offense. He was a rabid copier and filled countless notebooks with breakdowns of plays he had seen on film.

Across the street from our home was the Veterans Market, a combination grocery store and meat market, which we veterans ran. I helped out because I seemed to be the only one who knew anything about meat cutting. After all, I had worked as a butcher at Bazley's Market back in Mansfield. I arranged for us to buy a big wooden meat cooler and counters and drove to Cincinnati and found some saws, knives, and other utensils. I was soon delegated the official meat cutter and found myself running the Veterans Market butcher shop. Pretty young brides would come in not knowing diddly-squat about cooking, so I would teach them about different cuts of meat and how to prepare them. One of my specialties became fairly popular. I would grind up a piece of ham and squeeze it into a clamp that shaped it into the form of a drumstick. I then inserted a stick in the drumstick so it could be held easily. One day I was explaining to a young lady how to prepare these, and Anne happened to drop in. Later she told me that I really didn't know how to cook those ground ham drumsticks. She was probably right, but in any event, I knew more than the young bride, and after all, I was the official meat cutter.

My teammates elected me captain of the football team, the undefeated team that beat Texas Tech in the Sun Bowl. This was the third undefeated football team I was a part of. Things were about as good as they could get. I was running the meat market, playing football, and going to school all at the same time. My grades were good, and I seemed to be doing well in premed. I was eventually inducted into three honor societies, including Omicron Delta Kappa, and was elected president of both ODK and the Education Honorary, Kappa Delta Pi.

At this point I had been the team's first-string center for some time. In most games, I played a full sixty minutes—center on offense and linebacker on defense—and had developed into a real nitpicker about proper technique. Each week during the season, Sid would grade and give awards to the most efficient lineman, the most efficient back, etc. I managed to win the award fairly consistently. As graduation neared, Coach Gillman offered me a graduate assistantship with a monthly stipend of two hundred dollars. Of course, I accepted!

Since I had graduated at midyear, my assistantship began with spring practice. I thought I knew most everything about the game of football. But

Anne in Miami, Ohio, 1946

Still playing center, now at
Miami University

I won first-team All-American honors in 1947.

at the first practice session, I was rudely awakened to my ignorance when one of the running backs asked me what he was supposed to do on a certain play. I had no idea. I quickly learned that I didn't know nearly as much as I thought I did. It was a great experience for me to have that opportunity to find out how ignorant I was.

Later that spring, George Blackburn, Miami's backfield coach, invited me to accompany him on a trip to Dayton, where he was to speak at a football banquet. He bragged on me so much that by the time we left that night, I had been offered a job as head football coach at the brand new Dayton Fairmont High School. That was pretty heady stuff! I was offered thirty-five hundred dollars a year and was told that I could hire a former teammate, H. Wayne Gibson, as backfield coach at three thousand a year.

It was decision time—whether to take the job with Sid as graduate assistant at Miami or the one as head coach in Dayton. I didn't know what to do. A former coach of mine and a good friend, Frank Claire, gave me this advice: "Paul," he said, "I'll tell you what. You go to Dayton and you coach your head off for five or six years—you'll have a fantastic record. Then, if you're lucky, you can come back to Miami as a graduate assistant." Nothing could have been more clear than that, and fortunately, I made the decision to remain at Miami with Sid.

Something very special happened at the end of spring practice. Colonel "Red" Blaik, head football coach of the United States Military Academy, had seen the Miami offense and was quite impressed. Coach Blaik was a graduate of Miami of Ohio, as were Paul Brown, Weeb Ewbank, and eventually, a host of other coaching legends. In fact, the school became known as the Cradle of Coaches, a term coined by one of Miami's former sports information directors, Paul Kurz. A particular play that our offense ran quite often, and one that Colonel Blaik especially liked, was a variation of a speed sweep that Fritz Chrysler of Michigan

Miami was known as the "Cradle of Coaches." Honored on this poster are (clockwise from top left) John Pont, Red Blaik, Paul Brown, Ara Parseghian, Paul F. Dietzel, Carmen Cozza, Weeb Ewbank, and Bo Schembechler.

had developed. Sid adjusted this play and transformed it to fit the T formation that we used. The only man we blocked in the play was the defensive end on the play side. All of the other defenders were screened off by offensive linemen running across in front of them at top speed. All in all, it was a fantastic play. Colonel Blaik liked it so well that he asked Sid to join his staff and coach the offense for Army's team.

Coach Gillman accepted the invitation and became one of Colonel Blaik's assistants. In those days, Army was riding high, and this move was a major advancement for him. Upon Sid's arrival at West Point, Colonel Blaik suggested that he might bring one of his former young coaches to the academy to work with the plebe line. So Sid mailed me a letter written on a yellow legal pad. I'll never forget that letter. It read simply, "Mum's the word. Do you want to be the plebe coach at West Point?" Anne and I were all set to move to New York City, where I planned to attend medical school at Columbia University. We had already rented a room across the George Washington Bridge in Shanks Village. But when

I was offered the chance to join Colonel Blaik's staff at West Point, my medical career quickly went by the wayside.

Anne and I had made friends with a wonderful couple, Dick and Ginnie Henke. About the time I was torn between medical school and West Point, I ran into Dick down at the square, just below the old water tower in the middle of Oxford. After describing my dilemma, he replied, "Well, Paul, I'll tell you what I think. I don't know who can do more with young men than coaches. I've known lots of other people here, but if I ever knew anyone that I thought should be a coach, it's you!" After I'd thought long and hard about what Dick had said to me, Anne and I moved to West Point, where a very interesting and exciting part of our lives began to unfold.

## On to West Point

On my first visit to the United States Military Academy at West Point, Coach Gillman met me at the airport and drove immediately to the campus, where a parade was in progress. At West Point, military reviews and parades are held on most Saturdays during the school year, and these are open to the public. I was lodged at the Hotel Thayer, named after the father of the academy, Colonel Sylvanus Thayer. It is an old, established hotel overlooking the Hudson River and within a short walk of the parade grounds. At the Thayer, I was introduced to Colonel Biff Jones, who became a friend and mentor, and in a curious way, helped change the course of my life.

Later that day, I was escorted by Sid to the football office and had my first meeting with Colonel Blaik, and to my surprise, I was introduced once again to Biff Jones. After a while, I was invited to attend a parade being held to honor an army colonel who was retiring that day. His name just happened to be Biff Jones. So for the third time in as many hours, I was introduced to Colonel Jones. With a big smile, he asked, "Paul, are you getting tired of being introduced to me?" I smiled back and replied, "Not really, Sir!"

The Army football team had a good season that year. In addition to coaching the plebes, I was assigned to scout Navy and attended all their home games. Navy didn't win a single game that whole year, but going into the Army-Navy game, Army was undefeated. Obviously, Army was very heavily favored.

Navy had a fullback who hadn't played all season because of a lingering case of mononucleosis. Supposedly, he was very good, and by the time of the game against Army, he had regained his health and was ready to dress out and play against us. Another fine athlete in Navy's arsenal was a little scat back named Pete Williams. Unfortunately for Army, in the week prior to the big game, many of our players came down with the flu, and it was unclear to the coaching staff just how many of them could be counted on to play. On the opening play, the ball was pitched to Pete Williams, who veered to his outside, reversed field several times, and scored. He must have run four hundred yards to make that touchdown. Next came the turn of that fullback who hadn't played all year. We never managed to stop him. How do you defend against someone you've never seen in action? He played the game of his life that day; it was indeed a career game, a stellar performance. To our surprise and chagrin, the game ended in a 20–20 tie. Winless Navy had tied undefeated Army. Great for Navy, not good for us.

At the end of the season, Colonel Blaik called me in and said, "Paul, didn't you play basketball?" I said, "Yes, Sir, all the way through school, and I even played a little at Miami—not much to talk about, though." He said, "Good. Would you like to be the plebe basketball coach?" I accepted the offer and got to work with some really good talent on the plebe basketball team. There was a young man named Bailey who had a great two-handed set shot from the middle of the floor, and a big center named Ed Tixier. Each day, I would ask the varsity coach, Johnny Maurer, what his plans were for his practice session. Johnny always took time to show me the particular play he was going to put in. On one occasion, he introduced me to a set offense with two guards out in front. One guard sets the screen up, then moves around the screen and sets up another, then shoots. If the shot is unsuccessful, the ball is brought back and the entire process is repeated. This seemed like a play my plebes could run, so I put it in. We won eleven straight games before my "coaching" caught on and we started losing. But I soon found I really didn't like coaching basketball, because the coach has so little control over what takes place on the court.

It was during basketball season that Sid Gillman was offered the head coaching job at the University of Cincinnati. When Sid had been at Miami, his teams had consistently beaten Cincinnati. He took the job, then offered me a spot on his staff as defensive coach. As much as I enjoyed coaching for Colonel Blaik, I wanted to go with Sid.

I went in to talk with Colonel Blaik and told him I thought I'd like to go to Cincinnati with Sid. "Well, Paul, you don't need to go to Cincinnati with Sid," he said. "You're much better off right here. Why don't you stay here? I'd sure like to have you stay."

In retrospect, I think my response may have been a little insulting, though I didn't mean it to be. I said, "Coach Blaik, I have so much I need to learn from Sid." That was a pretty dumb thing to say, I know, but I went with Sid and became the Bearcats' defensive coordinator. I had been at Army in 1948. In 1949 and 1950, I was the defensive coach at the University of Cincinnati under Sid Gillman.

# The Cincinnati Bearcats

The two years at Cincinnati were good ones. I learned a lot as the Bearcats' defensive coordinator and gained a great deal of valuable experience. I recall a game with Kentucky when they had an outstanding quarterback, Babe Parilli. But Babe was not the only great player on that Kentucky team. The Wildcats had a pair of very fine ends and two All-Americans, Gene Donaldson at guard, and tackle Bob Cain. Kentucky was an all-around solid football team, and they drilled us; in fact, they drilled several other teams, too!

On another occasion, we traveled to California to play the College of the Pacific. They had a great line and three extremely fast running backs. Pacific's quarterback was Eddie LeBaron, who was a fine ball handler and was known to possess a very strong arm. On the very first play, LeBaron executed a double spin fake, hid the ball, and unleashed a long bomb for a touchdown. At one point, Pacific attempted to pound in a score from the one yard line. Twice, the fullback dived over the top and the ref signaled, "NO." On the third try, the ref took the ball from the fullback in the air and signaled "NO" again. After the players unpiled, he put the ball down, and amazingly, it was over the goal line and in the end zone. Strangest thing I had ever seen. We got stomped.

In those days, I was a big fan of the comic strip "Terry and the Pirates," drawn by Milt Caniff, who happened to be a Sigma Chi and an alumnus of the Ohio State University. The Burma-Chinese border area was the setting for the strip, which featured Chopstick Joe, the Dragon Lady, and of course, Terry. In one story, Chopstick Joe claimed that Chinese Bandits were the meanest, most vicious people in all the world. I liked that and thought I might use the idea to inspire my players. I cut the strip out of the newspaper and posted it on the team's bulletin board. At our next practice, I told the fellows, "From now on, we're going to play like Chinese Bandits!" So the Bearcat defense became college football's original Chinese Bandits. Little did I know that in another place at another time, a second team of Chinese Bandits would emerge and gain a measure of fame beyond anything I could have imagined.

After my second year at Cincinnati, I was greatly surprised to get a phone call from Bear Bryant, head football coach at the University of Kentucky. He asked if I would be interested in becoming an assistant of his. Since Kentucky was a member of the Southeastern Conference, the job would be quite a step up. Though I had been impressed with the quality of the Kentucky team, I found it hard to reach a decision. After a visit to Lexington, I told Coach Bryant that I could not leave Sid, and I turned down his offer.

I returned to Cincinnati, and after some agonizing reflection, I realized that my decision to remain with Sid and the Bearcats was a mistake.

University of Cincinnati football staff in 1949. Left to right: Paul F. Dietzel, Joe Madro, Sid Gillman, George Blackburn, Bill Schwartsberg.

I had been associated with Sid for quite a long time and felt that I needed a change. Bear Bryant was widely respected as an outstanding defensive coach, and defense was not one of Sid's strengths. I called Coach Bryant and said, "Coach, if you haven't filled that job, I've been thinking about it, and for a nickel, I'll take it." Coach Bryant retorted, "Hell, Paul, I've got ten cents! Come on down here."

This time as I walked through the door to his office, he waved a contract in his hand. The Bear greeted me with a terse "Here, sign the contract." He wasn't going to let me change my mind again. Hello, Wildcats!

## Two Years with the Bear

I was hired in 1951 by Coach Paul "Bear" Bryant as the offensive line coach at the University of Kentucky. Babe Parilli was still the Wildcat quarterback, so I knew we were going to have an outstanding passing attack. We had a big halfback from Elder High School in Cincinnati named Bob Fry. Bob was about six feet four, weighed 210 pounds, and could really run. He was a fantastic athlete. We decided to move him to offensive tackle. One day in the shower after practice, I remarked to my buddy

University of Kentucky football staff in 1951. Standing, left to right: Vic Bradford, Charles McClendon, Paul F. Dietzel, Jim Owens, Buckshot Underwood. Seated: Ermal Allen, Paul "Bear" Bryant, Carney Lasley.

Jim Owens, a former Oklahoma All-American and our end coach, "Boy, I wish I had more players like Bob Fry." From a nearby stall, Bear growled, "Hell, if I had more Bob Frys, I wouldn't need you!" Right!

While I was at Kentucky, we played in the Cotton Bowl against Texas Christian, coached by Dutch Myer, who ran the short punt formation, now called the shotgun. It was a wide-open attack. The Horned Frogs were a good football team, and I thought Coach Bryant did a spectacular job of defending against them. Since the closest back they had to the line of scrimmage was three yards deep, Bear just backed our defensive linemen off the line of scrimmage two or three yards and then dared them to run against us. Well, we won the game, and it was a great experience because the Cotton Bowl people were very hospitable. They even invited our coaching staff to go to the Varsity Club, a nightclub catering to the show business people and prominent folks in town. We went there for dinner and dancing. It was a very lovely place. We thanked them as we were leaving, and they said, "That's all right, just sign this." We thought that was the normal thing to do. We decided to play a joke on Bill McCubbin, one of our assistant coaches. I took some stationery from the Varsity

Club and had a letter typed up the next day that read: "Dear Coach Mc-Cubbin. We appreciate you coming to our club and we're so happy that you have taken advantage of our hospitality. I thought perhaps you'd like to keep your account up-to-date. Here is the bill for last night for $375.00. We do hope you will visit us again." We were all waiting in the lobby for McCubbin to get this note from the Varsity Club, and when he opened it, I thought he was going to faint. He said, "What's this? What's this!" And we said, "Well, you know, you signed the bill, and we really appreciate it." We let him sweat for quite a long time—and he really did sweat. Meanwhile, we were living in tall cotton. The team and coaches were housed at the brand new Shamrock Hotel, and it was fabulous. It was especially nice that we won the game.

Kentucky is known as the bourbon capital of America. Sometimes after work, the football staff would stop at a local tavern to sip a Bonded Beam or two, the drink of choice. Since I was new to the staff, I figured I ought to go with them. Anne soon put a stop to this. She always had a fine dinner ready and didn't want to wait around until I decided to come home.

No, she wouldn't put up with that, but she did put up with other things while we were at Kentucky. For instance, I was expected to use my own car when I went on recruiting trips for Coach Bryant. This meant that Anne would be left without a vehicle, since we owned only one. When I was away with the car, she would tirelessly pull our young son, Steve, to the grocery store in his little red wagon.

Our entire coaching staff attended the national coaches meeting, which was held that year in Cincinnati. J. T. Langley (one of the staff) and I wandered into a sporting goods hospitality room where they were serving free drinks and pretzels. The bartender asked me, "What'll you have?"

I wasn't fond of scotch, but I said, "A scotch and soda, please." I knew I could sip a scotch and soda all night long and toss it at the end of the evening because I really don't like scotch.

"Fine," said the bartender. "And what about you?" he asked, turning to J.T.

"Well, I don't know. Scotch, I guess," replied J.T.

"Anything in it?" the bartender asked.

"Oh, Coke, I guess," J.T. answered. Ugh! I've never heard of scotch and Coke before or since.

After Anne and I had been in Kentucky for about a year, we bought a very small house on Cardinal Lane. The living room was only large enough for Anne's grand piano and one chair. Every evening, I'd go down and work on the basement. I installed a nice asphalt block floor with a shuffleboard court inlaid in it. Then I built a false ceiling and a wood-paneled wall to block off the furnace and the washer and dryer. The basement had a solid concrete block wall at one end that I didn't know what to do with. J.T., who was a fine artist, suggested that we paint the wall so it looked like a wall was being built there by the Seven Dwarfs. He painted Sleepy dozing on the floor, Dopey dropping concrete off a trowel as he was hanging from a hook, and Grumpy frowning. It was fantastic—I wish I had taken pictures.

Coach Bryant and his wife, Mary Harmon, never hosted a staff party at their house so we always had staff parties at our little house, especially after we finished that neat rec room. At one of these, Coach Bryant was there but without Mary Harmon. We said that we were going to play charades. He didn't know about charades, so we explained it to him, and he really got into it. One charade he was acting out was "Fordyce on the Cotton Belt." (He was born near Fordyce, Arkansas, and played on the Fordyce High School football team.) We said, "That's not a book." But he said, "Oh, yeah, that's a book." Anyhow, that was a big laugh, and we had a great time.

On a recruiting trip with Charlie McClendon, one of Bear's graduate assistants, we spent an evening with a prospect and his parents up in northern Kentucky. When we left their home at about ten o'clock that night, we decided to drive over into Cincinnati to get something to eat. From Newport, we crossed over the bridge into Ohio. As we were going through an intersection, another vehicle ran the stop sign and plowed into us. It hit us so hard that the hood of my beautiful Pontiac Torpedo was ripped right off, and both of us were thrown out of the car. As our door flew off, I saw Mac tumbling end over end across the street, and I tumbled out right behind him. When the police finally arrived, they asked if I was by myself, and I said, "No, I was with Charlie McClendon." Meanwhile, Mac was in a daze and just walked off as they took me to the hospital. Mac came to, wandered back to the site of the wreck, and asked, "Where's Paul? Where's the guy that was in the car?" He was told I'd been taken to the hospital, but no one knew which one. Well, Mac finally found me. Had we not been in good physical shape, we would have been badly hurt. The next day, the Cincinnati newspaper stated that Kentucky assistant coach Paul Dietzel and a "companion" had had a bad accident. That took some explaining. The next morning, I called Anne, and she borrowed a car and came to get us. She had pillows in the backseat, and Mac and I sat there surrounded by those pillows. Every time we hit a small bump, we'd say, "Oh, no, don't hit another bump!" We were really sore and beaten up. That was one of the first of many memorable experiences Mac and I shared. We maintained a solid friendship in the years to come.

Handball at Kentucky was a murderous thing. The courts were really small, and the way we played, the object was to hit the other fellow in the back with the ball. When we got four guys on one of those small courts, it could be dangerous, but we had a great time. It was during those good times together that Mac and I decided that whoever got a head coaching job first would have to hire the other as his first assistant. That eventually came to pass much later on.

Coach Bryant assigned me to scout the University of Tennessee football team, coached by the renowned General Bob Neyland. Tennessee was our big rival, and Bear had never beaten them. As fine a record as Babe Parilli had in his four years at Kentucky, he never managed to throw a touchdown pass against the Volunteers. To help our defense prepare for Tennessee, I created a "Volunteer" team of some really good redshirts and other athletes who had transferred to Kentucky. I even ordered some orange jerseys with white numerals for them to wear at our practice sessions. During the last ten minutes of every practice, I'd have the "Tennessee" team run a series of single-wing plays (the single wing was the formation used by Tennessee). Our "Volunteers" developed into a pretty good-looking football team and really helped the Wildcats prepare for Tennessee's balanced-line, single-wing formation.

John Griggs was Kentucky's All-American linebacker; he was a fine young man and an outstanding football player. Coach Bryant decided to move him to defensive end and place him on the strong side of our line against the Vols' single wing. Tennessee ran many plays that looked very similar, a practice that helped confuse the opponent's defense. For example, they would snap the ball to the tailback, and the blocking back and fullback would start to the strong side; the guards would also pull. The first time someone would chop the defensive end, and the guards would pull around the chop. The next time, they would run at the defensive end and fake in his direction, but then the blocking back would block him out and they'd run off tackle. And they also had a running pass from that formation. For someone who had not played defensive end, it was extremely complicated. It was very difficult to determine which of these plays was coming at you. As carefully prepared as we had been by my "Tennessee" team, it was the first loss to a team that I had scouted. Tennessee really drilled us. It was a crushing blow because we hardly slowed them down. They were more difficult to defend against than any other team we had played. General Neyland was indeed an outstanding football coach.

After the game, all the coaches were gathered outside the shower room, contemplating what had happened. Coach Bryant asked each of us, "What do you think we did wrong?"

Each one answered, "Coach, I don't know."

Finally he came to me and said, "What do you think, Pablo?" (He called me Pablo because he said we couldn't have two Pauls on the same staff.)

I said, "Coach, maybe it was a mistake to move John Griggs from linebacker to defensive end."

He really blew up then and demanded, "Why in the hell didn't you say that before the game?"

And I said, "Coach, you just asked me what I thought, and I told you."

I figured I was gone, especially as I thought back to one of the first meetings I attended when I joined Bear's staff back in the spring. We were discussing how to block a certain sweep. Our end coach, Jim Owens, showed how they blocked it at Oklahoma. He had been an end. The end would drive into the defender and try to force him back as the play materialized. And Bear said, "Well, we could do that. But I think we should block it this way and force the end to the inside. What do you think, Pablo?"

I said, "I just don't agree."

He shouted, "WHAT?" and threw the chalk down. He always threw the chalk down when he got angry; most the time it would miss the chalkboard tray and splatter. Then he said, "What do you mean?"

And I said, "Well, we always hooked the end." Then I got up and demonstrated how we could hook the defensive end to force him out the back side. I explained that the other way, all you do is force him into the play. But the way Coach Owen suggested, by the time the ball carrier reaches the defensive end's position, the defender is chasing the play from the rear.

Then Coach Bryant said, "OK, we'll try it."

Just about then we took a break. In the restroom, backfield coach Ermel Allen told me, "Man, that was great."

I said, "What's that, Ermel?"

He said, "That's the first time anyone has ever disagreed with the Bear in a meeting." Bear was such a dominant person that most of his coaches were afraid to oppose him. I didn't know any better because when I coached for Sid Gillman, everyone had a chance to say what he thought. If we thought Sid was wrong, we'd say, "Sid, we don't agree with that." Sid would always listen to everyone. But after Bear's reaction to what I said about John Griggs following the Tennessee loss, I felt that I was gone. The Tennessee game was the last game of the year.

On Monday, Coach Bryant called me and said, "Come on down to my office." I *knew* I was gone then. Bear said, "Pablo, I want you to go down to the Sugar Bowl with me and scout Oklahoma."

I said, "Huh?"

He said, "Yeah."

"Gosh, Coach, we don't play them," I observed.

"We might play them later on," he explained, "and I'd like you to scout them."

So Bear, the governor, and I went to the Sugar Bowl. We had a great time, and Bear couldn't have been nicer. I guess it was his way of apologizing.

I really enjoyed my two years at Kentucky, and I learned a great deal. One thing I learned about Bear Bryant was that, with him, you better be on time. If there was a meeting with the squad at 6:00, the team and the staff would be seated five, ten, even fifteen minutes before 6:00, because everyone was afraid of being late. If any of the players arrived late, they never came in to the meeting. They just sat down on the floor outside the room, waiting to see what was going to happen to them. I really liked Coach Bryant.

In my second year as one of Bear's assistants, our preseason fall practices were held in the small town of Millersburg. We ate, practiced, and lived in a school there. This was one of the toughest preseason camps I had ever seen. Phil Cutchens was defensive backs coach. He didn't have very many players to work with, and the few he had were small. In a meeting one day, he said to Coach Bryant, "Coach, if I keep having these kids tackle each other, they're really great kids, but I don't know whether there will be anything left by the time we get ready for opening game." It was tough!

Years later, there was a movie called *The Junction Boys,* which was about Bear Bryant's infamous preseason camp at Junction, Texas. About half of Coach Bryant's Texas A&M squad never made it through the ordeal. It was one of the toughest camps anyone could imagine. My son, Steve, saw the movie on television and called me during a commercial and asked, "Dad, was it really that bad?" I told him, "Well, Steve, you know this is television, and they can't show it as bad as it really was—they had to clean it up a bit." Oddly enough, one of the Kentucky players who had been through preseason at Millersburg was quoted in a newspaper as saying, "That preseason camp at Junction City would look like a Girl Scout camp compared to what we had at Millersburg." I thought that was rich.

Coach Bryant was a real stickler for loyalty. At a Kentucky statewide coaches' meeting, he asked a high school assistant coach what offense they were running at his school. This fellow told him that they were still running the "same old offense," and even though he wanted to modernize the offense, the head coach was old-fashioned and would not change. Coach Bryant was quite disturbed, to say the least, that an assistant coach would speak this way in public about his head coach. The Bear told the man that he was going to get him fired, and indeed he did.

There was no love lost between Coach Bryant and Kentucky's fabled basketball coach Adolf Rupp. The Bear liked to tell the story—which was true—that when Rupp won a championship, he was given a new Cadillac, and when he won one, he was given a cigarette lighter.

Right after the 1952 season, I received a call from Colonel Blaik, asking me if I would like to come back to West Point to be his offensive line coach, the job that Sid Gillman had when he left Miami back in 1948. Of course I was really thrilled, but Colonel Blaik needed to know right then. Coach Bryant was out of town and I tried to find him to talk with him about it, but I couldn't locate him. Since Colonel Blaik needed an answer, I told him I would take the job. When I saw Bear a couple of days later, he said he didn't mind that I took the job, but he hated to read about it in the newspaper. I apologized and told him that I had made every attempt to contact him but had been unable to. I really don't know if he believed me or not. Either way, after two years at Kentucky with the Bear, I was on my way back to West Point.

## Back to the Academy

When I went to West Point as Colonel Blaik's line coach in 1953, it was immediately after the cribbing scandal (involving allegations about players cheating on tests); the academy had forced dozens of cadets to resign, and it had decimated the Army football team. All of those stars, all those great players—the entire A squad, as the varsity team was called at West Point was gone, and quite a few of the B squad, too. What we had left were walk-ons and the remaining B-squad players. We were starting over.

Vince Lombardi was the backfield coach. I really liked Vince. I've been asked many times since, "How does he compare with other coaches you have coached with? How does he compare with Sid Gillman, Red Blaik, and Paul Bryant?" And I would say, "Well, I'm not sure Vince is a better coach than any of them, because they were all top-notch coaches. But the one thing that's different about Vince is that I've never been around anyone as intense as he was."

There was a sergeant at West Point who made and sold steak cookers, which were actually little more than oil drums cut in half, with hinges attached so the contraption could be opened and closed and a grate inside that could be raised and lowered. But they made great grills. Vince had one, and he told me I had to get one. So I did, and he taught me how to

The Hudson River as seen from Trophy Point at West Point

grill a steak. I still like to do them the same way as he did. Of course he said the steak had to be at least two inches thick as a starting point. Then you put the steak right down in the fire, sear it well, raise it up, and cook it for about five minutes more on each side, which should make it about medium rare. Vince was exceptionally good at this.

During the 1953 football season, Colonel Blaik invited me to attend the New York Writers' Luncheon, which was held at Leone's restaurant each Monday. The restaurant was fantastic, and I got to know some wonderfully talented writers, including Til Ferdenzi, Allison Danzig, Tim Cohane, Red Smith, and Willard Mullin. They were a great bunch. Years later when I returned to West Point as head coach, they were among my best friends.

Those luncheons were almost always attended by one or two players of the New York Giants. Vince had left West Point and was now the offensive coach for the Giants. Early in the year, I asked the Giant players, "How do you guys like Vince Lombardi?" At first they'd hem and haw and wouldn't say much. Then they'd finally say he had to be the dumbest coach they'd ever been around. "He doesn't know anything. All he does is ask questions." One of the Giants' linemen said, "You know, I'm a guard, and Vince asked me, 'Do you shift your weight from one foot to the other foot when you know you are going to pull without tipping it off, and what is your first step?' He would ask us all these trivial questions." But as the season progressed, these same players said, "You know what? Vince used to ask a lot of questions, but he doesn't anymore. Now he tells us what to do." That's what Vince did. He would get all the information he could from the guys who were playing the game. He'd get it altogether in his mind, and then he would tell them what they were going to do from then on. He really absorbed a great deal of knowledge and added it to what he already had. I think the players were impressed by the fact that when he picked their brains, he was really figuring out what he wanted them to do.

My son, Steve, had been born at West Point Hospital on January 27, 1948, my first year as plebe coach, and now he was about five or six years old and going to preschool on the post at West Point, ready to start kindergarten. But by 1953, when our daughter, Kathie, was born, the army no longer allowed civilians the use of West Point Hospital, so we had to take Anne to the hospital at Cornwall on the Hudson. That involved a harrowing ride over the Old Storm King Mountain Highway in the middle of the night. Kathie was born at five o'clock in the morning and weighed nearly nine pounds.

Back in 1951, on my first tour of duty at West Point as line coach, we were assigned a house in the Army Athletic Association Circle, where most of the coaches lived. In this pleasant area of the post were 8 or 9 two-story, four-bedroom duplexes. There was a very nice play area for children and a little creek that flowed through the grounds. As we were

My son, Steve, at five and a
half years of age and daughter, Kathie, at ten months, May
1954

moving in, Anne asked me if I had met the guy next door. I said, "Yes,
that's Doc Blanchard." She replied, "Have you seen him? He's out there
unloading the car, and he's got on shorts. I have never seen anyone with
such big legs."

Well, Doc Blanchard did have a set of legs under him. Doc was my
next-door neighbor, and he had been hired to coach the plebes. As we were

getting ready to play Navy that year, we were still having a hard time rebuilding after that cribbing scandal. Navy, on the other hand, had a really good team that year. They were coached by Eddie Erdelatz and employed a five-three defense with the front five linemen stunting either left or right. Their stunt was really flat, so they would entertain the man they were lined up over and then would actually stunt into the man next to him. Basically, you couldn't get to their linebackers, who were making all the tackles. The rest of the Army staff was convinced that you couldn't run against them—it just seemed impossible. But in

Kathie at age three

studying Navy's films, I observed that their linemen would take the first step in their stunt or slant and, if the play was going the other way, would plant their feet and come right back out of the stunt. Our coaches thought that Navy had inside information on what we were planning to run against them, and with their speed, we'd be stopped cold. Well, I just knew there had to be a way to run on them. So I devised a zone blocking scheme in which the center and the right guard charge off to their right, shoulder to shoulder, and the right tackle and end then charge to their left, shoulder to shoulder, and create a funnel-like hole. If one of our linemen didn't make contact with one of their linemen, he would continue right on and block the linebacker. We had two running backs, Pat Eubell and Tommy Bell. They were both in the two-hundred-pound range, both straight-ahead runners, but very tough. All we did in that game was run right through the funnel created by our blocking scheme.

Steve at age seven

One of Doc Blanchard's favorite phrases was "Holy doodad." I've never known where he came up with that, but I decided to name this zone blocking scheme, "doodad blocking." We just handed the ball off on a dive to one of those two running backs, and he would squirt right through the hole that had been created. Navy couldn't take the ball away from us. We went up and down the field and beat them handily. I was so proud! The thing that made me most proud was that I was so thrilled for Colonel Blaik. He had stayed the course. He had vindicated himself. He never lost his desire to bring West Point back. When we beat Navy, it was the indicator that we had come back. I was proud of myself because I had invented something new that had never been thought of before. I felt that I had contributed something good to the game that I loved so dearly and that had given me my chance in life.

The next Monday, Colonel Blaik asked me to come to his office. The Colonel was at his desk with General MacArthur's picture hanging on the wall right behind him. Several of the young assistant coaches referred to him as "El Rojo Grande," The Big Red. El Rojo invited me in and said, "Well, Paul, since you're a line coach, I thought you might like to have this little book, written by Pot Graves, who was the Army line coach many, many years ago." I said, "Thank you, Sir." And I immediately wondered why he was giving me this. There was a paper clip about halfway back in the book, and so as I sat at my desk, I opened the book at the paper clip. There in detail was my "doodad blocking," diagramed many years ago by an Army line coach by the name of Pot Graves. I thought to myself, "Well, so much for something new in football." I learned a great lesson that day. There is nothing new in football, just a rehashing of things that have been done before. Zone blocking is now universally used by college and pro teams.

Each summer, before the start of football season, Colonel Blaik would invite the New York sportswriters to an area near West Point called Bull Pond for several days of recreation and relaxation. He called this the "Bull Pond Encampment." We fished, slept, drank and ate, and engaged in a flood of bull sessions, mostly about football.

Gene Leone of Leone's restaurant in the city owned a large piece of property adjacent to Bull Pond. His daughter had married a much-decorated army major, Tom Messero, who happened to be Army's B-squad football coach. Gene loved West Point and was a true and loyal friend to the coaching staff. There was always a special "Gene Leone Night" at Bull Pond. He entertained us lavishly with a seven-course dinner, complete with his finest crystal, candelabra, and silver. It was a wonderful affair, and one we greatly appreciated. We always knew we would see several Susan Hayward movies because Tim Cohane, the sports editor of *Look* magazine, was in love with Susan Hayward. We always enjoyed her movies. She was a beautiful woman. We always had good meals, but the night with Gene Leone was the high point. My time at Bull Pond with all those writers served me in great stead because later on, when I later became head coach at the academy, I already knew them all, and they were always very supportive of me.

Back at Kentucky, things had come to a head. Bear Bryant and Adolph Rupp were really not very close friends. After Kentucky had won the national championship in football, Leo Peterson, the head of the Associated Press, came to present the plaque to Bear Bryant and the team. It was to take place in the field house right before a Kentucky basketball game. Of course Adolph Rupp and Kentucky basketball were very, very big. A platform had been erected at the end of the arena, and the coaching staff, including Coach Bryant, athletics director Bernie Shively, and the captain of the team and I were sitting on the platform. Just as Mr. Peterson stood to make the presentation, the Kentucky basketball team came out for their pregame warm-up. When they did, the crowd erupted and totally washed out the presentation. That was a real slap in the face to Coach Bryant.

Once when I served as Coach Bryant's line coach, I returned from a recruiting trip to Pennsylvania, where I had collected a great deal of film and information on a number of prospective players. It was Saturday afternoon, and I was sitting in the office going through some of the film. Coach Rupp came by and stuck his head in the door and said with that Kansas twang of his, "Paul, what are you doing?"

I answered, "I've been on a recruiting trip, and I'm just going through some of the film to check on some of these athletes I've been studying."

He walked over to the window and looked out toward the bowling alley parking lot across from the field house, where our offices were located. He said, "Well, Bear's not even here."

And I said, "I know he's not here. I'm working for Bear, but I'm also working for myself, and I really need to do my job."

He said, "Well, Paul, that's very commendable, but I want to tell you something. If you fool around with turds, you're liable to come out smelling like a turd." That was crude, but that's what he said.

Back at West Point, the Navy game was history. I was working in my office one day when I got a call from Bernie Shively, the athletics director at Kentucky. He was a fine man, and he and his wife, Ruth, had been awfully nice to Anne and me. He said, "Paul, I can't tell you anything over the phone, but you know Coach Bryant has left and gone to Texas A&M, so get down here as fast as you can." I said, "Yes, Sir!" I knew what it meant. I was thrilled at the prospect of a job in Kentucky, as Anne and I loved Lexington. We had a lot of good friends there, and we had been hoping to go back someday. So Anne drove me to the airport at Newark. I took the red-eye special to Lexington and arrived there at about two o'clock in the morning. I went to the hotel but I couldn't sleep, so I sat around wide awake, then took a shower, shaved, and went out to the president's office on campus.

Bernie met me on the steps of the president's office and said, "Paul, I'm really sorry I'm going to disappoint you, but we've already hired a coach."

One of my favorite people in the coaching ranks was Paul Brown's assistant with the Cleveland Browns, Blanton Collier. I had spent a lot of time with Blanton, and he had taught me a lot of things. He had such a wonderful football mind. I said, "If it's anyone besides Blanton Collier, I'll be really unhappy. But if you hired Blanton, then all I can say is that you got yourself a really good man."

He said, "That's good of you to say because that's who it is."

Bernie explained that when he called me, Blanton had turned down the job. But Blanton's wife, who was from Paris, Kentucky, right down the road from Lexington, was very tired of the weather in Cleveland and had talked him into taking the job. So Blanton had called Bernie back that morning and said, "If you haven't hired someone, I'll take the job." Bernie said that Blanton had called him while I was flying down and had been given the job.

I don't know when I've ever been more disappointed about a job. To make matters worse, the other three varsity coaches on the Army staff got head coaching jobs elsewhere. I was the only one left. Bobby Dobbs took the job at Tulsa, George Blackburn took the job at Cincinnati, and Paul Amen took the job at Wake Forest.

Several years earlier, Charlie McClendon and I had made a pact that whoever got a head coaching job first would hire the other as first assistant. These three fellows had all gotten head coaching jobs and none of them had a staff, and I knew that I could get Mac on with any of them. At the time, he was an assistant coach at LSU, and I had learned that LSU had just fired its head football coach and its athletics director. I called Mac and said, "Listen, which one of these coaches would you like to work for?"

"Paul," he replied, "I'd like to stay here at LSU. Why don't you apply for the head job here?"

I said, "Mac, I don't know anything about LSU. I don't even know where LSU is."

"Well," he said, "it's a good job, but they aren't going to hire any of the present coaches."

Then he started naming all the members of the board of supervisors, none of whom I'd ever heard of. Finally he said, "If only you knew somebody who knows Biff Jones."

As a matter of fact, *I* knew Biff Jones. He had been the LSU coach when Huey Long was governor. Once at halftime during a big game, Long had shown up at the door of the dressing room with his body guards and told Herman Lang, the assistant trainer—a great fellow—that he wanted to talk to the team. Herman turned to Coach Jones and said, "Captain Jones, the governor's out here. He wants to talk to the team."

Biff shouted back, "Nobody talks to the team but me!"

Needless to say, the governor was not happy. Biff took out a match cover, wrote "I quit at the end of this game" on it, and signed it. When he went out for the warm up at the end of the half, he handed it to LSU's president and said, "I quit at the end of this game."

Huey came stomping over to the president and said, "I want that coach fired!" And the president replied, "I can't fire him. He already quit."

I had met Biff Jones three times at West Point back in 1948. When Biff retired, he moved to Washington, D.C., where Colonel Blaik had put him in charge of obtaining legislators' appointments for prospective West Point football players. After Sid Gillman bragged about my organizational ability in 1953, Colonel Blaik put me in charge of recruiting, so I was in constant contact with Biff over the telephone. Mac said, "Boy! If Biff Jones would recommend you—"

So I called and asked Biff about the LSU job, and Biff said, "Funny you should ask. The chairman of the board of supervisors, Lewis Gottlieb, called and asked if I would take the LSU coaching job. I told him absolutely not. He said, 'How would you like to become our athletics director?' I told him that I was retired and enjoyed being retired. Then Gottlieb asked me, 'Well, who can we get as coach?' And I said, 'Well, you might look into this young coach that Colonel Blaik has as an assistant, Paul Dietzel.'"

Then Biff said to me, "Act surprised when Buck Gladden calls you. He's chairman of the search committee. And by the way, when you look at Lewis Gottlieb, you're looking at seven votes on the board of supervisors."

Buck Gladden did call, and then I had to break the news to Colonel Blaik, just after he'd lost his other three varsity coaches. Unfortunately, Colonel Blaik was in bed with a throat infection, but this was not something that could wait. I went to his lovely home on Lusk Reservoir, where, as fate would have it, Anne and I were to live some years later. Colonel Blaik's sweet wife, Merle, led me into the bedroom. When I walked in, the Colonel, who was always way a step ahead of everyone, said, "Not you, too!"

I told him LSU had invited me down for an interview. Then he said, "You can't go. I need you. You're the only varsity coach left. You just can't go."

So I said, "OK, I'll tell them to withdraw my name."

But then the Colonel said, "Now, that's me talking to you as the AD and head coach. But now I'll tell you man to man. Go down, and if you can get that job, you take it." I have never forgotten that. I respected Colonel Blaik so very much, and his words meant a lot to me.

When Anne and I flew down to Baton Rouge, Charlie Mac picked us up at the airport. With him was Oliver P. Carriere, a judge from New Orleans who was on the board of supervisors. He got me in the backseat of the car and started interviewing both Anne and me. He asked Anne one question she didn't appreciate. "How many times have you been married?" he asked.

Anne exclaimed, "Are you kidding? One time—to Paul!"

The next day, I was to meet with LSU's board of supervisors. Charlie Mac prepped me and gave me all the information he had about the board members. General Troy H. Middleton was the very strong president of LSU, and he had called Coach Blaik to get a recommendation about me. The interview must have gone well. The board offered me the job at $12,500 a year, with no perks. I asked if the university could pay for our move, since I had been a poor assistant football coach for seven years. They said no but raised the salary to $13,000 to make up for it.

Next stop, LSU!

# IV
## Into the Tiger's Den

LSU's football program had languished for several years. At the time, Boxing was the big sport at LSU; the team was nationally recognized and had a colorful and very successful coach. It was decided that I would be introduced to the LSU "family" at a boxing match in the Cow Palace, the J. M. Parker Coliseum. The place was absolutely packed; I was stunned. I had never been associated in any way with an intercollegiate boxing program, and all this was very new to me. Blondie Bennett was the ring announcer. He was extremely exuberant as he announced the names of the boxers: Bobby Freeman, "Moo Moo" Chambray, Crowe Peele, and on and on. When I stepped into the ring to be introduced, the crowd went ballistic and cheered for a good five minutes. I was shocked, but gratified, too.

LSU football coaching staff of 1958. Kneeling, left to right: George Terry, Bill Peterson, Charles McClendon, Carl Maddox. Standing: Abner Wimberly, Raymond Didier, Pop Strange, Paul F. Dietzel.

I don't remember a word I said, but later one of the assistant coaches told me that I had said exactly what the crowd wanted to hear.

A month later, Jim Corbett was hired as LSU's athletics director. He had been a sports information director at Southeastern University in Hammond, Louisiana, and was working for NBC Sports in New York when he was hired by LSU. Jim Corbett was a fantastic talent and would eventually become a very close friend. Joe Kahill (a former sports information director at West Point who later assumed the same role for the New York Jets) had told Jim when he asked about me, "You'll like Paul Dietzel."

As it turned out, I was quite lucky—first of all, to have Jim Corbett as athletics director, and secondly, to inherit my predecessor's entire staff. All but one of my assistants were older than me. When I asked Charlie McClendon his opinion of the staff, without hesitation he said, "They're great. It's a great staff." Just as he and I had agreed, while we were Bear's assistants at Kentucky, Mac immediately became my first assistant. Everything was coming together. I was able to hire just one new coach. I selected my old buddy Bill Peterson. Bill had served as head coach at Mansfield High School back in Ohio and had won several state championships there. He became our offensive line coach. Bill and his wife, Marge, were close and loyal friends to Anne and me.

Dr. Marty Broussard, the fabulous LSU athletic trainer

The rest of the staff had all been extremely successful high school coaches. Carl Maddox coached the offensive backs, while George Terry was assigned to the defensive backs. Abner Wimberly was our end coach; Pop Strange coached the freshmen team. Our athletic trainer was Dr. Marty Broussard, who had been nicknamed the "Dour Cajun." Older players warned younger ones not to go into Doc's training room with a minor ailment; apparently, that was not a wise thing to do. Marty's training room was always immaculate, with clean starched sheets on all the tables, and he ran it with an iron hand. Herman Lang was his gem of an assistant, and at the time I was hired, had been at LSU for thirty-three years. Herman was a wonderful fellow, ever so loyal to the players, to LSU, and to me. The players and the staff loved him. After the games, he always came to our house to help Anne with the refreshments. In my first year there, I presented Herman with an LSU blazer with the number "33" imprinted boldly on it to honor his years of service.

The press faithfully showed up for our postgame functions, and it was always difficult to get them out of the house when the party ended. Because of LSU's night games, these get-togethers wouldn't get started until about ten o'clock; that made a short night of it because in the morning I was on duty as head usher at the University Methodist Church on campus. Dr. Bill Trice was the marvelous minister there, and he and his wife, Leora, were our next-door neighbors.

Troy H. Middleton was the President of LSU. An alumnus of Mississippi State University and a retired army general, he was a man with very strong beliefs and values. He had served under General George Patton, who once said of him, "Troy Middleton is the only general I've ever had who never made a mistake." More than once, General Middleton told LSU's board of supervisors that he didn't need to be president of LSU, and if they didn't like the job he was doing, they could hire someone else. I've been told he said it much more colorfully. With General Middleton, Jim Corbett, and a great staff, I was at the right place at the right time. I was indeed very fortunate.

I spoke at meetings all across the state, and I recruited, recruited, recruited. John David Crow was a Louisiana native and an outstanding football player, sought after by a number of colleges. I learned that he had just left the state in a brand-new Oldsmobile and was headed for Bear Bryant's Texas A&M Aggies. Coach Bryant was a very tough recruiter who did whatever it took to land players he wanted. Having been his line coach at Kentucky, and having recruited for him in Ohio and Pennsylvania, I knew how he recruited. We could not allow talented Louisiana athletes to leave the state, and that became my number-one recruiting priority. So I called Coach Bryant and told him that I was happy to be at LSU and looked forward to games we had scheduled with him. I also told him how much I appreciated all he had done for me and how much I had learned as a member of his staff. Then I said, "Coach Bryant, I don't really care what you and your staff do recruiting in Texas, Arkansas, or wherever. But in Louisiana, there are some things that you are doing that are not legal. I want you to know that in the future, if any of your coaches break the rules in Louisiana, I'm going to turn you in to the NCAA. Coach, I'm very fond of you and grateful that you treated me so well when I was on your staff, but if you continue to use that private airplane to haul Louisiana athletes and their parents to College Station, I will turn you in."

Coach Bryant protested, "Now, Pablo, you know me."

I said, "Yes coach, I do know you. I worked for you, remember? I have told all of my own coaches, 'If you cheat, you're fired!' I mean that. If they cheat, I'm going to fire them."

Herman Lang, revered long-time assistant athletic trainer

Then the Bear said, "Well, OK, Pablo." And we never lost another athlete to Texas A&M.

As I began my tenure as head coach, I made a number of changes. I had a stream of visitors, one of whom was a former high school star now on the LSU team. He informed me that he had come in for his money. I asked, "What are you talking about?"

He said, "I get forty dollars a month."

I said, "Where does that money come from?"

He said, "Right there from that lower drawer of that desk where you're sitting."

"Oh, I wondered what that was," I said. "I turned that into the treasurer because I didn't know what it was for. By the way, you can tell any of the other players who had such arrangements that those payments are over with. They're over with for you, too."

Unfortunately, he quit the squad, and so did a number of his teammates. I took over the job with slightly more than seventy players on scholarship; by the time fall preseason practice rolled around, the squad had shrunk to thirty-seven.

A new set of rules was set in place. Since a number of players were cutting classes, a class attendance system was inaugurated. Our guidance counselor created a card for professors to use to report the names of athletes who cut classes. Those who did were automatically enrolled in SSC-600, Supervised Stadium Climbing at six in the morning—all sixty-eight rows. A curfew was imposed and closely monitored, and facial hair and long sideburns were eliminated. Dining at Broussard Hall's training table was quite an incentive and a treat; those who broke the rules were denied this privilege. Ike Mayeaux, the athletic dormitory supervisor and food director, was a benevolent dictator. He would stand at the head of the chow line, snap his fingers, and exactly five players would enter the line. Not four, not six, but five. The food was fantastic, with steaks served at least three nights a week. We had several dorm monitors, one of whom was Boots Garland, who checked the players in at curfew. Years later, he confessed that from time to time he looked the other way when some of them snuck out after curfew to meet their girlfriends. Boots was a very popular fellow. When some of Ike's favorites were "taken off the table" for rules infractions, Ike would show up at their doors after hours with something for them to eat; he couldn't stand to see them go to bed hungry.

I had heard that in previous years there had been problems with the athletes and their automobiles. With the start of fall practice, all of the football players were required to park their vehicles under the stadium and surrender their keys to the staff. Nowadays, that would be a tough rule, but it was pretty tough back then, too.

That summer Anne and I were invited to a dinner party across the river at the home of Horace Wilkinson Sr., a true gentleman. Many prominent LSU supporters were also there, among them a well-known high school coach and a high school principal. After dinner, the ladies retired and I found myself backed up against the unlit fireplace and surrounded by more than a dozen Tiger boosters. They made no bones about asking how I planned to raise money to pay the athletes. I told them bluntly that I would never pay athletes to play football for LSU. They insisted I couldn't win at LSU without doing so. I replied bluntly, "If you think I'm going to pay my players, you've got the wrong coach!" With that, I stormed out.

My approach to life and to coaching has been molded by my association with some of the great football coaches of all time. In addition, I have always been vividly impressed by the words of General Douglas MacArthur that are emblazoned above the door of the gymnasium at the United States Military Academy:

> Upon the fields of friendly strife
> Are sown the seeds
> That upon other fields, on other days,
> Will bear the fruits of victory.

One army general stated while serving in Korea that the only problem with former athletes was that you had to hold them back by the shirttails, whereas some of the more academically inclined recruits were more interested in "correct procedures" when the situation called for leadership by action. General Douglas MacArthur also said that in football, a boy becomes a man by experiencing the exhilarating awareness of physical hardness.

It has been my experience that it takes courage to be an athlete. On an athletic field, each person is judged on personal merit rather than on social standing. On the football field, no one is rich and everyone is broke, and there is no "I" in team.

Reverend Pat Murphy was our army air corps chaplain when I was stationed on Tinian in the Marianas. He told me, "There is no one outside of a boy's father who can have as much influence on that boy as his coach." That places a great responsibility on every coach, and that's why I have always had a simple philosophy about coaching. A coach is responsible for training the most priceless possession that a mother and father will ever have, their son. So the coach must treat each player exactly as he would treat his own son. I have found that America's high school football coaches do just that, and in my regard, they are among the finest people in the world. I think it is very important for every coach to remember that he is a role model for young people. He should be cautious of the face he presents to the general public and should always be aware that the things he says will be believed and repeated over and over again.

Many people seem to question whether paying the price for anything is worthwhile. Many adults are poor examples who seem to try to do as little as possible and only what feels good. This tug-of-war that a boy's conscience undergoes, and the test of his sense of values is the subject of a little poem I wrote early in my coaching career. It emphasizes my philosophy. I call the poem simply "Sissy":

Is it a Sissy to be the first guy on the practice field?
Is it a Sissy to be the toughest tackler on the squad?
Is it a Sissy to knock your opponent on his butt, pick him up,
    and say, "Get braced, Buddy, 'cause that's how
    the *Chinese Bandits* do things!"
Is it a Sissy to say *no* when your buddies ask you to join them in
    abusing your body by dissipation,
And the only excuse that you can say is, "I don't think that'll help
    me to be a Champion"?
A Sissy to teach a Sunday School class like Jerry Stovall or a
    Sissy to believe in God?
Yes, it takes a real Sissy to be the toughest guy on the field,
    but not as *tough* in the classroom,
A Sissy to wear a *"man's haircut"* rather than a haircut that looks
    like a girl's?
A Sissy believes the *team* comes first before any personal
    glorification.
Only a Sissy has courage enough to be a member of the team
    rather than one of the creeps who every local
    bartender knows by his first name.
He's definitely a *Sissy* if he respects Mom and Dad and honors
    their wishes,
And he's not only a Sissy, but a stupid one too, if he "guts it out"
    rather than joining the *ever-growing ranks of quitters.*
And, of those who get to play, you'll note that the Sissy'll lay it on
    the line anytime the teams asks.
If that's being a Sissy, Thank God for Sissies.
I'm hunting for Sissies
Because Sissies are the timber from which
*Champions Are Fashioned!*

To be a successful head coach, a person must put together a great staff, pay them well and expect each one to pull his own weight. Whatever jobs are assigned, allow the staff to work out the details themselves; in other words, avoid micromanaging. Always insist on outstanding job performance, and give credit when credit is deserved. When a game is won, publicly give all the credit to the players and staff; when you lose a game, take the blame.

A head coach should do his best to make his assistants' wives and families part of the "team." Include them in get-togethers and other activities as often as possible. Their loyalty to the cause is imperative and invalu-

Longtime assistant Bill Shalosky and I in a staff meeting

able. In my opinion, *loyalty* is the most important word in the English language. It is a virtue beyond measure. As you expect loyalty from others, always remember that others expect loyalty from you. When I first arrived at LSU, I felt that to succeed in the tough Southeastern Conference, I needed to try to be another Bear Bryant. I soon learned that this would not work—it was not me. You just have to be yourself. If you are insincere, your players will know it.

It is best not to have volumes of rules, but the ones you have must be consistently and fairly enforced. If one of your down-the-line reserves breaks a serious rule, it might be a temptation to dismiss him. How-

My sweet daughter, Kathie,
with Girl Scout cookies

*Gleason Photography*

ever, if you do, and then a star breaks the same rule, he must also incur the same penalty.

Anne and I enjoyed our new home on Meadow Lea, a street that had just been completed. We were among the first families to build there. After our 1958 championship, a group of boosters headed by board chairman Lewis Gottlieb, had a swimming pool installed in our back yard. At the time, our daughter Kathie was about four years old. One day, Jake Staples, who was part owner of Bob and Jake's Steak House, came riding his horse out into our very quiet subdivision. Kathie was out front playing, and Jake stopped to say hello. He asked Kathie if she would like to ride the horse. Kathie, who had never been on a horse, said, "Yes, Sir." She told him that she could ride. When Anne looked out the window, there was Kathie riding this big horse by herself down the street.

Our house was next to a large undeveloped lot, and one day Kathie came in and told Anne there was a big worm out by the pool. Anne went out and, with a shovel, chopped the head off a water moccasin. Anne warned Kathie not to touch them because they would hurt her. She bought Kathie a little snake book that Kathie carried around for quite some time.

Behind our garage was a huge old oak tree in which I decided to build Steve and Kathie a tree house. One day while I was building it, I walked out to the tree to figure out what piece of lumber I would use next. Since it was extremely hot, I was in shorts and clogs. Just as I was ready to take another step, I heard a rattle. I was about to step right on a six-foot rattlesnake! He couldn't have bit me, though, because being scared silly, I jumped high in the air. Out with the shovel and off went its head, followed by a proper but secret burial.

In our garage, I installed a set of weights and created a training program for Steve and some of his neighborhood friends, Brent McCoy and Jimmy and Don Cast. I made a large chart with each of their names on it so I could keep a record of their progress. The kids loved it, and so did I.

Our first few months in Baton Rouge passed quickly. Soon football season was about to begin and the first game was just around the corner.

# Lean Years in Tigerland

LSU's opponent in the opening game of the 1955 football season was none other than the Wildcats of the University of Kentucky. After my great disappointment in missing out on the head coaching job at Kentucky, you can readily imagine my level of motivation in preparing the Tigers for that game. It was also Blanton Collier's first game as head coach at Kentucky.

In all my coaching years, I cannot remember ever being more ready for a game. I was charged up and so was the team. Joe May, a future track coach at LSU, returned a Wildcat kickoff for a touchdown. LSU won the game, but it was almost the only game we won that first year. After the game, the entire Kentucky staff, and Coach Adolph Rupp, the Wildcat's basketball coaching legend, came to our house for an after-game party. Of course, I knew everyone on Blanton's staff and had coached with them under Bear Bryant. One of my assistant coaches made the fatal error of telling a Kentucky coach that since the Wildcats had installed the professional approach to passing, Kentucky just wasn't very tough anymore. What a terrible mistake that comment turned out to be—in the ensuing years, they always gave us a physical beating. This is a good example of why an opponent should never be baited; doing so very often comes back to haunt you.

In my early, lean years at LSU

The win over Kentucky was exciting and fulfilling, but LSU won only two other games that season, finishing with three wins, five losses, and two ties. Another dismal year followed. Our record in 1956 was three wins and seven losses, followed by a break-even season in 1957, with five wins and five losses. In my first three years as LSU's head coach, the Tigers won only eleven games, lost seventeen, and were tied twice. During these bleak times, the team was blessed with some good athletes, but just not enough of them to compete in the toughest football conference in America. Although our players gave their best, our SEC opponents just outmanned us and wore us down, week after week. We simply lacked sufficient overall depth to win consistently.

In those days, LSU's traditional rival was Tulane's Green Wave, coached by Andy Pilney. But it was the game with Ole Miss in 1957 that would eventually lead to our emergence onto the national scene as a football power. The Rebels had an outstanding, homegrown coaching staff, headed by Johnny Vaught. They also had lots of fine, talented athletes. For example, Coach Vaught actually played three quarterbacks in most games. That year in Oxford, LSU led 12–7 at one point, but our first team was totally exhausted from playing every minute of the first half. In the third and fourth quarters, we were completely overcome and dominated by the sheer depth of the Rebel squad. The game ended in a heartbreaking 14–12 loss for LSU. But help was on the way.

The next week, as the team was returning from an away game, which we lost, our plane circled Tiger Stadium. From high above, we were pleased to see more than twenty thousand fans watching our freshman team win. In the winter of 1957 and the spring of 1958, I made a number of changes. First, I invited Milo Lude from the University of Delaware to campus to teach us the intricacies of his wing-T offense, which our staff then taught to our squad in spring practice. Secondly, I asked the head coach of the Iowa Hawkeyes, Forest Evashevski, to help out at our annual spring football clinic. Later, he was overheard commenting that he thought the Tigers were a "skinny, ragtag outfit." He was apparently less than impressed. That year, Forest's Iowa team was ranked in the nation's preseason top five. We, of course, were unranked.

Thinking back, I recall so many fine young men who gave absolutely everything our staff asked of them. Some of the names come flooding back: Joe Tuminello, Win Turner, Matt Burns, Bill Smith, Jimmy Taylor, Billy Cannon. Remembering all their names would be nearly impossible, and I'm certain I would overlook many deserving ones if I tried to do so. However, I must mention three more. Few athletes can measure up to Enos Parker, a talented tackle on one of my earlier teams. He also served as president of the LSU student body and led the campaign to raise money to purchase LSU's second Bengal tiger, Mike II. On that same squad was

President Richard M. Nixon with LSU president General Troy H. Middleton and his wife, Jerusha

a great fellow and fine athlete by the name of Earl Leggett, who in that era was considered huge at 260 pounds. Another Tiger, Bill Smith, was a great punter and as good an end as I've ever coached.

For three consecutive years, the LSU team had played hard but hadn't won with any consistency. These rebuilding years were not easy. I was not certain that I could weather the storm of complaints from disgruntled fans and alumni. Sometime during the 1957 season, I received a most memorable letter from a supportive leader of the university. It read: "Dear Paul, I've heard that there are some rumblings on Third Street." (The "Third Street quarterbacks" were the "experts" who called the plays on Monday that they think should have been called in Saturday night's game.) "I just want you to know," the letter continued, "that I like the way you are running our football program and I am running this University." The letter was signed, "Troy Middleton, President, LSU." That was a great boost to my morale, and I needed it.

By the opening of the 1958 football season, LSU had not experienced a winning season since 1953 and had not won a bowl game since 1944. But that was all about to change. The tide had turned, and the Tigers had finally come of age.

## The 1958 National Champions

The 1958 LSU football team would finish its season unbeaten and untied, the first Tiger team to claim such an achievement in fifty years and, so far, the last. The Tigers finished the season with a win over Clemson in the Sugar Bowl and were collegiate football's undisputed national champions. The 1958 Tigers were the last of the four unbeaten football teams with which I was to play a part.

In the months of planning and preparation prior to the season, the staff and I constantly discussed and evaluated strategies that would enable us to play more of our athletes. With some fine players returning and an outstanding freshman class moving up, we decided upon a unique system that we all felt would work. It took advantage of three facets of the game: the three allowed time-outs, the out-of-bounds punt, and the running of out-of-bounds plays. The result was the creation of LSU's revolutionary three platoon system.

Our eleven best athletes were called the "White Team," because they always wore white jerseys. This was our primary team playing both ways, on offense and on defense. In their practice sessions, half the time was spent on offense and the other half on defense. Next, the staff selected the remaining best offensive players. They were named the "Gold Team," because LSU's colors are purple and gold. However, the press quickly shortened the name to the "Go Team," and that name stuck. Finally, the de-

The White Team

The Go Team

fensive unit was chosen from the remainder of the squad. Quite naturally, I named this squad the "Chinese Bandits," as I had called my defensive unit when I coached for Sid Gillman at the University of Cincinnati.

I've always felt that it takes a certain type of athlete to excel on offense; I refer to these players as "square," and by that I mean solid. In addition, they must be highly intelligent to execute their many assignment changes while on the move. On the other hand, a defensive player has got to be "round," and by that I mean extremely aggressive—someone who plays with complete abandon.

Our strategy for each of the squads was simple. The White Team would play the first half of each quarter; then the Go Team and the Bandits could be platooned in the second half of each quarter. Therefore, all thirty-three members of the three platoons were going to play in every quarter of every game. Our scheme worked perfectly. During the 1958 season, the White Team averaged thirty-five minutes per game, while the Go Team and the Chinese Bandits split the other twenty-five minutes almost exactly between them. Our practice schedule generally worked like this: the White Team divided its time on offense and defense equally; the Go Team spent three-quarters of its time on offense, and actually had more offensive plays than the White Team; the Bandits spent at least 75 percent of its time on defense, and had very few offensive plays that it could run.

The Chinese Bandits

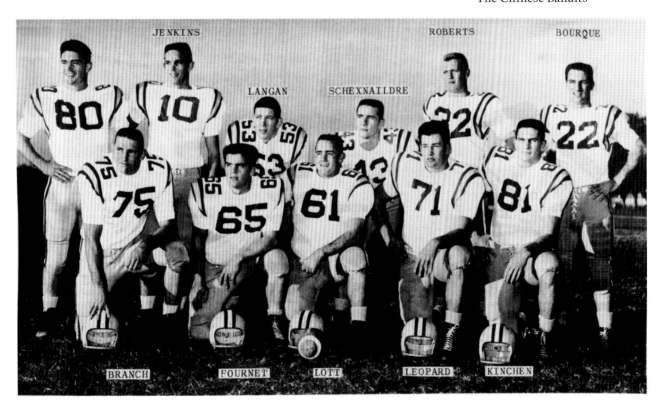

TV personalities and coaches prior to the LSU-Rice game in 1958. Standing, left to right: Lindsey Nelson, Red Grange, and NBC president Tom Gallery. Seated: Coach Jess Neely of Rice and Coach Paul F. Dietzel of LSU.

Amazingly, no player on the three teams weighed over 210 pounds, and the entire right side of the White starting line were all sophomores. Three-fourths of what was to become our starting backfield were born and raised in Baton Rouge: Billy Cannon of Istrouma High, Warren Rabb of Baton Rouge High, and Johnny Robinson of University High. That threesome lived in Baton Rouge and worked out most of the afternoons in the summer of 1958, polishing their ball handling for the intricacies of the wing-T that we had introduced during our spring practice. When fall practice began, Rabb, Robinson, and Cannon taught the rest of the squad how to run the wing-T.

The season opened on a miserable, humid, rainy night in Houston against the Rice Owls, who had regularly beaten us in past years. Some of the staff wondered if we should even try to use our new, intricate wing-T. But I remembered one of Sid Gillman's old sayings: "All weather is football weather!" We ran the wing-T and beat a good Rice team, 26–6. We didn't show everything and saved a few surprises for our next game, which was a very special game for me, when we traveled to Mobile to play Bear Bryant's first Alabama team.

Although the end zone bleachers collapsed at halftime, the game was most memorable for what happened on the field that day. Early in the game, Billy Cannon burst through a hole in the Tide's defense and ran over several Alabama players and a hapless official as well. He was finally collared near midfield. As he was trying to escape, the ball popped out and right into the hands of an Alabama player, who took off for our goal line. It was only through the tremendous efforts of Max Fugler and Dave McCarty that he was knocked out of bounds at the three yard line. The White Team had played halfway through the quarter, so I took a calculated risk and put in the Chinese Bandits. Alabama was in position to score, but the Bandits were fresh and eager. The Bandits held, and on fourth down Alabama was forced to kick a field goal from the three yard line. This fine defensive stand taught our staff a lesson and became the Bandits' cornerstone for the coming games. We beat Alabama, 13–3. After the game, the Bear was quoted as saying, "I've never seen a team with such raw speed. They just knocked our butts off!" Coach Bryant was absolutely right.

Our next game was back home in Tiger Stadium against Sammy Baugh and his passing circus from Hardin-Simmons University. They gave us a fit, but we eventually prevailed by a score of 20–6. The following week, we traveled to Florida to play the Hurricanes of Miami, a pretty good team. In that game the Tigers really came into their own. LSU won by forty points. On one particular play, I called a "counter-crisscross," a double reverse. Scooter Purvis, a member of the Go Team, reversed the field several times and scored a touchdown. He must have run ninety-five yards for that touchdown. It was a spectacular run by a great young athlete. Winning is always great, but when you win like that, it's even better!

I began to think that maybe we had a pretty darn good football team. The Miami game helped "make" the Chinese Bandits; you could feel their confidence and pride grow. It was in the game against Kentucky that they came into their own. Prior to the Kentucky game, Jack Sabin, owner of the Goal Post restaurant in Tiger Town, bought three thousand Chinese coolie hats from a supplier in New Orleans. He advertised that the first students who came to the restaurant would get a coolie hat. The Goal Post was swamped, and three thousand rabid LSU students showed up at game time proudly wearing those hats.

Had I planned the whole affair, or if we'd had a publicity agent in Hollywood fashion the script, it could not have been more spectacular. I had asked the public address announcer to introduce the Chinese Bandits when they first entered the game. Midway through the first quarter, when the Bandits replaced the White Team, the announcer proclaimed to the sixty-eight thousand fans, "Here come the Chinese Bandits!" At that moment, three thousand coolie hats appeared in the student section. On the first play from scrimmage, the Kentucky fullback was hit in mid-air as he dove over the pile on an off-tackle slant. The ball was knocked out of his hands, and Gus Kinchen, a Bandit end, recovered it. Since the Bandits did not have any offensive plays yet, Gus just downed the ball. As the Bandits returned to the bench, the announcer then proclaimed to the cheering throng, "And here come the Chinese Bandits right back." The ovation for the Bandits was deafening. From that moment on, the

The Chinese Bandits grounded the Hardin-Simmons Cowboys' aerial attack, and Durel Matherne scores from the four yard line.

Don Purvis scoots in for a spectacular score as the Tigers storm past the Miami Hurricanes.

Chinese Bandits were electrifying. The next Monday night, Tommy Lott, the 185-pound middle guard on the Bandit team, had been moved to the White Team because Ed McCreedy, the White Team guard, had suffered a slight injury. Tommy stopped me before practice and asked me whether this meant that he would not get to play with the Bandits anymore. I assured him that it was just a temporary move because McCreedy was in-

The masked Chinese
Bandits

jured and couldn't practice that night. Tommy said, "I'm sure glad, Coach, because I want to play with the Bandits."

A freshman lineman asked one of our coaches if he could try out for the Bandits in his sophomore year. One of the members of the Bandits asked me if it would be possible for them to wear a special kind of arm-band, or different kind of socks, to designate the fact that they were the Bandits. They got in the habit of coming to and from practice together, and eating together in the Broussard cafeteria. It was not in any way a joke, as there wasn't any joking about the Bandits. The fierce amount of pride they generated within themselves was almost unbelievable. It was hard for the coaching staff to understand how the Bandits could play so well. Individually they didn't seem good enough athletes to be capable of the outstanding play we were getting from them. Collectively, however, they were ferocious. They gang-tackled as if they had invented it. We graded each player on every play. When the ball carrier was down, any player who was not within a yard of him got zero on the play. We began to notice that on many occasions opponents' running backs took to the turf rather than face the onslaught of the Bandits' gang-tackling.

After the win over Kentucky, I received a long-distance call from Fred Huddleston, a popular Memphis disc jockey. Fred told me that he had written a chant for the Chinese Bandits and asked if I would like to use it. I said yes, and he mailed me a copy. I took the musical score to the LSU

Band Director, Mr. L. Bruce Jones, and he had his assistant Tom Tyra make an arrangement of it for the Tiger Band. At a pep rally before the Florida game, the student body learned to sing the chant. On the night of the Florida game, when the Bandits entered the fray, they were accompanied by the strains of "The Chinese Bandit Chant":

> Chinese Bandits on their way,
> Listen to what Confucius say:
> Chinese Bandits like to knock,
> Gonna stop a touchdown, chop, chop!

As the chant rocked Tiger Stadium, the Tigers socked Florida. Another win!

In our seventh game, we faced our old archrival that we had not beaten during my tenure at LSU. Both LSU and Ole Miss were undefeated. At game time, the Tigers were ranked number one nationally, and the Rebels were number six. It was the biggest game in the United States that week and was the first time in many years that two nationally ranked, unbeaten southern teams had played each other that late in the season. Tremendous tradition was involved on both sides, and tickets were at a premium.

This game went a little further in explaining why the Bandits had been so spectacular. As we graded the game films, we discovered that on each of the first six plays, we could count nine men who had made aggressive contact with the ball carrier before he was brought down. They weren't piling on or hitting after the whistle but swarming the ball carrier to bring him down. It was one of the greatest exhibits of pure desire that I ever witnessed in football. Time after time, all eleven Bandits would be in on the tackle. That's why coaching the Chinese Bandits was one of the greatest thrills I've ever had in sports.

Someone—I have no idea who—flew over the campus and dropped leaflets that said, "Go to Hell, LSU." We were getting a taste of our own medicine. Enthusiasm had really picked up in Tiger Town, and it was impossible to get a ticket. The level of excitement was at fever pitch. It was really fantastic. The action on the field in that game was as exciting as could be, despite the low score. Our two excellent quarterbacks both ran for touchdowns. Warren Rabb went in on a bootleg for the first, and Durel Matherne ran the same play for the second. During the game the Rebels were unable to complete a single pass. Our defensive effort was truly amazing. There was wild celebration in Tiger Town as we finally beat Ole Miss, 14–0. Ole Miss had not been shut out in its previous fifteen games.

Next, we played Duke in Tiger Stadium. Duke had a really fine football team and racked up eighteen points against us, the most anyone scored on us that year. (Incidentally, their quarterback, Bob Brodhead, became LSU's athletics director many years later.) Despite the Blue Devils'

The 1958 national champion-ship squad and staff

best efforts, we scored every way that it is possible to score. We blocked punts, we got a safety, we ran punts and kickoffs back for touchdowns, and we intercepted a pass for a touchdown. We ended up beating Duke 50–18. I felt bad that we had beaten them so soundly, because Bill Murray, their excellent coach, was a good friend of mine. It really wasn't a matter of trying to pour it on, though. They just made costly mistakes. The next morning, I went to the hotel where the Duke team was staying and tried to cheer them up at their breakfast, but I don't think I was very successful.

The following week we traveled to Mississippi State. I think there had been a high school football game in the stadium a couple of nights before under rainy conditions, and the field was torn up quite badly. The footing was terrible; we were ankle-deep in the mud. State had a big, strong team, and they were ready to slug it out with us, whereas our main strength was speed. We had a tough time trying to do anything. They had scouted us well. One of our key plays was the "218 counter," in which our great left tackle, Lynn "Blue" LeBlanc, would pull and trap the first defensive lineman past the center. Our fullback, Red Brodnax, would fill the hole where LeBlanc had pulled out. Then the ball would be handed off on a little cross-block to Billy Cannon. Every time we tried to run this play in the first half, State's defensive tackle would follow LeBlanc down the line and tackle Cannon before he could get started. This was one of our big plays, and it wasn't working at all. So at the half, I got Warren Rabb, the quarterback, and Red Brodnax, the fullback, and said, "Listen, we're going to call 218 counter. When you turn, Warren, hand the ball off to Red, and we'll just see whether we can get him squeezed out of there. Don't tell the rest of the team what you're doing." We ran it on the first play of the second half. Red broke for about thirty yards, and the next time we ran it, we got down very close to the goal line but then became stymied. On fourth down, Rabb rolled out on an option pass and hit Billy Hendrix, who made a spectacular catch. He just reached up with one hand, pulled the ball in, and then skidded across the end zone in the mud. That tied the score at 6–6. The Bulldogs had scored earlier but missed the extra point. When dependable Tommy Davis came in for us, though, he very calmly booted the ball right through the uprights. Tommy was the finest punter, field goal kicker, and kickoff specialist I have ever coached. LSU won the game, 7–6. It reminded me how lucky you have to be to have an undefeated season. Had we not made that extra point, we would not have had a perfect season. We were very happy with the win.

Then came our traditional game with arch rival Tulane to end the season. Tulane had had a good year but not one of their best. It's difficult to get ready for a team that you know you should beat, but we were helped by a comment from one of the Tulane players, Boo Mason, a younger brother of Tommy Mason. Tommy had been a halfback for Tulane and later played in the pros for quite a long time. Boo was a smaller version of his brother. He was a good halfback. He made a comment to one of the New Orleans writers, probably in jest, that LSU would choke and Tulane would win. As I always told our players, you can say something jokingly to the press, but when it comes out in print, there's no way to add the chuckle that goes with it. Anything you say is right there in black and white. I took that clipping and had it enlarged and reproduced. I had dozens printed so that each of our players would have one in his locker, and one was posted in front of every urinal and at every shower door. Our players got really tired of looking at that clipping all week.

It was a tight game in the first half, but in the third quarter, we broke loose. When our score reached into the thirties, I decided not to run it up on Andy Pilney. I told the White Team they had played enough and then started the Go Team in the fourth quarter. However, it didn't take them long to score. The Bandits then kicked off. According to the substitution rule in those days, a player could enter the game and come back out twice in each quarter. After coming out the second time, however, he couldn't reenter in that quarter. The Bandits almost immediately took the ball away from Tulane, and the Go Team had to go back in, since the Bandits were not prepared to run any offensive plays. The Go Team scored, but then the Bandits were ineligible to return to the game because of the substitution rule. Defense is not the Go Team's game; in fact, they had hardly ever lined up on defense. So, late in the fourth quarter, the only good option was to send in the White Team. We became trapped by our own substitution plan. Our travel squad was composed of thirty-four players—three teams and one kicker. When the White Team went back into the game, I told them not to score. I said, "Just run dives." I should have said, "Run dives and fall down." But Rabb handed the ball off to Cannon, and he scored a touchdown. Wham, just like that! It was embarrassing. We won the game, 62–0. Of course, the Tulane fans were very upset and thought that we had run up the score intentionally. The following Monday, I had to speak to the New Orleans Quarterback Club. I apologized to Andy and attempted to explain what had happened. The Tulane fans did not buy the explanation. They were mad, and frankly, I could understand why.

After the regular season ended, we prepared for the Sugar Bowl. During one practice session, we ran our third-down passing drill. In this drill, our three teams competed against each other. The drill was done at full speed. This was the only time that we had a full-speed drill in preparation for a bowl game. The drill was intended to approximate game conditions as closely as possible. Each team was given the same number of opportunities to play on defense against the other two teams. The teams were scored when they were on defense, and the team with the winning score got to go to the showers immediately after the drill. The team in second place had to run around the field three times, and the losing team had to run to the top of the stadium, sixty-eight steps. Avoiding a run to the top of the stadium is pretty good incentive, but when you have good teams in competition, their pride is also at stake. I'm a great believer in pride.

The manager kept score on a big blackboard with each team's colors: white, gold, and red. The chains were marked for third down and five. The defense was scored as follows:

1. Pass not thrown
   Run for less than 5 yards         0
   Run for 5 yards or more          +1
2. Pass thrown
   Incomplete                        0
   Complete less than 5 yards       +1
   Complete for 5 yards or more     +1
   Complete for TD                  +2
   Intercepted                      −2
   Fumble                           −2

Obviously, the team with the lowest score is the winner. We began this drill that particular night by putting the Go Team on defense first. Their score after ten attempts against them was five. The Go Team usually spent very little time on defense, so the score was to be expected. The

White Team was on defense next, and after ten attempts their score was a minus three. This is a good score, indicative that they were doing a fine job. Then it was time for the Chinese Bandits to take their turn. Melvin Branch, an outstanding Bandit end, wrapped himself around the quarterback's neck so many times that the quarterback thought they were roommates. The drill got a little rough, and frankly, there was a bit more contact than I'd intended. After eight attempts, the Bandits already had a score of minus six and had won without using the rest of their attempts. So I told them, "You guys go on in before you hurt someone." The true significance of this drill was that the team that had started the season more or less as our third team had just won the day. Physically, they had demonstrated that they were better than a match for our other two teams combined against them. They had been stronger and actually superior in that particular drill. The White Team was totally embarrassed, and as a consequence, many challenges were made. I was standing at the goal post when players of the White Team, who came in second, were circling the field three times. Every time they ran by, the Bandits were waiting and taunting, "Now don't worry about it—you're getting better. Don't let it get you down!" The White Team was getting madder and madder. I can remember Billy Cannon and Johnny Robinson saying, "Coach, we're gonna have this drill again tomorrow night, aren't we?" I'm not very smart, but I'm not that dumb. We would have left it all on the practice field. That's why there was a sign over the gate to our practice field that read, "Proving Grounds."

We were invited to meet Clemson in the Sugar Bowl. They had lost only to Georgia Tech and South Carolina during the season. Although they were an excellent football team, the national press joked that the nation's number-one team was playing "lowly" Clemson. Members of the press constantly asked Clemson coach Frank Howard, "What do you think you're going to do against the Chinese Bandits?" He said in his drawl, "Well, I got a bunch of one-armed bandits on my team. We'll make chop suey out of those Chinese Bandits. They've got this little tackle, Bo Strange, who is listed at about 195 pounds." What Coach Howard didn't know was that Bo was very strong, very quick, very smart, and very fast. During the game, their big tackles, who weighed 240, would knock Bo off the line of scrimmage, but before the ball carrier could get there, he'd recover and make the tackle for no gain. Bo was an excellent football player.

In the first quarter, Warren Rabb broke his hand and had to leave the game. He said "Coach, I don't know—I can't grip the ball." So Durel Matherne had to play on both the Go Team and the White Team. All year Durel had been handing the ball to Donnie Daye and Scooter Purvis, who, if you average their height, would be about five feet five inches, and that's being generous. Durel was not used to handing the ball off to Billy Cannon at six feet two inches or Johnny Robinson at six feet one

The Associated Press presents the national championship trophy in 1958.

inch. The first two or three times he handed the ball off, he hit them right in the knee, at the height where he was used to holding the ball for Daye and Purvis. It was my fault, not Durel's. We lost the ball on fumbles several times. Besides, our team had never been really interested in playing Clemson. We finally ended up winning the game 7–0. I was just happy the game was over and most of the team was coming back the next year.

After the game, I walked out into the deserted stadium. I waited until everyone had left. My biggest fan, my rock, was still waiting for me, as she always was. I remarked to her almost prophetically, "Anne, if you take all of the plaudits, save all of the clippings saying how great I am, and put them in a box, and then take out one clipping every time someone says or prints something derogatory about me, at the end of my career, the box will be empty." That turned out to be so very true.

In the Sugar Bowl game, the Bandits did their share again. Although our opponents scoffed at them, it was the Bandits who took the ball away from Clemson in the clutch. Our opponents in the 1958 season averaged 2.87 yards per carry against the Bandits, whereas the White Team allowed 3.4 yards per attempt that year. How the Bandits accomplished what they did, I do not know. Only the facts remain. They were a rare group of young men who played like champions throughout the season. They were a great pleasure to coach because of their tremendous enthusiasm. I shall never forget them.

A marvelous thing took place at our football banquet. Red Brodnax was picked as the most valuable player. Red was such a fine, tough football player yet so humble. He was durable—a great blocker and a fine runner. He had given up being a running back for the good of the team when

Above: Anne in 1958. Right: I receive the Coach of the Year award.

he was moved to fullback, more of a blocking position. But he never complained, and I was so pleased when he received the award.

The season ended with national recognition and many honors for the Tigers. Billy Cannon, Johnny Robinson, and Warren Rabb were all named First Team All-Southeastern Conference. I don't think that three players from a single team had ever achieved that in one season before. A fine bunch of young men and a great team had brought the SEC championship and the national championship to LSU. I find it almost unbelievable that, even after a half century, the names of those three platoons are as familiar today to Tiger football enthusiasts as they were in 1958—the White Team, the Go Team, and the never to be forgotten Chinese Bandits.

I was greatly honored by being named National Coach of the Year. At the time, I was the youngest coach ever to receive this award, which was made by the widest margin of votes ever recorded.

## Another Winning Season

My tenure as LSU's head football coach was to continue for three more very exciting years. The 1959 season turned out to be somewhat of a repeat of the championship year. We began ranked number one nationally, and since most of the previous years' players were returning, expectations ran high. The press kept us constantly in the national eye with our photos in newspapers and magazines, along with an overdose of unrealistic media hype. This constant stream of publicity had a bit of a negative effect on the players. In grading our 1959 weekly game film, I detected that the White Team was not covering kickoffs with as much zeal and all-out abandon as they had the year before.

The Kentucky game loomed, and I asked Bill Peterson, our line coach, to set up two projectors in our meeting room. One projector would feature the kickoff coverage of the '58 team against Miami, while the other featured the kickoff coverage of the '59 team against the same opponent, whom we had played just prior to the Kentucky game. As usual, the play-

With All-American Billy Cannon in 1959

ers arrived on time for our Friday night meeting. They sat and waited silently, sensing something in the air. Pete cranked up both projectors simultaneously with images of both teams side by side on the screen. All present were quite shocked. The 1958 White Team covered the kickoff like a mob of mad men, while the '59 White Team seemed content to allow teammates to make the tackle. This was a vivid lesson to the team, to the coaches, and especially to me. We managed to beat Kentucky again that year, 9–0.

There wasn't any question about the Ole Miss game being a big one, because the Rebels were again undefeated. They were ranked number three, and we were number one. We were in effect playing for the national championship again. Tiger Stadium was predicted to have the first sellout in the history of the 67,500-seat stadium (the official attendance was actually 67,325, the closest we had come to a sellout in the expanded stadium). In an attempt to keep preparation for the game as normal as possible, I was determined to maintain our regular weekly schedule. Getting ready for the really big games is easy, because the players are highly motivated by what they read in the papers and hear on radio and TV. Ole Miss helped us out on Thursday before the game by dropping "Go to Hell, LSU!" leaflets on the Ole War Skule campus. Players and students alike were infuriated. It was a first in the history of LSU football when three thousand of our students marched on the practice field to cheer our team.

On the night before all home games, I invited the visiting teams' coaches to a steak dinner at the famed Bob and Jake's Steak House. Since all of our assistant coaches were out scouting high school games, I found myself hosting Ole Miss coach Johnny Vaught and several of his assistants alone. Earlier in the day, the Ole Miss team was having its walk-through practice on the field where the PMAC is now located. The stadium field had already been painted in preparation for the game, and we would not allow them to practice on it. However, LSU students had discovered that the Old Miss team was practicing, and they had surrounded the field, shouting, "Go to Hell, Ole Miss, Go to Hell!" and "We're Number One!" When the Ole Miss assistant coach who had supervised their practice came into Bob and Jake's, he was steaming mad! When we asked him what was wrong, he growled through clenched teeth, "Well, I thought we were ready before, but now, after the taunts of the LSU students, I am positive. Our team is livid." Hearing that, I thought to myself that those students had unknowingly given the Rebels a real battle cry. I had learned long before that you don't taunt an opponent. But the deed had been done, so the Tigers would just have to get fired up, too!

That night after our team movie (which happened to be *Kiss Me Deadly*, selected by the senior film committee), we had our usual Hershey bar treat, took our team walk, and then returned to Broussard Hall. After I got home, at 2:00 A.M. our bedside phone rang. It was the LSU switchboard operator, who asked Anne to put Coach on the phone. The operator was very agitated and pleaded with me, "Coach, you've got to come to campus right away and settle down a mob of rowdy students. There are hundreds of them chanting, 'Go to Hell, Ole Miss, Go to Hell!' No one else can handle them. You've got to come over here and quieten 'em down." So I dressed and, equipped with my bullhorn, drove to the practice field.

The operator was right. There were hundreds of boisterous students proudly vocalizing their support of the Tigers. When I showed up, they gave me a cheer and shouted even louder. Finally, I was able to settle them down a bit and said, "You know, I just put your team to bed a couple of hours ago." Another cheer. "Let me tell you what I told them before I sent them in." An even louder cheer. I said, "Just try to remember how hard it has been to get where we are now. Every team we play would like nothing better than to knock us off."

"No! No!" they shouted.

And I added, "No team wants to beat us more than Ole Miss. They remember what happened to them last year."

"Yea! Go to Hell, Ole Miss! Go to Hell!" they chanted.

I continued, "You know how much we depend on your cheering us on."

Another chorus of "Yea! Yea! Go to Hell, Ole Miss!"

"But," I said, "Don't wear yourselves out tonight—or this morning." Laughter. "Save your voices for the game! Besides, right now we are only a short block from Broussard Hall, where the team is in bed and asleep, I hope. Do you think they can rest with all this noise and bedlam? So I ask you to go back to your rooms and get some sleep so that you can be stoked up for the game. Your team will need you tomorrow night, and the team needs to be rested and ready for the Rebels. Goodnight!" They quietly left the field and I was able to return home. I didn't get much rest the remainder of that night, but I hadn't been able to sleep anyway.

I didn't feel it was necessary to say much to the team before the game. The heat and humidity that night were stifling, and atmosphere in the chute leading into Tiger Stadium was absolutely electric.

The Tigers were indeed fired up for the game. In fact they were so fired up that they fumbled four times early in the game. The Rebels' Bob Khayat came in and kicked a field goal. (Bob Khayat is now the chancellor of Ole Miss.) That field goal held up for a long time. Coach Vaught had decided that the best way to beat LSU was to let the Tigers have the football. He had great confidence in his fine defensive team and decided to give the ball to LSU and allow us to fumble some more. So they started punting the ball back to us on first down. We'd punt it to them and they'd punt it right back. Finally, on a third and seventeen on the Ole Miss forty-two, the Rebels punted to Cannon, who was standing on his own five yard line. The ball traveled forty-seven yards in the air. It took a high bounce, and Billy was eyeing it. We had a rule that you don't handle a punt inside the fifteen yard line. When Billy took the ball at the eleven, I shouted, "No, no, no!" But as Billy started up the field, I started yelling, "Go, go, go!" It was one of the greatest efforts in the history of college football. As local sportswriter Dan Hardesty described it, "Cannon grabbed the ball and crossed the eleven yard line and started an incredible, absolutely unbelievable run to glory. First one Rebel and then another tackled Cannon, sometimes singly, sometimes two or three grasping at him simultaneously. He ran over them, through them, around them, or outran them. Those he could not elude, his teammates removed from his path. Total bedlam erupted in Tiger Stadium."

But the excitement was not over, as ten minutes remained on the clock. The Rebels took the ensuing kickoff and pounded it down the field toward the LSU goal for nine minutes and forty-two seconds. Vaught had used quarterbacks Gibbs, Franklin, and Brewer. Now Doug Elmore took over. Elmore's run on a keeper was stopped by the fine White Team linebacker Donny Daye at the LSU two yard line. Then Rebel Jim Anderson hit right guard for no gain.

It was fourth and goal from the two—win or lose on one play!

Elmore took the ball on "student body left," and as he tried to cut toward the goal line, Ed McCreedy got to him and slowed his momentum, which allowed Warren Rabb to make a head-on tackle, and in came Billy Cannon to finish off Elmore at the Tiger one. The goal line was one yard away, and now it was LSU's ball. During the week of this monumental game, Walter Stewart of the *Memphis Commercial Appeal* had written: "Both teams are very fast, very talented and will probably nullify each other. But somewhere during the game, a great athlete will make the difference." Walter Stewart had called the shot before it happened.

With only eighteen seconds remaining, the students and fans were delirious. We lined up, ran a quarterback sneak, and the clock ran out. The score was LSU 7, Ole Miss 3. Thousands of spectators stood in stunned disbelief. No one left the stadium. Several people were reported to have suffered heart attacks. The players were exhausted—they had literally "left it on the field." Everyone was completely mesmerized. Fred Russell, that wonderful, talented writer from the *Nashville Banner*, said in his postgame write-up, "This is the fullest and finest football game I've ever witnessed in my thirty-one years of reporting." The LSU fans were beside themselves. To this day, Cannon's punt return is broadcast over and over again before every Ole Miss game.

The Tigers had bested a fine Ole Miss team and defended their number-one ranking. But danger lurked in our next game, which would be in Knoxville against a strong Tennessee Volunteer team. They were coached by Bowden Wyatt and came into the game with a 4–1–1 record. The weather in Knoxville was very different from that in Baton Rouge—we went from a hot, humid night in Louisiana for the last game to a bitterly

Billy Cannon's famous run

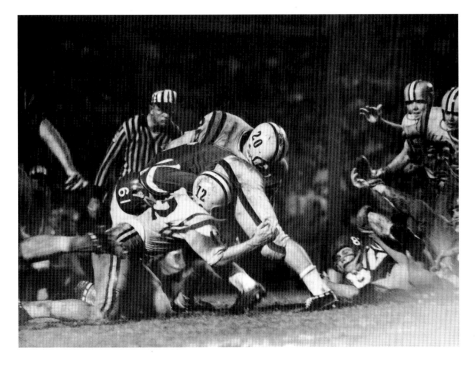

Warren Rabb and Billy Cannon stop Doug Elmore one yard from the goal line.

*Photo by Jim Pitts*

Billy Cannon accepts the Heisman Trophy with his father and his coach.

cold afternoon in Tennessee for this one. Our staff scoured the town for long underwear and long socks for the players; both items were somewhat new to us as game apparel. Bandit cornerback Andy Bourgeois said he felt like a professional wearing those long socks. We played a fine game, gaining 335 yards and allowing Tennessee only 112. However, their linebacker, Cartwright, intercepted two of our passes, one of which was returned for a touchdown. Scoring again after an LSU fumble, Tennessee led 14–7. Although we had a measure of success with the rollout pass to our fullback, we had gone to the well too often. Yet we finally scored again, making it a one-point game, 14–13.

Some might say that the thing to do so late in the game would be to kick the extra point to tie and hope to get down to their goal line one more time. But I felt differently. Being ranked number one nationally, I didn't feel that we should settle for a tie. We went for it. We ran our best back on our best play for two points: Billy Cannon ran off tackle to the right side. But Tennessee was ready for that play and stopped Cannon right at the goal line. Billy insists that he made it into the end zone, but the head linesman ruled otherwise. And that was how the game ended: Tennessee 14, LSU 13. Our long winning streak had come to an end and, with it, our first-place national ranking.

It was difficult for all of us to take that loss the way champions should, but our team did. After showering and dressing, the players and coaches and I boarded our bus and waited for the trainers and stragglers to get on.

Then, an amazing thing happened. Tennessee's athletics director and legendary former coach, General Bob Neyland, stepped onto the bus and asked if he could address the team. I replied, "Sure, Coach, absolutely." He then told the players, "Men, I just wanted to tell you that you are the finest-coached and best football team that's ever played on this field." With that, General Neyland turned and stepped off the bus. For a moment we remained in silence. I cannot adequately describe how much his comments meant to me.

When our airplane arrived back in Baton Rouge, we had a tough time landing because the airport and runways were packed with LSU fans who had come out to cheer us and show their support. That was very special and greatly appreciated by players and coaches alike.

At the end of the season, the Sugar Bowl Committee "double banked" us. They invited Ole Miss to the bowl and then publicly announced that they were daring LSU to accept the challenge and replay the Rebels. The players and coaches all wanted to go to a different bowl, but because of tremendous political pressure, LSU accepted the challenge to play Ole Miss in the Sugar Bowl. An old saying among coaches is "Never replay a team you've already beaten in the same year." That adage would be drummed into my mind forever. I would never allow myself to repeat that mistake again.

Our team was not easily motivated for the game. Why should they be, since they had already beaten the Rebels? I don't think our players ever developed a real interest in the game. Making matters worse, our fine right halfback Wendell Harris was out of the game, Johnny Robinson had broken his hand in practice, and Warren Rabb was in poor shape.

The Sugar Bowl was a sellout, and Ole Miss really came to play—after all, they had something to prove. The Rebels were determined to redeem themselves, and they certainly did. We were beaten convincingly.

From the beginning, I felt that it was a mistake to replay Ole Miss. As it turned out, agreeing to play in the Sugar Bowl was a serious failure on my part. But I also thought it was wrong for some folks at LSU to insist that we play in that game. We quickly found out that we were not ready to face Ole Miss again, but they were more than ready for us. It was a sour note to end a fine year. When all was said and done, LSU concluded its 1959 season ranked number four. Rebuilding time had arrived again.

## My Final Years as LSU's Head Coach

Many of the talented players from the 1958 and 1959 squads had graduated. The time had come to retool. In preparing for the 1960 season, our staff and I decided, for the good of the team, to switch several key players from their former positions to different and unfamiliar ones. It made little sense to have both Wendell Harris and Jerry Stovall line up at left halfback. Both of these young men were outstanding athletes and fine running backs. Both, by the way, were also class acts. Wendell was left-handed, so to execute the running pass, it was practical for him to be at right halfback. I discussed this change with him at great length, and he agreed that moving to right halfback would be best for him and for our team. Although somewhat reluctant at first, Wendell grasped the idea, and after quite a bit of hard work and effort, developed into a "natural" right halfback. Jerry Stovall remained as our primary left halfback. Jimmy Field, a former high school halfback, was switched to quarterback. It took Jimmy a bit of time to get a feel for the new position, but he eventually developed into an outstanding quarterback. He was a very talented athlete and a team leader. With these and a few other changes in our lineup, we were ready for another year.

We played Texas A&M and beat them 9–0, followed by a win over Baylor, then a tough game against Ole Miss, which ended in a tie—though I really felt that we had lost that game. The next week we played South Carolina, and Lynn Amedee came into his own as the Go Team quarterback. Lynn was an excellent passer and threw for three touchdowns against the Gamecocks. The Go Team also had two other outstanding backs, Charley Cranford at fullback and Donnie Daye at right halfback. The left halfback slot was manned by a wonderful, slashing running back, Bo Campbell, who has always been a winner. We then beat Mississippi State 7–3, Wake Forest 16–0, and Tulane 17–6. Even though we had not had a spectacular year defensively, we allowed only fifty points our en-

Outstanding halfback Bo Campbell dives for another hard-fought touchdown.

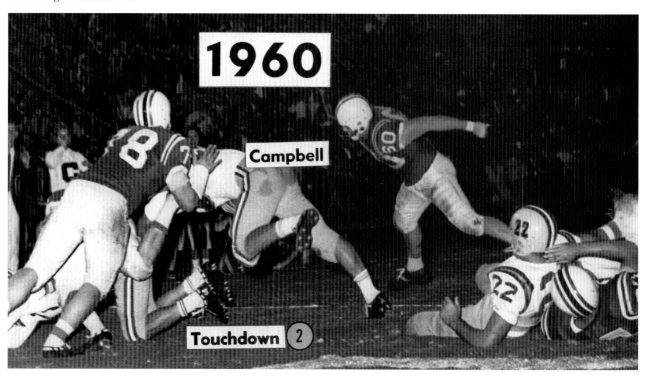

tire season, which was quite remarkable. Our 1960 squad was another outstanding team.

As 1961 rolled around, many of our best players from the 1960 season returned. All in all, I really think that this squad was the deepest and strongest of any in my tenure as head coach at LSU. Our team had matured, and we were ready for the opening game against Rice. At least we thought we were ready. We lost the game because we were not in sync as a team. It wasn't the players fault, it was mine. I felt that I had done a poor job preparing the team to face the Owls. But when someone asked me about it afterwards, I said, "We've lost the battle, but we haven't lost the war."

The next week we beat Georgia Tech 10–0, and Bobby Dodd, their remarkable coach for many years, was quoted as saying, "LSU is the toughest place to play." Then he was asked, "What about South Bend?" And he said, "It's harder to play at LSU than South Bend." He concluded by adding, "I've never seen a team better prepared."

The LSU fans were constantly on my case because when we were backed up behind our fifteen yard line, we would always punt on third down. The fans always wanted to go for it. Every time we lined up to punt, the fans would protest. But punting on third down was good football because of the kind of defense we had.

Interviewed by Bill Stern of Mutual Radio.

We played position football. Late in the Georgia Tech game a key play occurred that would prove that point. Tech was backed up deep in its own territory, and Bobby Dodd, who also usually punted on third down near his own goal line, waited until fourth down to kick. I think Bobby did it to needle me. But their fine punter dropped the snap. We recovered, took the ball in to score, and ended up beating them 10–0.

During my tenure as LSU's head football coach, I participated in a weekly television sports talk show, the *Monday Night Quarterback Club.* The program featured two popular local personalities, Bud Montet and John Ferguson. John was our announcer on the LSU radio network, and Bud was the sports editor for the *Baton Rouge Morning Advocate.* People would call in with questions, and then John and Bud would fire these questions at me and I would answer them as best I could. In the beginning of the show after the Georgia Tech game, I said, "Now I think that all of you folks understand why we kick on third down when we're backed up. I believe Bobby Dodd taught us a really good lesson, don't you agree?"

Most people didn't know that I had a secret weapon on the *Quarterback Club.* It so happened that Anne's mother, Mrs. Wilson, lived with us at the time (actually, she lived with us for twenty-five years). "Nannie" was a loving, wonderful woman and a fine cook who baked the best apple pie you ever put in your mouth. I never knew what else we were going to have for dinner, but we would always have a pie and I loved them.

Getting back to the *Monday Night Quarterback Club,* though: if anything controversial happened during the game on the previous Saturday, I made sure a question would be asked about it on the program. My purpose was simple: to answer in a positive and honest manner any questions that might arise over a controversial strategy or decision. To get exactly the question I wanted asked, I would have one sent in from Ethel Wirtz, which was Nannie's maiden name. I didn't use the name Wilson on the air because someone might catch on. In would come this question from Nannie, and Bud or John would say, "We have a question from Ethel

On NBC's *Today* show in 1962. Left: Dave Garroway. Right: Jack Lascoulli.

Wirtz. She wants to know . . ." Then I would explain what I was thinking and would usually end up saying something like, "Well, it didn't particularly work, and if I had it to do over again, I wouldn't do the same thing. But at the time, it seemed the right thing to do." In this way, I tried to eliminate controversy harmful to the success of our football program. The television show became a positive tool that I used to the advantage of LSU football.

When the time came for us to play our archrival, Ole Miss, once again, the Rebels fielded a big, tough team. During the season, they had outscored their opponents 240 points to a mere 13. When the Ole Miss team arrived on campus, hundreds of LSU students surrounded their buses and greeted them with the traditional, "Go to Hell, Ole Miss! Go to Hell!" The Rebel players fumed but were helpless to retaliate. That night, our staff had Johnny Vaught and his staff out to Bob and Jake's for a grand steak dinner with all the trimmings.

Once again, after the students' taunting, the Rebels were very ready, but so were we. We won the game, 10–7. Wendell Harris scored all ten points. Bill Truax, who is about six feet six, kept one of our drives alive by catching a pass that was down at his ankles. After we beat Ole Miss that night we were ranked fourth in the nation. I thought we had about as good a team as I'd ever been associated with. Afterwards I was quoted as saying, "I hope the '58 and '59 teams will forgive me, but this has to be one of the greatest victories I've ever experienced."

We wrapped up our regular season in 1961 with wins over Mississippi State and Tulane. Once again we were the Southeastern Conference champions, and as in 1958, I was named the Southeastern Conference Coach of the Year.

As conference champions we were invited to play the University of Colorado in the Orange Bowl. There were a number of black athletes on the Colorado squad, and since LSU was not allowed to compete against teams with black players, the university's board of supervisors was forced to draft new rules allowing us to accept the Orange Bowl bid.

I've often pondered what the administrators, students, and fans of those venerable southern universities and colleges of the 1950s and 1960s would have thought of the racial mix of athletic teams just a few decades later. Many would have been astonished. I know that I would have been. There were no black athletes on my football teams at LSU during my tenure there as head coach, nor had I encountered any black athletes in my earlier years as an assistant coach at Cincinnati, Kentucky, or West Point. After the war, when Anne and I returned to Miami University in Oxford, Ohio, there was only one black football player on the entire squad, a substitute halfback by the name of Bill Harris, who was quite a fine fellow. When the process of desegregating college athletics began in the 1960s, few could imagine how it would unfold. By the time I became athletics director at Indiana University and then at LSU, black athletes were very much a part of both schools' many fine teams. Black athletes have come into their own, and collegiate athletics are better for it. We've come a long way.

## Army Beckons

LSU's opponent in the 1962 Orange Bowl, the University of Colorado, was a very fine football team, coached by Sonny Grandelius, who had enjoyed a heck of a career.

As we were preparing for that game, Army fired head coach Dale Hall. Since I had coached at West Point on two occasions, once as plebe coach and once as line coach, the academy's athletics director called and asked if I would be interested in the job. When Colonel Blaik retired several years before, I never remotely considered applying for the position, because you never want to follow a legend, and Colonel Blaik was definitely a legend. Red Blaik was an outstanding coach who'd had a remarkable run at Army. Besides, Army had never hired a head football coach who was not an alumnus of the institution. It was usually someone who was in the army and stationed at the academy who was chosen to coach the football team. When the athletics director called me, I pointed out that I was not a graduate of West Point. He said they had decided to go in a different direction. So I asked him to let me think about it.

We had a great football team at LSU in 1961, and many players were going to be coming back, so I would be leaving LSU with an excellent program in place. I called the West Point athletics director back the next day and asked, "Who's on your short list? Who are you interested in talking with?"

He said, "We've got it down to three. They are Murray Warmath, who has just been named the Coach of the Year at Minnesota, where he had a national championship team; Vince Lombardi, who is assistant coach for the New York Giants; and you." I said, "Well, that's a very heady group. I'm quite honored to be in the company of those two fellows, but if LSU finds out that I'm even thinking of another job, they'll probably fire me." I had been offered quite a few jobs in previous years. When you're a winner, everyone wants to hire you, and I had a very strong winning record.

I immediately spoke with Jim Corbett, our athletics director, and said, "Jim, Army has asked me to apply for the head coaching job, and I've told them that I can't be a candidate if I'm just one of several prospects on their list. But if they would really like to hire me, then I'd like to talk with them."

And Corbett said, "You know you've got a long contract here, Paul."

"I know that, Jim," I said, "and if this is going to be a major problem, or if LSU will not release me, I'll just tell West Point right now that I'm not interested in the job."

Jim Corbett and I celebrating the 1962 Orange Bowl bid

And he said, "What would it take to keep you here?"

I replied, "If I stay at LSU, I do not want a raise in salary." At the time, I was making $18,000 a year. "I don't want people to think they had to buy me to get me to stay. It really doesn't have anything to do with money at this point. The academy won't pay me any more than I'm making here. But if LSU will not release me, I'll just tell them to take my name out of the hat."

He said, "No, if you want to go, there's no way we would want you to stay. It wouldn't be good for either of us." So I talked with the Army officials, superintendent General William Westmoreland, and athletics director Colonel Hank Adams.

The week before the Orange Bowl, Notre Dame had fired its young coach, Terry Brennan. Just after that was announced an Associated Press writer asked if I would give him an interview about "preparing for a bowl game." I told him I'd give him one hour, before I went to practice. At the end of the interview, as he turned to walk out the door, he asked, "Wasn't it strange that Notre Dame fired Terry Brennan?"

I said, "That's very sad. That sure won't help Notre Dame's image."

He agreed, and I went to practice. When I got home, Anne said, "Call AP right away. They have called four or five times." I called, and they wanted me to elaborate on my "blast" at Notre Dame. There was never any mention of the one-hour interview.

Although I had been offered other head coaching jobs, I was never interested in any of them because I felt that I had the best job in the country. In one particular interview, I had stated, "I'll never leave LSU." Later, I certainly regretted saying that, but at the time, I was young and meant it. Those last four seasons at LSU were awfully good years because we didn't lose many games—our record in those years was thirty-five wins, seven losses, and one tie.

As we prepared to face Colorado in the Orange Bowl, the rumors were flying. Colorado was a very good team, and they arrived in Miami a few days before we did. They made it known that they were not worried about that little scrawny southern football team from LSU. Compared to Colorado, we were rather small. The Buffaloes were a big, fine-looking football team. Coach Sonny Grandelius had got together some awfully good recruits.

Some interesting things happened before the game. One night, our entire staff attended an Orange Bowl party at a Miami yacht club. Sitting across from us was Arnold Palmer and his wife, Winnie. I was so pleased to have a chance to talk with "Arnie." He wanted to talk about football, but I wanted to talk about golf. We really hit it off. We had an interesting conversation, and he was one of the nicest people I'd ever talked with. He was down to earth. I had always admired him, but now I really liked him. He wished us good luck.

When you're on the road preparing for a bowl game, you try to find things to do with your team to keep them occupied and out of trouble. We decided to take the players to a different restaurant each day for lunch. One place I remember well was called King Arthur's Court. It happened to be where Eastern Airlines housed and trained their stewardesses. I always tried not to dine with the players, because they don't eat their food—they inhale it. If I tried to keep up with them, I would surely have round-the-clock indigestion, so I always ate before or after them. At any rate, getting ready for a big game seldom engenders a healthy appetite.

As soon as some of the players finished their meal, they went outside. Since there were so many hostesses in the vicinity, I decided I would go out with the players just to make sure that no one got "lost." Our team was wearing their neat purple LSU sports coats with a Tiger emblem on the pocket. While we are standing outside talking, Arnold Palmer came in the other door of the restaurant. Seeing our players, he asked, "Aren't you members of the LSU team?"

"Yes, Sir, Mr. Palmer," they said.

Then he said, "Where's Paul?"

Our team manager, Greg Guirard, came running outside and said, "Coach, Arnold Palmer is in here and he's asking for you."

I went back inside and greeted Arnie. "Arnold, great to see you," I said. "What are you doing out here?"

He told me he'd come by for lunch and then remarked, "Boy, you sure have a good-looking bunch of men."

And I said, "Thank you. Would you like to say something to the team?"

He said, "Sure." So he offered them a few well-chosen words.

As we walked outside together, I told Arnie, "You have just made my day! My players now think that I know Arnold Palmer!"

He said, "Well, you do."

I said, "Well, you just made me into a big wheel." That was one of the good things that happened before the game.

Some of the comments in the Miami newspapers prior to the game really belittled LSU. Several of Colorado's star players were quoted as saying that they were not used to playing teams with such small players. They acted as if it would not be much of a game for them, since we were not nearly as strong as most of the teams they had played and beaten during the year. But the day before the game, the headline in the Miami newspaper read: "Coach to Give Team a Goodbye Win." It was really a shock to our players.

We always entertained the team with a movie on nights before games. Our "movie committee" of seniors always selected what we would see. I saw *Patton* and *Butch Cassidy and the Sundance Kid* so many times that I could just about quote the dialog. About halfway through the movie, there was always a break during which we would give the players a Hershey bar. As soon as the projector was turned off, the players would start chanting, "Her-shey! Her-shey! Her-shey!" When the movie was over, we always had cookies and milk in their rooms for them before they went to sleep.

But this night was unusual because of the newspaper article, and I decided to do what I always did with my players—tell them the truth. I said, "Fellas, you all read the newspaper article about whether Paul Dietzel is going to take the job at West Point or not. I just wanted to tell you that I don't want that to have anything to do with your attitude. Whether I stay at LSU or whether I go to Army is of no consequence. Just remember all those hours of practice that you've put in, and all the preparation for the football season in the heat and humidity of the summer. Think of all of the summer letters we sent you telling you what you should be doing each week in your workouts. Think back to all the times you felt you were about to die during two-a-days. You just can't throw all that away. This game is about you, it's not about Paul Dietzel. It's about you and LSU. We've had a great year, and we have to cap it off with a win in the Orange Bowl. This Colorado team has taken us very lightly. They think we're just poor, skinny southern wimps and that they are the big bruisers from the Big Eight. I want you to realize how much you've put into this, what a fine record we've had. This game is for you, not for anyone else—you and LSU. You'll remember it for the rest of your lives!"

That night when we got back to the hotel, as Anne and I were walking across the lobby, we met LSU president Middleton and his wife, Jerusha.

They had been extremely nice to Anne and me. He said, "Paul, I want to talk to you. How about coming up to our room."

I thought, "Uh-oh." So we went up to his room, and General Middleton said, "Paul, I hear you're thinking about West Point."

I said, "Well, General Middleton, yes, they've offered me the head coaching job."

Then he asked, "Paul, why haven't you come to talk to me?"

I answered, "General, I was getting ready for a bowl game, but that's not an excuse. I talked with Jim Corbett, and I presumed that he had spoken with you about it."

General Middleton then said, "Paul, you know Jerusha and I are very fond of you and Anne, and you have done a superior job here at LSU. We appreciate that, and we don't want to lose you. However, the Army football team is the mirror of the United States Army. West Point has got to have a good football program. They did have a fine one, but in the last few years, it has suffered a great deal. If they want you at West Point, you have got to go!" What a wonderful statement from a splendid man. I've never forgotten that, and if I had any doubt at all, that was the deciding factor. I made up my mind I was going to West Point. Having been there two other times, and since West Point was my very first job right out of college, I had a very warm spot in my heart for the academy.

The next day, we beat the stew out of Colorado. They had an All-Amer-

A sweet victory ride on the shoulders of Dennis Gaubitz and star quarterback Jimmy Field after winning the 1962 Orange Bowl.

ican defensive guard who lined up against our center, and he would play like a linebacker. He would run from side to side in the direction the play was to go. So instead of firing out and missing this quick fellow, we had our center, Dennis Gaubitz, set there as if he were preparing for a pass, and whichever direction the middle guard would go, Dennis would pull behind the line and meet him at the hole. He was not accustomed to having someone spotlighting him like that. During the season, he had made lots of tackles, but I don't believe he made a single one against us. The Colorado players found out that size isn't everything. We were so much faster than they were that we ran circles around them. The final score was LSU 25, Colorado 7—a very fulfilling victory for us. I was thrilled that we had won the game, especially since I knew it would be my last time to coach the Tigers. I would leave Baton Rouge with a heavy heart knowing how much I would miss LSU, my players, and the many wonderful friends Anne and I had made.

## A Coach's Wife and Family

As wife of LSU's head football coach, Anne experienced her fair share of traumatic incidents. One I recall quite vividly occurred at a game we were playing against Vanderbilt in Nashville. The Tigers weren't doing very well. Anne was in the stands sitting by Nell Rabenhorst, wife of Harry Rabenhorst, LSU's assistant athletics director and former very successful basketball coach. Seated immediately behind the two ladies was a man who repeatedly shouted, "That stupid Dietzel!" This guy was probably an LSU fan, but I have never been absolutely sure of that. In any case, he obviously believed that when a team doesn't play well, it's always the head coach's fault. The man's outbursts continued and were spiced up with a touch of vulgarity. Somehow he learned that Anne was my wife, and then he poured it on: "What a stupid call! Dietzel is an imbecile!" Worse still, he began to poke Anne in the back. This guy was making a complete nuisance of himself, and finally Nell turned around, and in her tiny southern voice threatened, "Mista, if you punch Mrs. Dietzel one more time, I'm going to smack you with my umbrella." And you know what? The fellow stopped.

As I came out of the dressing room after the game, I was told that this fellow had been harassing Anne, and I didn't like that at all. In fact it made me very angry. I can understand someone harassing me, but I don't want anyone harassing my sweet wife. So I went hunting. I said, "Where is that guy that was being ugly to my wife?" Athletics Director Jim Corbett grabbed me by the arm and said, "Paul, forget it. I've already taken care of him." I don't know what he had done, but Jim had a pretty good temper so I assume he had a few words with the guy.

As coach at LSU, I received two tickets to all the games, so when Anne wanted to take Kathie, Steve would go to the game with our good friends Jo and Karl Cast. At that time, LSU had a family plan, and for ten dollars you could sit with your whole family in the end zone. The Casts had two fine boys, Don and Jim, and they would take Steve along to the game with them. During the 1959 Ole Miss game when we were behind 3–0, Steve turned to Karl, white-faced, and asked, "Will my daddy get fired if he doesn't win this game?" What a terrible thing for my son to think and worry about.

The seats for LSU's president and other dignitaries were on the fifty yard line in little boxes on the sideline at field level. This is actually the worst place in the whole stadium from which to see a football game. Anne's seats were also near the fifty yard line, immediately behind the team. Whenever the team would stand up, spectators seated behind them had to stand, too, or miss much of the action on the field. To eliminate this problem, I had the players' bench built into a trench. Thereafter, when the players would stand, the fans behind them could remain seated with full view of the action on the field. Then I had the benches painted so that each of the three teams sat in designated places according to their assigned colors—white for the White Team, gold for the Go Team, and red for the Bandits. Each player's position was lettered on the bench. I explained that I wanted them to remain seated and in their designated places so I could find them if I needed to send someone in. I didn't want to have to search all over for them. I would always know exactly where they were. When they went in the game, they always went in as teams. When they came back out, they sat down in their places on the bench, which was now several feet below ground level.

From time to time, a coach's wife is subjected to situations ranging from the unpleasant to the ugly. One day, a lady came up to Anne in the grocery store and said, "Aren't you Anne Dietzel?"

Anne said, "Yes, I am."

Then the woman said, "Oh, I just wanted to tell you how terribly sad we are to hear that you and your husband are not getting along and that you are getting a divorce."

Of course Anne said, "That's the craziest thing I ever heard of, and it's not true!"

We were playing Kentucky that week, and Anne had told me about the conversation. So at game's end, I took Anne's hand and we walked together across the field to shake hands with Blanton Collier, Kentucky's coach and a good friend of ours. Since this was an unusual thing for us to do, there was a picture in Sunday's paper showing Anne and me walking across the field, hand in hand, to shake hands with Blanton. We were determined to put that rumor to rest because it was the most nonsensical thing we had ever heard.

I recall a very funny story about a coach's wife who was asked if in all the years of their marriage, she had ever considered divorce. She answered,

"No. Murder yes, but divorce never." And that's the way we laughingly put this thing off. I truly believe that most people don't realize how difficult it is to be the wife of a coach, especially a head coach.

I have been very fortunate and blessed to have had Anne as my wife. She has been a perfect coach's wife.

# Record as LSU's Head Football Coach
# 1955–1961

Rebuilding years
1955–1957
11 wins, 17 losses, 2 ties

National championship year and beyond
1958–1961
35 wins, 7 losses, 1 tie

Southeastern Conference championship
1958 and 1961

Southeastern Conference Coach of the Year
1958 and 1961

National championship
1958

National Coach of the Year
1958
(awarded by the widest margin of votes ever recorded,
and awarded to the youngest coach so honored)

Bowl games:
1959 Sugar Bowl
defeated Clemson, 7–0

1960 Sugar Bowl
lost to Ole Miss, 21–0

1962 Orange Bowl
defeated Colorado, 25–7

# V
# Return to the Point

We prepared to leave Baton Rouge and move to West Point to take the coaching position at the academy. It was difficult to leave because we had some great friends in Baton Rouge. Some of our dearest friends gave us a going-away party. The party was planned by Ruth and Chuck McCoy, our neighbors from down the street. Their children played with our children; they are just wonderful people and have remained great friends through the years. Others there were Luther and Marjorie Jordan, Bill Hughes, Jo and Karl Cast, and Bill and Jane LeBlanc. There were also about a dozen others who were among our best friends. Someone had made a mule with ears and a tail that moved at the same time. It was about five feet long and about three feet high, and I carried that thing around for years until it finally fell apart. On the blanket you place over the mule before putting on the saddle was a big *A* for Army on a gray background. Underneath, it read: "FROM COONASS TO MULE ASS." It was a wonderful going-away party. It truly was hard for Anne and me to leave LSU and so many of our dear friends.

We moved into Colonel Blaik's former home at West Point, which he had designed himself. It was a very nice big house, three stories in fact, and near Lusk Reservoir, a beautiful setting with a great view. It was a lovely home with a fine back yard. The Army Athletic Association, a private organization that supports the academy's athletic program and is financed primarily by gate receipts from the football program, had begun some minor renovations to the house, which were completed soon after we moved in.

I found the football offices to be in a rather

From the *Dallas Times Herald:* "The Army Wants You."

sorry state. Before accepting the job, I had asked General Westmoreland if the offices could be renovated. He agreed that they would be, but after several weeks, nothing had been done. In a meeting with the general, I reminded him of his promise. That was on a Friday, and early Monday morning, a bevy of workers and several army officers showed up and work on the offices began in earnest. Soon the offices were beautifully transformed.

Before the renovations began, our wonderful secretary, Harriet Demarest, who had been there for many years, had to shout for the coaches to come to the phone, since their offices were across the hall. She had interesting names she would call out, like "Georgy Porgy" for George Terry. For me, she called "Coachy Woachy," which I told her would just not work. She really was a wonderful lady.

Anne and I were invited to the superintendent's home to celebrate my birthday. The entire coaching staff and their wives were invited, along with the athletics director, the chief of staff, the dean of academics, the commandant of cadets, and all of their wives. We were on pins and needles and not really sure how to act. The general's wife, Kitsy, was a beautiful woman, very friendly and very nice. She stood in front of the grand piano, welcomed us, and said, "Happy birthday to you, Paul. I hope that you will be successful and happy here at West Point." Then she looked directly at me and said, "There's one thing you'll need to understand right from the very beginning." And with that, she turned around and flipped up her skirt to reveal a pair of black panties with "BEAT NAVY!" printed in bright gold letters across the backside. You talk about breaking the ice!

Kitsy appointed Anne to the Altar and Hospital Guild. Anne's responsibilities included decorating the Cadet Chapel with flowers and supervising cadet weddings, which were traditionally held in the chapel.

The cadet will earn and save most of his pay as an army private while he is attending the academy. In four years, he will save enough money for at least a good down payment on a Corvette. About a month before graduation every year, the parking lot would be filled with brand-new Corvettes. In addition to a new car, many of the cadets acquired new brides as well, and right after graduation, there would be a series of forty or fifty wonderful weddings. Most of them wanted to be married in the beautiful Cadet Chapel. Anne was in charge of all these weddings, and she had some very interesting experiences. For instance, there were the guests of an Oriental cadet who could not speak English. Using sign language, Anne had to figure out which side of the chapel they preferred for the bride's family. Another time, the bride and groom were at the altar, but the groomsman had dropped the ring. Anne, very quietly snuck up, almost on her hands and knees, got the groomsman's attention and held up the ring, and he sidled over and retrieved it. There were some fantastic weddings. I have no idea how many there were, but there had to have been a lot of them. At the busiest times, weddings were held every thirty minutes, and that meant getting them in, getting them married, getting them out, and getting the next group in. The newlyweds then left under the traditional crossed sabers. The weddings were beautiful, and Anne did a tremendous job supervising them.

One year for Thanksgiving, Anne decorated the front of the chapel with fruit, vegetables, and corn shocks. She had just finished when Mrs. Spears, the wife of the chaplain of West Point, called and said, "Anne, have you heard the news? I'm sorry to tell you, President Kennedy has been shot in Dallas." They commiserated for a moment, and then Mrs. Spears said, "Anne, I really hate to ask you, but we're going to have to take all those decorations down and put some palms there, since the whole nation is in mourning." Several weeks later, Mrs. Spears said, "Anne, that was such a beautiful arrangement you had prepared before the president died—would you mind putting it back up again?" Of course Anne agreed, and back up went the fruit, vegetables, and corn shocks.

Family time together in the backyard of Quarters 1000 at West Point

We never had to worry about our kids walking anywhere on the Post at night. We could give Kathie and Steve each twenty-five cents, and they could walk down to the movie theater on the post, which was in the first level of the cadet gymnasium. They could get in for fifteen cents, have a bag of popcorn for ten cents, and walk home afterwards. We didn't have to worry about them at all. I thought that was a real plus about being at West Point. The kids attended the school on the post for the elementary and middle grades. Since there was no secondary school on post, Steve attended high school in Highland Falls. I didn't think that was quite as nice as going to school on the post. When we left Army and moved to South Carolina, Kathie was far ahead of her class there because the academic program at West Point was excellent, even in grade school. Cadets taught the children's Bible classes on Sunday morning, and Kathie loved that—she was about ten years old and really liked those handsome cadets.

Steve was involved in a serious accident during his sophomore year at Highland Falls High School. At football practice one evening, Steve was playing end and went out for a pass. Unfortunately, when he made his cut across the middle, he ran into Coach Nicola-

West Point superintendent General Westmoreland (left), myself, and General Omar Bradley at an Army football practice.

copalous, a very large man. Steve broke his leg—a compound fracture of both bones—which really hurt him athletically, as he was in a cast for six months during the cold winter at West Point.

In my first interview with General Westmoreland for the head coaching job, I told him and athletics director Hank Adams that, since the army was integrated, I thought West Point should have black athletes, and they readily agreed. Later, after I had settled in at the academy, I received an invitation from sports commentator Howard Cosell to appear on his live TV program in New York City. Howard told me to come early so that we could have a drink or two before the show to loosen up a bit. I did get there early, and we went across the street to a bar where apparently he was well known. At that time I did not drink, so I had my usual club soda while Howard downed several double martinis. We arrived at the studio shortly before broadcast time. An attractive young lady came onto the set and powdered Howard and was about to powder me, but I politely declined. The director counted down "Five, four, three, two, one," and Howard began: "Today we have on our show the new football coach at the United States Military Academy at West Point, fresh from a remarkable tenure at LSU, Paul Dietzel." Then he said with gusto, "Coach, I'm sure the Army fans would like to know why you don't have any black players on the Army team."

Although totally surprised by this question, I replied, "Funny, you should ask me that, Howard, because you did not mention it before the camera came on. It just happens that we do have the first black player

coming into the academy this summer. His name is Gary Steel. His father is an army warrant officer, his mother is the head nurse in a Philadelphia hospital, and he is an honor student. But we did not recruit him because he is a black athlete. We recruited him because he is six feet four, weighs 210 pounds, and he can fly!" Howard was quiet for a moment and immediately changed the subject.

When the program was over, I said to Howard, "That was a sorry thing to hit me with. Why didn't you warn me in advance? I wanted to knock you off your chair!"

Howard simply replied, "Oh, Coach, I had to be spontaneous!"

At West Point, I didn't have access to a television show like the *Monday Night Quarterback Club* in Baton Rouge, so I decided to create one. It was called "A Quarterback Club" and was held on Monday nights in the academy's auditorium. Since the club was not broadcast or televised, I took questions directly from the live audience. (Of course this meant I could get no help from "Ethel Wirtz"!) The senior cadets could come, and all the officers and enlisted men on the post were invited. We had good crowds, and I would make sure that the more controversial issues were addressed. I would even draw diagrams of plays being discussed. I thought the club was helpful because it got the fans' criticisms out in the open. If you're in the coaching business, you can't escape public criticism, and I didn't really try to. I made sure the tough questions were asked so that I had an opportunity to explain our side of the story.

It didn't take long for me to realize that I had been brought to West Point to beat Navy. Unfortunately, I arrived at the academy at a time when Roger Staubach was a sophomore at the Naval Academy. It was just my luck that my team had to face Staubach for three long years. And Navy had a very fine team besides. The first year we played, I knew how good Roger Staubach was and I made up my mind that we were not going to give him a chance to throw the ball. We decided to put pressure on him with all kinds of blitzes and rushes. That turned out to be a serious mistake. We were able to force him out of the pocket, but in spite of the pressure, we still couldn't tackle him. He was a tremendous runner and had a knack for getting away from rushers. Once when we chased him out of the pocket, he took off to one side and threw a pass that we batted right back into his hands. He reversed field, ran to the other side, and completed a pass. I knew we were in trouble. Navy managed to beat us pretty badly that day. When I came out of the Army dressing room after the game, there was the largest group of writers that I had ever faced, all with their pencils poised. I said, "Well, gentlemen, I just want to tell you one thing. You have just looked at the poorest-prepared Army team that you've probably ever seen. I did a terrible job getting Army ready to play Navy." And they all agreed, so most of them turned around and left. Some did have a few questions, but I thought there wasn't any sense in beating around the bush: I had done a lousy job getting the team ready to play.

In one of those early years, we played Duke at West Point. I think they beat us by one point. Duke's coach, Bill Murray, a good friend, met me after the game. He said, "You know, Paul, we've got two very lousy teams, and yours is lousier." He was right. But we did play well against Penn State, which had a fine record. Our Army players knew many of the Penn State players and were confident we could win, and in fact we beat them at West Point that year. We shouldn't have, but we did.

The next year, we took our Army team to State College for a game that turned out to be very interesting in many ways. During the off-season, I had the idea that it would be great to be able to listen to our quarterback while he was on the field. So I paid a visit to the Army "spook school." I took one of our helmets and talked to one of the geniuses who worked there. I told him, "I'd like to see if you can put a small radio transmitter in the quarterback's helmet. We can take some of the padding out, run a wire through the helmet into the nose guard, and place the microphone in front of the quarterback's face." The transmitter was installed. I don't believe this had ever been done anywhere before. Now I would be on the sideline with one side of my earphones listening to the play the quarterback called and the other earphone connected to our coaches up in the press box. As soon as our quarterback, Rollie Stichweh, called a play, I would relay it to our coaches in the press box. They could then see exactly what happened on a play and why it did or did not work. In addition, if our quarterback audibled to change the play at the line of scrimmage, we would know. We would be able to hear the change and see why he made it. We could then determine whether or not a change should have

Shaking hands with President
Dwight D. Eisenhower at West
Point in 1962

*U.S. Army photograph*

been made. It worked really well, and no one else knew we were doing it. It wasn't illegal at the time. Though such technology soon would be banned in college football, it's widely accepted now, and most college teams and all pro teams have much more sophisticated electronic communication systems today.

But when we went to State College to play Penn State, as we were warming up, Rollie said, "Coach, I'm hearing somebody giving instructions about parking." Rollie's transmitter was picking up a signal from someone out in the parking area outside the stadium, so we figured we had a problem. We had to change our frequency.

Penn State was really upset with us because we had beaten them the previous year. A young man came up to me at our Friday walkthrough in the stadium and said, "Coach, could I talk to you on the radio? I'm with the local station for the students here at State College." I told him he'd have to wait until the players got off the field and into the shower, but then I'd be glad to talk with him. When the workout was over and I went up to the press box with the young man, he said, "You know, Coach, last year you beat Penn State at West Point and really ruined their season, and they have not forgotten. Tomorrow, they're not planning on just beating you, they want to humiliate you!"

I said, "Is that right?"

He said, "Yes, Sir, they're going to beat you as bad as they can."

Well, I took that into consideration. As we did at LSU, we always took the Army team to a movie the night before a game. There was only one theater in State College, and featured that night was a movie called *The Leopard.* It had to be among the sorriest movies I've ever seen. After the film, we left the theater and got on our buses. As we boarded, a mob of Penn State students began pounding on the buses and yelling, "Go to Hell, Army! Go to Hell, Army!" It was a big scene, but they didn't do anything except make a lot of noise and pound on the buses. We went to our hotel, and as usual, I took the team for a short walk. We strolled to a quiet place where I could talk to them. I told them about the young man from the State College radio station who had told me that

Speaking with Attorney General Robert Kennedy at a Washington, D.C., luncheon

*City News Bureau*

they intended to humiliate us. I said, "Fellas, I'll tell you one thing: nobody humiliates the United States Army!" I could see their backs stiffen just as mine had.

We had scouted Penn State rather thoroughly; they had a fine running attack, but they couldn't throw the ball. They never even tried to throw the ball—they just ran and ran and ran. They had some fine backs, and they were a big, strong football team. George Terry was one of the best men I've ever known, an excellent scout, and without any question, one of the better defensive coaches anywhere. I said, "George, you know these guys can't throw the football. Why should our secondary play for a pass when we know they aren't going to pass? What I think we ought to do is bring our corner men right up on the line of scrimmage and bring our two safeties right up just outside our two linebackers. We'd be playing with eleven men on the line of scrimmage."

We told our troops that State wouldn't throw a pass, so we'd play a goal-line defense the whole game. Although Penn State was heavily favored and ranked number four in the nation, they were stymied. They finally threw a pass in the fourth quarter, but the receiver was so far be-

The Corps of Cadets salutes
Paul F. Dietzel.

yond everybody on the field that he had to stand and wait for the ball to
finally come down, like a wounded duck. He caught the pass and scored
a touchdown, but the game ended in our favor, 21–7. They could not run
against our eleven-man line—that really was something! But what had
got us really cranked up was the comment made by that young radio announcer the night before the game. It's true: you should absolutely never
try to bait your opponent. You have to be very careful about what comments you, your coaches, or your players make. Things that are said or
done before the game have a tendency to come back and haunt you. Beating Penn State that year was one of the great upset victories of my coaching career.

We played Notre Dame in New York City and were holding our own
very well until about the middle of the third quarter. Notre Dame had
some fine personnel and was coached by Ara Parseghian, my old Miami
teammate. They were big and fast and strong. The Army players don't
have any spare meat on their bones. If a cadet gets injured, it takes a long
time for him to recover. Cadets get up every day at 5:50 in the morning,
and because of the academy's rigorous daily schedule, it's very hard for
them to recover from any kind of injury. There is very little rest time for
cadets. We had three of our starters knocked out of the game. They were
simply hit very hard and were badly bruised.

The next week we played Pittsburgh, which was ranked number three
in the nation. The game was played at West Point. I realized that the Pitt
game would be followed by Navy. There was no way that I was going to let

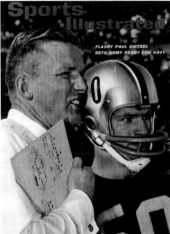

Dietzel with Army linebacker Dick "The Thumper" Nowak on the cover of *Sports Illustrated* in 1962.
*Marvin E. Newman*/Sports Illustrated

Coach Dietzel on the Army Proving Ground in 1962
*Walter Iooss Jr.*/Sports Illustrated

those three players get reinjured and then be unable to play against Navy. So I held them out, and Pitt proceeded as they normally did to steamroll us. Five or six of Pitt's players, including Paul Martha, got into the pros the next year. Their coach was John Michelosen. They just lined up and ran right over us. To give you some idea, at the end of the first quarter, they were ahead 28–0. The score was the same when the game ended, 28–0. Pitt could have scored a hundred points, but after the first quarter, they backed off. After the game, I walked across the field to Coach Michelosen and said, "Johnny, you know you could have beaten us by a hundred points. I'll tell you, I really appreciate your not humiliating us."

He said, "Paul, if you coach long enough, sooner or later you're going to be on the other side of the field. I've been on that side of the field, too. It doesn't do you a bit of good to pour it on after you've already won the game."

I said, "Johnny, I don't know how long I'm going to coach, but I'll tell you one thing: I will never ever forget this. It was very generous." I appreciated it very much. Johnny Michelosen was a first-class coach, and a very fine guy.

Since we had held those three players out, we played a heck of a game against Navy the next week and finally beat them, by a score of 11–8, thanks to a late field goal by Barry Nickerson. That was a gold-letter day for West Point! Even though we tied Navy the next year, we had closed the gap with the Midshipmen. As Kitsy Westmoreland had indicated several years before, I was hired to beat Navy. Mission accomplished!

Lunching with Darrel Royal, Bud Wilkinson, and Ben Schwalder at a U.S. Army overseas football clinic.

Some of the finest experiences I have had in my coaching career occurred when I was invited to conduct football coaches' clinics for members of our armed forces who were stationed in Europe. In the late 1950s and early 1960s, many of the army and air force military bases had football teams that played against teams from other bases. Their coaches were soldiers who had played football in high school or college but had little or no experience coaching. These coaches would attend clinics that other college coaches and I conducted. It was very rewarding.

These men were most attentive students. After the clinics, we were free to travel Europe for a few days on our own. Following my third clinic, I took Anne and our two children on an unforgettable European vacation.

A couple of my fellow instructors were Bud Wilkinson and Gomer Jones of Oklahoma. At one air force clinic, we became acquainted with Colonel Sam Corollo, the athletics director for the air force in Europe. He invited Anne and me to dinner, and we met at his apartment. His girlfriend, who spoke very little English, joined us. In his apartment, he had a beautiful handwoven rug that Anne admired. Sam told her they were very cheap in Spain, about twenty dollars. So I gave Sam twenty dollars, he promised to send us one, and I promptly forgot about it. Sam's girlfriend drove a sports car and asked Anne to ride with her to the restau-

Anne and I during a break at an Air Force clinic in Europe in the 1960s

rant. It was a hair-raising ride for Anne, but the girlfriend assured her, "Don't worry! I have racing brakes!"

Fast forward to our Penn State game the next fall at West Point: a huge crowd, cadets all standing, and I was standing on a bench on our sideline sending in plays. Just as I sent in a play, I felt a tug on my pants leg. I looked down and saw an air force captain who said, "I've got your rug." I was incredulous.

I asked, "What?" and sent in the next play.

He said, "I've got your rug from Sam Corollo." This pilot had just flown in from Spain, and he delivered the rug to me during the middle of a football game at Michie Stadium. Hilarious!

I was selected to coach the North-South game in Miami along with Ara Parseghian. Ara was the head coach of the North team, and I was the assistant. I took three of our Army players with us to the game, which turned out to be a crazy one. In that game if you're behind, you keep receiving the kickoff. We got far ahead of the South team but kept having to kick off to them because they were behind. It was hot and humid in Miami, and our players from West Point and Notre Dame were used to cold weather. By the fourth quarter, our three West Point men were exhausted, but it was a great experience for us all the same.

During my career, I coached a lot of all-star games. The East-West game is an especially classy operation. A coach serves twice as an assis-

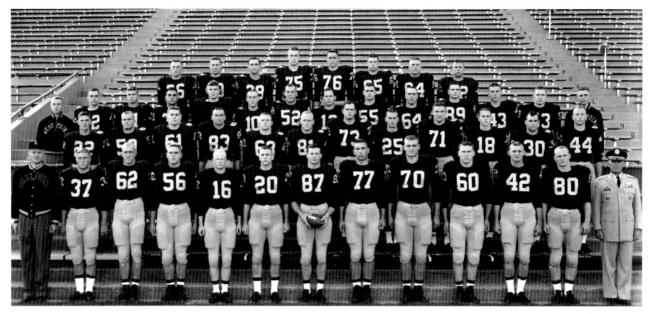

The 1962 Army squad with Colonel Paul Tuttles (right), Officer in Charge of Football

*U.S. Army photograph*

tant, and if he's lucky, he'll be invited back as a head coach. I went out the first time as Duffy Daugherty's assistant and the second time as Ara's assistant. The players and the coaches stayed at St. Mary's College, south of San Francisco. The wives and children of the coaches stayed at the Mark Hopkins Hotel in San Francisco. The Mark Hopkins is a fantastic hotel. When we could, we would drive into San Francisco in the evening, stay with our wives at the Hopkins, and then drive back for practice at St. Mary's the following day. One coach would always stay overnight at St. Mary's with the players.

One day it was Ara's turn to drive us back to St. Mary's. The East-West Shrine Committee provided each coach with a new white Oldsmobile convertible. We were in Ara's car, which had a sign on the side that read, "Shrine Football Game, Ara Parseghian, Coach." As we talked, I had a funny thought. I said, "Ara, it must be great to coach at Notre Dame, where all you have to do is have the padres sprinkle a little holy water on the recruits and tell them they have to go to Notre Dame."

He said, "Yeah, that's what everyone thinks, but it's not so. You know there are a lot of Catholics who don't like Notre Dame at all. We have a terrible time because everywhere I go to speak they'll ask me, 'Why don't you have a local boy on the Notre Dame team?' I go to Los Angeles, and it's, 'Why don't you have any Los Angeles boys on the team?'"

Just about then, as we were waiting at a traffic light in Haight-Ashbury, a guy running a jackhammer stopped what he was doing and came over and knocked on the window of the car. Ara rolled down the window, and the guy asked, "Aren't you Ara Parseghian?"

Ara said, "Yes, I am."

Renowned Army coach Earl "Red" Blaik talks with me and Army football captain John Ellerson.

*U.S. Army photograph*

And then the guy says, "I'm from Sioux Falls, South Dakota. How come you don't have a South Dakota boy on the Notre Dame team?"

Ara threw up his hands and said to me, "See what I mean?"

The next time I was invited to the East-West Shrine game, I was the East team's head coach. I had two assistants, Tubby Raymond of Delaware and Len Jardine of the Big Ten. On the East squad were two talented backs, a big fullback and a running back just about the same size. Our quarterback from Ole Miss, who ran the option, had been injured but still ran well. We had just put in the "veer" offense, one of the greatest offenses I've ever coached. The veer is one of my very favorites offenses because it's such fun. The players really enjoy it.

At a meeting of the coaching staffs and officials of the Shrine game to discuss the rules for the contest, officials coordinator Rip Engle commented, "We had a very dull game last year and we need to keep this game exciting."

I responded, "Well, you need to run the ball to make it exciting." I made that comment knowing that our opponents had two outstanding passers from the West Coast and several excellent receivers. I said that if they wanted to open up the game a little bit, they should let us take some bigger splits in the line. Of course the West squad coaches said they didn't want to do that, so I said, "Well, if you don't want to open the game, if you want less scoring, just keep it the way it is. But, if you open it up a little bit, it might make the game a little more interesting."

We argued one way, and they argued another, and finally Rip said, "I think we ought to do what Paul suggests. What's it going to hurt? Just let the linemen take a bigger split." So we agreed that we could split guards out a yard and the tackles out a yard and a half if we wanted to. It wasn't required but it was allowed. On the other side of the ball, the teams were required to stay in a straight defense with no stunting or blitzes. The defense was to be a straight "Oklahoma" 5-2 defense.

We ran the veer offense. using our option quarterback from Ole Miss and two big strong halfbacks very effectively. The West team couldn't stop the veer, and we ran up and down the field on them. We wore them out. The West offense did complete some passes but to no avail. As soon as we got the ball back, we'd take it the length of the field again. They couldn't slow us down. We certainly opened up the game, and we won it going away.

Before the game, I had told my two assistant coaches that if we won, I would take them to the Top of the Mark for dinner. From high up there the view is fantastic. Wow! San Francisco from the Top of the Mark! But guess what. The fog had set in so thick we couldn't even see the railings on the windows. So much for the Top of the Mark. We could just as easily have been in a handball court. But we didn't care because we had just won a great victory.

The same year, I was invited to coach in the Hula Bowl. Everything people say about Hawaii, is true: it's a wonderful, wonderful place. I'd go back there anytime. One of our halfbacks in the game was Larry Czonka of Syracuse. He was a horse of a player and a fine young man. He showed his stuff and was one of the stars of the game. Afterwards, we were having dinner in a beautiful atrium when an owner of one of the professional teams came over and said, "Paul, tell me: do you think that Czonka can make it in the pros?"

I said, "I'll tell you one thing. If Czonka can't play in the pros, I've never seen anyone who could." He was a fine athlete, very coachable, really tough, and big. His career with the Miami Dolphins speaks volumes.

* * *

As I mentioned before, our children were being taught by cadets in Sunday school. These cadets were members of a strong group called the Fellowship of Christian Athletes. FCA was a fine organization that I became very much involved with, and while coaching at West Point, I was elected its national president.

About this time, I became familiar with Hunter Mountain, one of the most popular resorts in the Catskills, which was about an hour and a half's drive from West Point. On one skiing trip to the mountain, I met the two owners, brothers Israel and Orville Slutsky, two of the finest men I've ever known. They had been contractors and had bought the ski area and then built the magnificent lodge there. They could not have been nicer to me. I invited them to visit West Point to attend our football games, and from time to time they did. In turn, when Anne and the kids and I would visit the mountain, Israel and Orville would not let me buy a single ticket for skiing or even pay for a meal—they insisted that we be their guests. Eventually, I took them with me to New York for the National Football Hall of Fame dinner, which would lead to far-reaching developments later on.

Anne and I had a little travel trailer at the time, and Israel and Orville let us park it at Hunter Mountain. I could drive over there late in the afternoon after work and spend the night in the trailer. It was wintertime, but there was a heater in the trailer. I'd have breakfast with Israel—"Izzy," as we called him—and then we would ski all day long. Late in the afternoon, I'd drive back to West Point. I also became friends with the man who ran the ski school, a little Austrian by the name of Carl Plattner. Man, could he ski! At one time, he had been the Austrian downhill champion. He and his wife, Margo, became our good friends.

Grossinger's is another resort in the Catskills. I spent a weekend there when I was invited to serve as judge for the Miss America pageant. More than one thousand people can be seated in the dining room; the food is kosher and absolutely delicious. I mentioned to Paul Grossinger, the resort's owner, that I was searching for a place to have the national FCA board meeting. He said, "Why don't you come over to Grossinger's?" So we had our board meeting at Grossinger's. There were about ten or twelve of us. We had a wonderful time, and the kosher food was fantastic. The board spent three days at Grossinger's, but when we checked out, the desk clerked told us, "No charge." Paul had covered our tab. I was overwhelmed and greatly appreciated his kindness and generosity. He was, by the way, an avid West Point football fan and attended many of our games.

After LSU won the national championship in 1958, I was invited to speak at the FCA convention in Estes Park, Colorado. I was under the impression that the convention would open on Tuesday, so the family and I arrived on Monday. I was quite shocked when FCA founder Don McClanen informed me that my talk was scheduled for that night.

I said, "You've got to be kidding! I'm not ready to do it."

"I think you are," he replied. "Just step up and say what you want to say."

I took the car and somewhat frantically drove up the mountain to a campsite where I worked on my speech. I have no idea what I said that night, but apparently it was all right. Branch Rickey, the professional baseball manager who helped players like Jackie Robinson and Roberto Clemente break into the major leagues, was there, as were baseball hall-of-famer and LSU alum Alvin Dark and Michigan State football coach Biggie Munn. It was a wonderful experience and made a great and lasting impression on Kathie and Steve. It made me start thinking about things which are truly important.

At the convention I also met and formed a lasting friendship with Frank Broyles, head football coach and later athletics director at the University of Arkansas. It seemed that we had many similar experiences and concerns. I will always feel indebted to Frank for the advice he shared with me. While I was coaching at Army, I would have the opportunity to help both Frank and my old friend Bear Bryant (who was by then head coach at Alabama) with placing some of their graduates who needed to complete some military service following ROTC. These included Frank's All-American safety Ken Hatfield—who went on to become head coach at the Air Force Academy, Arkansas, Clemson, and then Rice —and Bill Battle, one of Bear's players, who would later become head coach at Tennessee. I was able to help both these young men join our staff as plebe coaches.

A few months after that FCA convention, Don McClanen called and asked if I would come to Philadelphia and speak at an FCA fund-raiser in Philadelphia. I flew into Philadelphia, and Don met me at the airport. We drove to the hotel and went up to my room. I asked him who would be at the banquet and whether he had any suggestions for me. I told him I had my speech all ready. He said, "Paul, don't make that speech."

"But I've worked on this—it's a good speech," I protested. "I'll say the right things and even make references to a couple of verses in the Bible."

But he said, "No, just leave the speech here." We got down on our knees at the side of the bed, and Don prayed. He brought tears to my eyes with his prayer.

When it was time for us to go, he repeated, "Now, leave your prepared speech here." I did. I don't remember what I said when I went to the fund-raiser, but Don told me that it was by far the best talk he had ever heard me give. He said, "You were talking from the heart. It was not something you had practiced in your mind—it was from the heart. That makes all the difference in the world."

In Baton Rouge, I encouraged LSU athletes to attend FCA camps. In 1960, there were enough LSU players attending camp at Estes Park to constitute one full team enabling us to put on a demonstration for the campers, which were all high school athletes. The great LSU and pro basketball player Bob Pettit was also demonstrating his skills to the FCA athletes. He told the boys, "I practiced this hook shot from the corner for so many years that now it seems like there's really nothing to it." He proceeded to drill about six of them in a row with his right hand. Then he went to the other corner and did the same thing with his left hand. He was amazing, and yet he was one of the most humble athletes I've ever known and a fine Christian man. I've seen him many times since, and he's still a tremendous credit to anything he is involved with.

It had become traditional for the national board to hold a meeting at the summer convention. It occurred to the leadership that perhaps it would be possible to have more than one summer conference; eventually we offered several, and the FCA grew and grew. Today, I think nearly fifty conferences are held every summer; there is a chapter at almost every university and public high school in the United States.

The FCA has been very important in my life and has really changed my life. After that meeting in Philadelphia with Don McClanen, I decided that there was no way I could get up and talk to athletes or anybody about something unless I was living it. I've never lived up to what I think the Lord would have me do, but I have certainly tried. I have had some wonderful experiences because of people I met in the Fellowship of Christian Athletes.

At West Point, we had begun to recruit all over the country. I knew that would be the key to success for academy football. There are always some athletes who consider going to one of the academies because of a brother, uncle, or someone else who had been in the armed forces and been an influence on them. However, there are two things that make recruiting for academy athletics difficult. The first is the postgraduate obligation: those who attend one of the U.S. military academies must remain in the service for five years after graduation, and that discourages many good athletes from considering the academies. The other difficulty is the lure of professional football. It is true that professional athletes have become pampered and spoiled; the salaries they receive are obscene. Millions of dollars are often paid to young men who seem immature and who don't seem to know how to handle such sudden fame and fortune. As a consequence, they often make very poor decisions. But professional football seems extremely glamorous to the typical high school athlete, to the point that all he wants to do is go to college just long enough to become a star athlete so he can go into the pros and make millions of dollars and drive fancy cars. There is one major flaw in that way of thinking. Several years ago, I made an extensive survey of high school and college athletes. It is amazing how few high school football players will go on to play in college. An even smaller number, much less than 1 percent of the college athletes, will play in the pros. Yet the dream of going pro has made many

Shaking hands with President Richard Nixon in the Oval Office. Also pictured, left to right: Coach Bill Murray of Duke, Coach Joe Paterno of Penn State, Coach Duffy Dougherty of Michigan State, and Coach Bud Wilkinson of Oklahoma.

a promising recruit think twice about attending one of the academies.

Few have done it. Roger Staubach is one. But there aren't many Roger Staubachs around. The five-year obligation and the emergence of professional football have been the greatest challenges to college athletics at the academies and were the greatest obstacles I had to overcome as head coach at West Point. Yet in almost every state, there would be one or two athletes each year who, for one reason or another, had a yen to go to the United States Military Academy. There are some tremendous pluses to attending the academy. Where else can you be guaranteed such a bright future? Where else can you get paid to go to college as you do at the military academies? Where else can you graduate with enough money saved to buy a Corvette and get married if you want to? But most important, at the academy you get the finest education that can be found anywhere in the United States. This is not to say that you can't get a fine education at Carnegie Tech or Lehigh or MIT, because you can. But how many courses do they have at those schools in leadership? At West Point you learn to be a leader. You also learn to be physically competent. You get the most complete education at the academy that you can get anywhere. That was the premise upon which we recruited, and we brought in some fine athletes. In 1965, our Army team was just about as good as anyone around.

The first stop for recruits visiting West Point was the fabulous Friday night buffet at the Bear Mountain Inn. Early the next morning, they would be treated to the weekly cadet corps parade, which is very impressive; then they would have lunch with the cadets in the academy's huge mess hall. In the afternoon, there would be a variety of athletic events to attend: indoor track, basketball, wrestling, swimming, and, after dinner at the Thayer Hotel, hockey. After the hockey game, Anne and I would treat the recruits to doughnuts and hot chocolate at our house. They always seemed to enjoy the visit and the refreshments. This also gave our staff a chance to chat with the young men informally. After breakfast on Sunday morning, the recruits departed for home. The staff and I always did our very best to provide these prospects with activity-packed weekends; we wanted their impression of West Point to be positive and lasting.

We had good players on offense and defense, and of course we had the Army Chinese Bandits. I needed to find a thousand or so Chinese coolie hats for the cadets, and I thought John Martin of the Bear Mountain Inn might help. I was right: John bought enough coolie hats for the entire cadet corps. At our next game, the Rabble Rousers took over. The Rabble Rousers are the cadet cheerleaders. The officer in charge of the Rabble Rousers was a good buddy of mine. First the Rabble Rousers counted the number of cadets in each row. Then they got big brown paper bags and put the number of hats needed for each row into a bag hidden at the end of that row, where they remained until the Chinese Bandits went into the game for the first time.

I spoke with the academy's band director, Linn Arrison, who had arrived at West Point about the same time as I, and asked him if he would arrange the chant for the Bandit team. He agreed. By the time the Bandits went into the game halfway through the first quarter, the Rabble Rousers had secretly passed the coolie hats to the cadets. Every cadet in the stadium had a coolie hat. When the Bandits went in, the entire corps stood up with those coolie hats on, and the band played the Chinese Bandit chant. The spectators, as you might expect, were stunned. It was just electric. Of course, the Bandits played like mad.

General Westmoreland was sitting beside Dick Stillwell, the commandant of cadets. The "Comm" was a ramrod type of officer. General Westmoreland, without turning his head, said out of the side of his mouth, "Dick, why wasn't I informed of this?" And Colonel Stillwell said, "Westy, I didn't know anything about it." Of course, the commandant of cadets is supposed to know these things. The officer who was in charge of the

Rabble Rousers was called in and had the riot act read to him. But since it turned out to be such a fun thing for the whole corps, no one was seriously reprimanded. The next week, however, when we were scheduled to play Syracuse in Yankee Stadium, an order was issued that there would be no coolie hats worn in New York City.

During my times at West Point, Army football received generous treatment from the New York papers. The only difference was that in 1948, when I was the plebe line coach, Army football was on the front page. Four years later, when I came back as Colonel Blaik's offensive line coach, with Vince Lombardi coaching the offensive backfield, news of Army football had moved back to about page three. The New York professional teams had crept onto the front page. When I returned in 1961 as head coach, West Point football was back on about page five or six.

In hopes of remedying this situation, I decided to continue the Bull Pond Encampment that Colonel Blaik had started years before. I invited all the New York sports press, including Tim Cohane, Til Ferdenzi, Red Smith, Allison Danzig, the renowned sports cartoonist Willard Mullin, and Fred Russell of the *Nashville Banner.* Freddy had always been a great jokester. Years earlier, he arranged to have Vanderbilt coach Red Sanders put in jail as a joke and then confessed to the prank much later. I knew Freddy was flying up for our retreat, so I made arrangements to give him a welcome that would be a taste of his own medicine.

Right next to Bull Pond was a firing range where they fired the big howitzers. Bill Battle, in his uniform as officer of the day, met Freddy in New York City and drove him up to West Point. As they came by the firing range, some of our coaches, who were hiding, began firing off these big blockbuster firecrackers. Bill quickly stopped the car and said, "I didn't know they were firing here today. They didn't tell us they were firing. What's the matter with these people? Let's get out of here!" Then Bill jumped over a pile of dirt into a trench. Freddy was right behind him. I had our regular cameraman capture the entire "bombardment" episode on film. While our coaches were firing off the blockbusters, they threw handfuls of rocks and gravel into the air into the vicinity of Freddy and Bill. Bill apologized to Freddy and said, "I hope they don't get more accurate."

Freddy, by now, was pretty worried. After about five minutes of this "shelling," our coaches stopped. Bill said, "It's time. They only fire for a few minutes at a time, so let's get out of here while they've stopped, and I'll take you on out to Bull Pond." They get back in the car and proceed to Bull Pond, where Bill just drops him off without saying a word.

Freddy, of course, tells us about the shelling in vivid detail. Then I said, "I heard the firing, but I didn't know they were firing today or we wouldn't have driven you through there."

Fred Russell, *Nashville Banner* sports editor and a dear friend

"Well, they are firing, and we had to get out of the way," Freddy said excitedly.

Meanwhile, our photographer developed the film and spliced in the introduction that I had already prepared. That evening after dinner and drinks, we sat down for our movie like we always did. Everyone was prepared for our usual fare of one of Tim Cohane's favorite Susan Hayward films, but on the screen appears the title "Freddy Visits West Point." The next thing you see is gravel flying and Bill and Freddy running and jumping into the ditch. Every once in a while, you can see Freddy peeking out over the top of the trench. It was hilarious! The film concluded with, "This is the end. Happy you're here, Freddy!" We turned off the projector, and Freddy was completely flabbergasted! We laughed about it many times since. I'm sorry he's no longer around to share the memory, as he was a fantastic gentlemen, a splendid writer, and a wonderful friend.

Gene Leone, who had donated the Bull Pond property to the academy, often invited Anne and me and the kids to his home in Central Valley "for a little soup," which always turned out to be a feast. Steve and Kathie would ride his horses, which they dearly loved. Gene would prepare a "little" minestrone soup. He never used anything canned. There were always cases of fresh tomatoes, celery, onions, potatoes—in short, every vegetable known to man. We would begin the meal with shrimp rémoulade. Wow! It was as good as we had ever had at Leone's in the City. Gene's minestrone was absolutely delightful. Then Gene would bring out the main dish of veal parmigiana or something fantastic like that. It was funny how his wife, Mae, would follow Gene around the kitchen. Since he was a real chef, dirtying up pans and generally creating a mess didn't bother him. Mae would follow behind him and wash the pans as fast as he used them. Gene and Mae were wonderful friends whose company we really enjoyed.

We had recruited a fine bunch of athletes from all around the country. These players came from Ohio, New Jersey, Florida, Pennsylvania, Michigan, and Illinois. To find athletes who would come to West Point, we had to cover the country. One of the funniest things that happened when I was recruiting for Army involved a young man from Chicago, Fred Barofsky—a fine quarterback. Since he was quite a good prospect, I traveled to Chicago with Jim Valek, our backfield coach, who was responsible for recruiting Fred. Jim had made a reservation to take Fred and his parents to dinner, which was permitted at that time. There were not any great restaurants near Fred's home, so Jim chose what he thought was a good supper club, reported to have very good food. We were early and were seated at a table right at ringside for the evening's stage show. But when we entered the restaurant we had failed to notice that the performer that night was, of all people, Sally Rand, a renowned fan dancer. Young Fred was all eyes—he wanted to see this, and we were practically on the stage. Sally Rand came out and was dancing with her fans and, rest assured, she didn't expose anything improper. Still, Jim Valek spent the evening apologizing, assuring the parents that we did not know Sally Rand would be performing there. I don't know if it was because of Sally, but Fred became a cadet at West Point. He developed into a fine quarterback, but one day in practice, he suffered a mild concussion. Because of this injury, I was reluctant to play him.

General Douglas MacArthur, whom I visited often while coaching Army. The general gave me this autographed photo.

One of my fondest memories of West Point is of my personal relationship with General of the Army Douglas MacArthur. During my years as head coach of the cadets, 1961 through 1965, General MacArthur resided in New York City at the Waldorf-Astoria. He had very large quarters high in the Waldorf Towers. The general was an ardent Army football fan, and as the Army coach, I was in direct communication with him. Each year before the start of the football season, he invited me to his quarters to discuss the team's prospects. He always received a complete rundown on the squad from me prior to the meeting. But of course I couldn't see him without my military superiors, including the director of athletics and the superintendent of the academy.

We would ride to New York City in an army staff car and usually arrived at the general's apartment at about 10:30 A.M. for our scheduled 11:00 A.M. meeting. We were always greeted by the general's aide, a brigadier general, who showed us into the large and magnificent quarters. The entire apartment was very tastefully appointed with memorabilia that the general had accumulated throughout his long and distinguished career. Never before nor since have I seen such gorgeous silver pieces, huge vases, and decorations and awards from around the world. The general's aide described many of the pieces to us and explained what each represented.

Precisely at 11:00 A.M., the apartment's French doors would open and out would stride General MacArthur, General of the Army, dressed in his West Point bathrobe with the letter *A* on the breast. At the academy, the cadet bathrobe is a most noteworthy piece of clothing. Each year, the cadets at West Point wager their bathrobes on the outcome of the Army-Navy football game. The general was extremely cordial and friendly, and it was hard to imagine that this was the famous commander from the war in the Pacific and the military governor of Japan. He greeted each of us—superintendent General Lambert, athletics director Colonel Murphy, and me. He would address the superintendent and the athletics director tersely by their last names only and then indicate where we were all to sit.

**Letter 1:**

90 CHURCH STREET, ROOM 1303
NEW YORK 7, NEW YORK

23 August 1963

Dear Dietzel:

As the new season is preparing to get under way I send you this line of support and encouragement. I know full well that no coach can do more than realize the full potential of the material at his disposal and have every confidence you will do just that. I can do nothing to help except to give you my full moral support and that you can rely upon.

Good luck and every good wish.

Most cordially,

D. M. A.
DOUGLAS MacARTHUR.

Mr. Paul Dietzel,
Football Office,
U. S. Military Academy,
West Point, New York.

**Letter 2:**

90 CHURCH STREET
ROOM 1303
NEW YORK, NEW YORK

9 December 1963

Dear Dietzel:

This is just a line to say that in my opinion you did everything possible with the material at your command. Bad luck has dogged you for the past two years but the law of averages is sure to work sooner or later.

Your real problem is recruitment. Devote your full energy and that of your assistants to organizing and developing it. Therein lies the future of success or failure.

If not too much trouble, let me have a copy of Cahill's analysis of the potentialities of this year's plebe squad.

Be of good cheer for better things are coming.

Faithfully,

DOUGLAS MacARTHUR.

Coach Paul F. Dietzel,
U. S. Military Academy,
West Point, New York.

Letters from General MacArthur, 1963

General Lambert and Colonel Murphy would be seated at the side of the room, and then he would say, "Paul, you sit here," and point to one of the double settees facing each other in the middle of the room. Frankly, I was somewhat embarrassed. After we were seated, he would begin discussing the football squad's personnel, and it was obvious that he had acquainted himself with the entire team. He would say, for instance, "I note that you'll be starting Ski Ordway at defensive tackle. Even though he weighs only 185 pounds, he is quick and very aggressive just like his father was. And Chesnauskis will be good enough to make All-American at guard. Stichweh will be an outstanding quarterback, especially from the shotgun, which you plan to employ, and he is an outstanding leader." It was obvious that he had a fantastic memory. These meetings were an inspiration, as were the many letters and telegrams he sent to the team and me.

Prior to General MacArthur's final talk to the cadets at West Point, his aide told us that he had asked the general if he had planned his speech, and the General had replied, "No, I'm just going up there to talk to my boys!" And yet he spoke eloquently and flawlessly for forty minutes, without the benefit of notes. The day the General visited West Point to review the troops and speak to the corps was a Saturday, the same day I

General MacArthur speaking to the National Coaches Association. Left to right: General MacArthur, Paul F. Dietzel, AFCA president Johnny Michelosen, Eastman Kodak president Jerry Zarno, and Coach Bear Bryant.

had planned to hold our regular spring practice drill. Since we would not have time to change clothes, our squad went into the mess hall in full gear—shoulder pads and all. Anne was allowed to attend and was probably the only woman present.

At one corner of the huge mess hall, which accommodates the entire corps of cadets, there is a raised section called the Poop Deck, where the cadet officer in charge calls out the orders and announcements. General MacArthur made his address from the Poop Deck. He spoke to a very hushed corps of cadets. It was the finest speech I have ever heard. There was not a sound in that huge mess hall except the wonderfully modulated voice of one of America's greatest heroes. Even today, when I listen to a tape of that address, I am overcome with emotion. He ended his talk with the words, "As I cross over the river for the last time, my final thoughts will be of the corps, the corps, and the corps." He was referring to the corps of the past, the present, and the future. A few years later, when I took my turn as president of the American Football Coaches Association, General MacArthur was selected as the first recipient of the AFCA's Tuss McLaughry Award, named in honor of first president of the AFCA. General MacArthur gave a marvelous acceptance speech, and the coaches gave him an enthusiastic standing ovation. They cheered and clapped, and it seemed they would never quit. Finally, the general stepped back up to the podium and said, "The other day as I was leaving my hotel, a lady stopped me and asked where I was going. I told her, 'West Point.' She replied, 'A lovely place. Tell me, have you ever been there before?'"

That brought out a good laugh. But then the lady continued, the general said, "'You know, you look so much younger than your pictures. As a matter of fact, I hardly recognized you without your eye glasses, Mr. Truman.'" That really brought down the house!

The Army team of 1965 was one of the best teams I had ever had. We lost a very close game to Notre Dame in New York City and a heartbreaker to Texas in Austin, which was really decided by an official's call. We had a solid line, anchored by Bill Zadel at tackle, Sonny Stowers and Dick "The Thunder" Nowak at guards, Lee Grasfeder at center, and two excellent ends, David Rivers and Tom Schwartz. In the backfield, we had two fine halfbacks, John Seymour and Johnny Johnson. Our fullback was Donnie Parcells, a great young man. At quarterback was one of the finest athletes I have ever coached, Rollie Stichweh. The academy was primed for another winning season with an outstanding team in 1966. It seemed that Army football was back on track.

# VI
## South Carolina Calls

Quite unexpectedly following the 1965 season at Army, I received a call from Bob McNair, the governor of South Carolina, who said to me, "Paul, we really need you to come down here and become our football coach and athletics director." The University of South Carolina had just lost its coach, who had gone to Canadian football, but to me, the offer came out of the blue, at the very time that I was beginning to realize that the kind of football team I wanted to have at West Point might be impossible to produce in light of the recruiting obstacles there.

Frankly, I wasn't sure the academy needed to have the kind of football team I would have liked. I'm not sure how important it is for West Point to have a championship team. I think it's important for the academy to have a good team, but to get back to where Army football had been years before I thought was almost impossible, especially with the emergence of professional football. So I said to Governor McNair, "I might be interested in looking into that," but I wasn't ready to appear in person down in South Carolina. So I sent George Terry to scout the place. George was there several days, looked at everything, and when he came back, he said, "I'll tell you what, it's not a bad setup. It's kinda run down, but I think it could be a pretty good job, and besides, you'd be the athletics director." And there was one other factor in South Carolina's favor: I had met Frank McGuire, the Gamecocks' basketball coach, at an FCA camp several years before, and we were on friendly terms. So I told the folks in Columbia I'd talk with them. University president Tom Jones flew into La-Guardia along with the chairman of the school's faculty, and George and I went down and met with them. We talked and talked about everything. They were very positive, and I wasn't sure what to do. On the way back to the academy, I asked George, "What do you really think? I mean what do you really think about the situation?"

"Let's put it this way," he said. "You've got a real challenge here at West Point, and you'd have a real challenge at South Carolina. Both places present challenges, but at South Carolina, they'll let you take on the challenges." I had great confidence in George Terry, who was an experienced and very intelligent coach and a wonderful friend, and he reiterated that

South Carolina was willing to allow me to do what was necessary to get things going.

One of the hang-ups I had about West Point, and one of the things that helped me reach a decision, was the pattern that existed there of constantly changing the superintendent, the commandant of cadets, and the director of athletics. When I was offered this opportunity to go to South Carolina, I wanted to talk with some of the administrators at West Point to express my interests and concerns and to get their advice. However, we had a new superintendent, a new commandant of cadets, and a new athletics director. I'm sure they were fine people, but I did not know any of them at all, whereas the ones who had just left had become my good friends. I did go to the new superintendent, whom I had never met, and told him of my dilemma. I said that I really didn't know what to do and that we had a very fine football team returning next year. His response was, "Well, if you don't think you can do something for the benefit of the academy, then I think you should leave." I thought that was a rather cold comment, and there was no one else with whom I could discuss the

The South Carolina coaching staff. Standing, left to right: Scooter Purvis, Dick Weldon, John Menger, and Jacky Powers. Kneeling, left to right: Bill Rowe, Larry Jones, Paul F. Dietzel, Bill Shalosky, and Pride Ratterree.

situation. At that point in time, West Point's administration was in the process of making a major decision: whether or not to return to big-time football.

The cribbing scandal had left a very long shadow on the academy, and some of the people there as I was told later viewed me as another Red Blaik. But I was not another Red Blaik because I did not have good friends and West Point classmates who were high up in the army chain of command as colonels and generals. Colonel Blaik had buddies with clout that he could depend on, and I think many were worried that what had happened in the cribbing scandal might rear its ugly head again. But our team had turned the corner, Anne and I had many warm friends at the academy, and our Monday night program was most popular. The attitude of the superintendent was a real damper. The fact was that as a result of their transfer to new Army assignments, I had lost the key people who could have persuaded me to remain at the academy. So, taking George Terry's assessment into account, after a great deal of thought, reflection,

Lightening strikes at my first spring practice at South Carolina in 1966.

and prayer, I reached the decision to accept South Carolina's offer. In 1966, I became head coach and athletics director of the Gamecocks.

Before I accepted the job, I asked the board at South Carolina if I could recruit black athletes. I said that I hated to see so many South Carolina athletes becoming All-Americans in the Big Ten and the Big Eight just because USC did not recruit them and keep them at home. They said, "It is time."

We hired an outstanding black coach, Harold White, to handle academics and also hired the first women's assistant athletics director, as women's athletics were beginning to make great strides. In no time many fine black athletes were enrolled, but a tricky situation developed in our recruiting efforts. It came to my attention that a prominent black judge was going to give a local black athlete a car if he would attend USC. I called him and said, "Judge, I do appreciate your support of the university. I hear you're going into the automobile business?"

He said, "No, Coach. Where did you hear that?"

"You offered one of our outstanding black athletes a car, didn't you?" I asked.

He said, "You don't need to know that."

"But I do know it," I said. "And I didn't know how many black athletes we had, so I counted them. There were seventeen. When they see that athlete's car, they will want one, too. So you'll have to buy sixteen more cars."

"I can't do that!" he exclaimed.

"And then the other players will also want cars, so you'll have to go into the auto business."

"I can't do that."

"I know. And if you give any athlete a car, I can't grant him a scholarship. It is against the rules." End of conversation.

I had a number of very interesting experiences at South Carolina that, to this day, I recall quite vividly. One very memorable game was against the University of North Carolina at Chapel Hill. North Carolina had a great All-American running back named Don McCauley, and we had decided that in no way were we going to let that fellow run the ball against us. Each time he lined up with the strong side to the wide side field, we had our entire team stunting to that side, with the cornerback rotating up to the line of scrimmage. After the kickoff, on the very first play of the game, they pitched the ball to him, and he took off on their student body right. It seemed he had no place to go, so he planted his foot, reversed field, and ran for a touchdown. So much for great planning. That began the onslaught. At the start of the fourth quarter, North Carolina was leading 29–3.

We had quite a following at South Carolina, and a group of lawyers, doctors, and prominent citizens—all men—had decided to rent a bus and go up to the game. It was a big bus, and there were a lot of them on it. Since we were behind 29–3 going into the final quarter, in disgust they decided to leave. They left the stadium, boarded their bus, and headed home to Columbia. But as they were listening to the game on the bus radio, pretty soon we scored a touchdown, kicked off, knocked the receiver loose from the ball, and had the ball again. We quickly scored and were back in the game with seventeen points. The men barked to the driver, "Turn the bus around, we're going back to the stadium!" So they returned to the stadium, but since they had thrown away their ticket stubs, they couldn't get back in. Only one fellow had kept his stub, and he got back in just as we caught fire with the fine passing of Tommy Suggs and the outstanding receiving of Freddy Zeigler. Freddy was an amazing guy. He was not fast, had really big feet, and was slow afoot. But he could cut on a dime and catch anything in his vicinity. We went on to win the game, 32–29.

When this busload of loyal Gamecock fans returned to Columbia, they swore secrecy, each promising he would never tell that they had not seen our heroic comeback. The next week on my Monday night television program, I mentioned that a bus full of "loyal" fans had left the game at the beginning of the fourth quarter and missed seeing our victory because the gatekeepers at Kennan Stadium would not let them back in without their ticket stubs. I didn't identify any of them, and no one ever admitted to having been a part of that busload. It was really rather hilarious.

At that game Anne had a fainting attack because of her hypoglycemia and was taken to the Red Cross tent, where she missed most of the game. She could hear the cheering and could figure out what the cheering was for. She finally recovered after Dr. Billy Gause, our family doctor, administered a Coke and a candy bar. That game with North Carolina was quite a victory and truly one of the most unusual games that I can remember.

One of the Gamecocks' finest athletes was Warren Muir, an outstanding running back from Fitchburg, Massachusetts. We had recruited Warren to West Point when I coached there. Since plebes were not eligible to play varsity football, it was quite a pleasure to watch them play against other freshmen teams from area colleges, and watching Warren in these games, we could see that help was coming. Warren could stop on a dime, was very powerful, and had great speed. After I left the academy, he decided to get married, which meant he'd have to leave the academy. As

## carpet the cockpit

Be it known by all present that

_Anne Dietzel_

is a true "Rooster Booster", having purchased a "Piece of the Pad".

He has demonstrated his true allegiance to the Fighting Gamecock Football program by purchasing *4* square yards of synthetic turf in the drive to "Carpet the Cockpit."

By his generosity and love for the Fighting Gamecocks he has helped assure that Carolina Stadium forever remains the Football Showcase of the Southeast.

Paul F. Dietzel
*Athletic Director and Head Football Coach*

Thomas F. Jones
*President, University of North Carolina*

Date: _October 30, 1970_

Our campaign to install synthetic turf in the "Cockpit." The fans bought the "carpet" by the yard.

"The Roost," the new athletic residence hall overlooking the new baseball stadium

soon as I found out, I invited him to come to South Carolina, where he proved to be just as good as we had predicted when he was a plebe at West Point. He became an All-Conference and All-American player for the Gamecocks and was one of the best running backs I ever coached.

Another truly outstanding young man who played for us at South Carolina was safety Dickie Harris, a former halfback whom we moved to defense because of his size, 165 pounds. In Athens, against a powerful Georgia team, Dickie ran back a kickoff for a touchdown and a punt return for a touchdown and intercepted a pass for another touchdown. He was a sensational running back. He was selected first team All-American and was eventually named to the professional All-Canadian team. Though we lost that game to Georgia, the very next year, Dickie blocked a Bulldog punt on our way to beating them at home in Columbia.

I made a great mistake in coaching Dickie Harris. He was such a sensational ball carrier that the fans were on me all the time, asking, "Why don't you put him in on offense?" Well, we were nearing the end of the year and really wanted to go to a bowl. Our next-to-last game was with Wake Forest, which at that time was a very strong football team. So we decided to move Dickie Harris to tailback for the Wake Forest game. He was sensational and scored three touchdowns very rapidly. But on the third touchdown, he was injured and could not play against Clemson, our biggest rival. I knew that I shouldn't have played him on offense. Dickie weighed only 165 pounds, and as a running back he was always in great danger of injury. Though of course I regretted that he was injured, it taught me an important lesson: don't pay too much attention to what the fans think because they are gambling with someone else's money, so to speak. They can't be expected to understand the whole situation, and I was really sorry I allowed their opinion to influence my decision to play Dickie on offense. It was unfair to him.

Back in the early 1960s while I was still the head coach at LSU, Athletics Director Jim Corbett had called me to his office and told me that we needed to schedule an opening football game for 1966. Jim pointed out that we already had a pretty tough schedule for that year, so we probably needed to schedule someone we thought we could beat—a breather, in other words. There were six or seven teams willing to play us, since LSU paid a big guarantee. I picked South Carolina. So guess who we were going to play in the opening game of my first year at South Carolina. LSU! The game created considerable interest among Tigers fans who were still angry with me for leaving LSU and returning to West Point.

Two of our South Carolina coaches had previously planned a vacation trip to New Orleans for that summer. While there, Dick Weldon and John Menger along with their wives, Deanie and Ann, were doing what comes naturally at Pat O'Brien's famous bar, where Mercedes presided at the piano. Mercedes would belt out, "Where are y'all from?" Someone would yell back, "Ohio!" Without one second's hesitation, Mercedes would launch into "Beautiful Ohio" and Ohio State's "Down the Field!" For someone from New York, she would play and sing "East Side, West Side." But when Dick Weldon shouted, "South Carolina!" without missing a beat, Mercedes sang out, "Go to Hell, Paul Dietzel! Go to Hell!"

As we were preparing to fly to Baton Rouge for the game, unbeknownst to me, Anne and her mother started getting crazy phone calls from some demented person saying that he was going to blow up the plane and kill everyone on it. Since I was working day and night on campus, Anne did not want to bother me and did not tell me about the phone calls. She spoke to the sheriff, who said that since no crime had been committed, he could do nothing. However, one of our neighbors was an FBI agent named Jim Calhoun. He told Anne that they would tape the calls and attempt to trace them. The FBI instructed her to go ahead with plans to attend the game and told her there would be agents staying in our home with Anne's mother and Steve and Kathie. They would also be guarding the chartered plan and would have agents on board.

Nannie had quite a good time entertaining the federal agents. She baked them a cake and kept the coffee pot on. Once, she answered the phone, listened to the ranting of this nut, and suggested to him that he "go and get a cup of coffee." Since I was so involved in preparations for the game, Anne kept me oblivious to all of this.

In Baton Rouge on Friday night, one of our good friends, Jo Cast, had baked a german chocolate cake to celebrate my birthday. She came to the motel where the team was staying to deliver it to me, along with a knife to cut it. The FBI agents who were guarding us confiscated the knife and would not let her in until we identified her. Eventually, they got to sample that cake.

Immediately prior to kickoff, as we were waiting in the superheated visitors' dressing room, I told our manager to watch outside and tell me when LSU was in the "chute." Traditionally, LSU's coaches like to let the opposing teams come out first so they can be intimidated by the earthshaking ovation the LSU fans give the Tigers when they run onto the field. For a while, I thought we might be playing the game at midnight because Coach Charlie McClendon held his team in. Finally, the Tigers made their entrance and at that instant, so did the Gamecocks. Both teams went onto the field at exactly the same time. I had warned our team that the LSU cheerleaders place Mike the Tiger just outside the visitors' dressing room and get him to roar to scare opponents. I told them not to worry because Mike can't get out of his cage.

Close friend and accomplished pilot Roger Booco standing beside the *69 Gamecock*

Our Gamecocks took the opening kickoff and methodically marched down the field and scored. That really silenced the crowd. But in the end, the LSU team's strength prevailed, and they won by three touchdowns to our one.

After the game, we found that our plane was not at the airport because it had been sent to Atlanta for safety. When we finally got back to Columbia, the FBI asked Anne to listen to the tapes to see if she could identify the voice of this nut. By then, Anne had told me the whole story. They found the caller, but according to the FBI, he had not committed any crime. I don't know if charges were ever filed against him.

The *69 Gamecock* was a Cessna 220 purchased by the athletic department.

I had scheduled South Carolina as a "breather" for LSU when I was coaching there. The Gamecocks scored the first touchdown.

Preparing for the game of the year—Clemson

At South Carolina, the major event of the football season is the game with Clemson. At one time, it was played each year at the fairgrounds in Columbia and was called "Big Thursday." But Clemson did not want to play us in Columbia every year, so the game was eventually scheduled as a home and home series.

I doubt that there are any rivalries more intense than the one between South Carolina and Clemson. Both are state schools, and the alumni and fans of the two schools just don't like each other. Preparing for the Clemson game was always intense and exciting. Being carried off the field after winning the game and having your team sing the alma mater after the victory is beyond great.

South Carolina had never been very successful in many sports in the Atlantic Coast Conference, so it was truly awesome when, in 1969, we went undefeated in the conference and then won the university's very first conference championship in any sport. The Gamecocks had come a long, long way!

Anne and I really liked Columbia. It was only four hours' drive from a little ski cottage we had built in the mountains and two hours from the beaches of the Atlantic. Moreover, we had some very good friends in Columbia. Bob McNair was still governor. He and his wife, Josephine, became close friends of ours, and Anne and I enjoyed several very interesting trips with them. I remember one in particular that was quite remarkable. Bob had called in the morning and told me that they were going to Charleston for Congressman Mendel Rivers's funeral and asked

The team and I, along with sports information director Tom Price, sing the South Carolina alma mater.

if Anne and I would like to go along. We accepted his invitation. There were more prominent dignitaries at the funeral than I had ever seen in any one place. It was also the only time I had ever experienced a flyover of B-32s, which was absolutely deafening.

After the funeral, Bob invited us to visit his farm, which had been his family home. Then he said, "Why don't we go hunting tomorrow morning?" I pointed out that I was in my black funeral suit and I didn't have any hunting clothes to wear. He said they had plenty of things that would fit me. That afternoon the state patrol drove us to the farm, and Bob, who is not as tall as me, gave me some coveralls that came about halfway down my arms and halfway up my legs. Since I couldn't wear my dress shoes to hunt in, he loaned me a pair of goulashes. I couldn't get my shoes into them, so I wore them with just my socks on. I was a sight, I'm sure. We drove to a place called Southern Railroad's Camp, which had to be the finest camp I'd ever seen. Each couple had a suite of rooms, and we were served a wonderful dinner. I got up about 4:00 A.M. for the hunt. It was cold and drizzly and you couldn't see your hand in front of your face. Bob said, "Oh, it's a perfect day to shoot ducks!" Well, I didn't know anything about good hunting weather, one way or the other. After a light breakfast, we gathered in front of the lodge, where six pickup trucks with six pirogues and guides were waiting to take us to our blinds. This was my first time in any blind. The weather was terrible—very, very cold. "A perfect day, all right!" I thought to myself.

Captain Spell of the state police was assigned to hunt with me. When we arrived at our blind, I was handed a very old double-barreled shotgun. The captain had his own first-class equipment, and I had this antiquated borrowed shotgun. Captain Spell asked me how many times I'd been hunting, and I told him it was my very first time. He said, "Oh?" and I said, "Yes, and you're going to have to tell me how to do this."

I was then given two boxes of shells, and I noticed that the shotgun was very wiggly. I told the Captain, "You'll have to tell me what to do when the ducks come. Do you lead them, or do you try to shoot them right where they are?"

He said, "Lead them just a little bit."

We sat very quietly and soon I saw birds flying my way. "Are those ducks?" I asked.

"No!" he said. "Those are crows."

"Oh," I said.

He looked at me rather curiously, but he was really a laid-back fellow, a very nice guy.

Pretty soon here came some ducks. He said, "OK, here they come."

I said, "OK, tell me when to shoot."

"Shoot now!" he barked.

So I shot. The gun went BANG! I wasn't smart enough to know you were supposed to hold the shotgun tight against my shoulder. The backfire just about dislocated my shoulder, but I hit the duck and it fell right into our blind.

"Good shot," the captain said.

"Pure luck," I said.

Pretty soon another flight of ducks flew over. "Shoot!" the captain said, so I shot again. BOOM! Another duck fell. He said, "Are you sure you've never been hunting before?"

I said, "Captain Spell, I promise you I have never hunted, and this is the first time I've ever fired a shotgun."

After I bagged my second duck, more appeared. I reloaded my gun, and because I didn't know any better, I saved the empty shell casings. The next duck flew over and I hit it, but it fell into the water and started flopping around. The captain said, "Shoot him again." So I raised up and shot him a second time, but when I did, the gun barrel fell from the stock—it was really comical.

"You're sure you've never been hunting?" the captain asked.

I said, "Captain Spell, I wouldn't lie to you, I have never, ever been hunting." Then I told him, "When the next ducks fly over, you shoot."

He had this fine repeating shotgun, and as they got close, he fired. BANG! BANG! BANG! And he didn't hit a thing. More ducks appeared and he said, "You might as well shoot." So I did, and another duck came down.

I had knocked down four ducks with six shots (I had the spent shells to prove it), and Captain Spell had not hit one. We went back to the camp, and Captain Spell seemed a bit miffed—he thought I'd been pulling his leg. When the other hunters asked how we did, Captain Spell growled, "He did all right."

I gave back my two boxes of shells minus the six I'd shot, and they couldn't believe I'd only shot six times.

I said, "Well, yeah, I had beginner's luck, and I got four ducks."

They laughed and obviously did not believe me. By the time we got back to Columbia, the word had gotten around that I had fooled Captain Spell. That was not the case at all because I would never do a thing like that. However, the visit to the Southern Railroad's Camp turned out to be my first and last hunting trip. After all, how could I improve on that?

When I took the job at South Carolina, I realized that the football program had become an embarrassment to the university, its alumni, and the team's fans. It had to be rebuilt from scratch. The season prior to my arrival, the Gamecocks' record was no wins and ten losses. The team had never won a conference championship and had not received a bowl invitation in twenty-five years.

The athletics department was beset with problems, too. It was ill-equipped, completely lacking in adequate facilities, on NCAA probation, and bankrupt. In fact, the athletics department had operated in the red for fourteen years. But within nine years after my arrival, the department had been revitalized, NCAA probation problems had been resolved, and amazingly, the department was debt free. By 1974, over two and a half million dollars had been raised and devoted to capital improvements, which were in addition to the construction of a new football stadium, a new basketball coliseum, and a new athletics dormitory. Increased ticket sales and contributions to South Carolina's Gamecock Club provided funding for the projects. It has been quite a source of pride to me that student athletic fees were never increased during my tenure as athletics director.

No university rules or regulations or NCAA rules were ever broken

A great victory ride after beating archrival Clemson in the 1960s

during my entire career as a head football coach and/or athletics director. That emphatically refers to all rules pertaining to the recruitment of prospective student athletes. My steadfast rule to all of my staff, in each institution at which I was privileged to serve, was always "If you cheat, you're fired!" Not once was any of the teams I coached cited by the its conference or the NCAA for irregularities in the recruitment of athletes.

There were other positives at South Carolina as well. The university administration was wonderfully considerate and helpful. President Tom Jones and his special assistant, Hal Brunton, a true visionary, were rock solid in their support, and the many fans and friends of the Gamecocks were eager to help. My staff and I rolled up our sleeves and went to work. By my fourth season, the football team was undefeated in Atlantic Coast Conference play and won the school's first conference championship in

South Carolina's "G Boys," Ben Garnto and Benny Galloway, two fine running backs

any sport. The team earned an invitation to the 1969 Peach Bowl, ending a quarter-century bowl drought. Football scheduling was completed through the 1986 season, with a minimum of seven home games in all but two of those years. Home and home opponents included Oregon State, Michigan, Baylor, Southern California, Georgia Tech, Notre Dame, and many Southeastern Conference teams.

The combined sports teams in my last year at South Carolina posted a collective winning percentage of over 80 percent. Football season ticket sales increased from three thousand to twenty-five thousand, which was the limit of season tickets then available. The Gamecocks became one of the South's leaders in women's athletics in terms of funds expended, number of teams competing, and qualified coaching personnel.

While at South Carolina, I achieved my goal of completing twenty

In 1969 the Gamecock football team brought home USC's
first ACC championship in
any sport and garnered an invitation to the Orange Bowl,
the team's first bowl game in
twenty-five years.

years as a head football coach at major institutions. I announced my re-
tirement during the 1974 season. My 109 victories over the course of my
coaching career placed me at that time among the twenty winningest
coaches in America. That was accomplished at three different institutions whose programs had been in dire need of rebuilding. None of my
success as a coach could have been accomplished without the support of
great fans and cooperative administrators. I have been most fortunate.

When I accepted the positions at South Carolina, I signed a long-term
contract. I thought that when I reached the end of my coaching career,
I would retire from that aspect of the job but would remain as athletics director. But when the university officials found the new coach they
wanted, it turned out that he also wanted to be the athletics director. So,
a new coach and athletics director was hired, and suddenly I was no longer South Carolina's AD. I was appointed vice president for university re-
lations, with no change in salary.

After only one month in my new job, Steve, who was home from the Southern Baptist Theological Seminary in Louisville, said, "Dad, you've spent your life in athletics and you love sports. If you are unhappy with the situation, why don't you just resign?" So I did resign and was happy about it until I realized that I was fifty years old and jobless. However, I'd had many people tell me, "Boy, if you ever get out of athletics, let me know because we've got a job for you." Surprisingly, most of the telephone numbers of those people who made comments like that suddenly seemed to have been changed. When I did manage to reach someone, I usually got a very polite response that amounted to "Don't call us, we'll call you." I was in a tough situation. But there was one fellow I had known years before when he was a high school football coach in Kentucky. Eventually, he became a college coach and then athletics director at the University of North Carolina at Chapel Hill and then at Georgia Tech. His name was Homer Rice.

During this very trying time, Homer called me at least twice a week, and his comments were invariably encouraging and positive. "Don't worry about it, you have a lot of talent and a lot of people know you, and everything's going to work out fine. Just hang in there," he'd say. Homer's support and friendship meant a great deal to me and to Anne. But one particular phone call from Homer was to offer promise of happier days and an exciting new opportunity.

# VII

# A Commissioner and an Athletics Director

## Commissioner of the Ohio Valley Conference

Homer finally called me and said, "Now, Paul, I want you to act surprised, but you will be getting a call from Dr. Dero Downing. He is the president of Western Kentucky University and the chairman of the search committee to select a new commissioner for their conference." The Ohio Valley Conference was made up of eight fine schools—four in Tennessee and four in Kentucky. As Homer had promised, President Downing called and asked me if I would come for an interview. Anne and I drove to Western Kentucky, a beautiful college campus in Bowling Green. It's very near Nashville, and the conference office had been in Nashville for quite some time. The schools in Tennessee were Austin Peay, East Tennessee State, Middle Tennessee State, and Tennessee Tech. The Kentucky schools were Eastern Kentucky, Morehead State, Murray State, and Western Kentucky. I was very impressed with Western Kentucky and certainly impressed with Dr. Downing. He could not have been nicer—a very sincere country gentleman. To make a long story short, I was offered the job and accepted on the condition that the conference office be moved to Lexington, Kentucky. Dr. Downing remarked that since half the schools were in Kentucky and half were in Tennessee, there was no reason the office couldn't be located in Kentucky.

Anne's mother, Nannie, had lived with us for twenty-five years and was a joy to us and our children. She had helped raise Kathie and Steve and had been a part of our family for all of their lives. Anne and Nannie were impeccable housekeepers. My pet name for Nannie was "Speed-Ball." Nannie had a passion for keeping the laundry moving. One day I came home to shower and change for a speaking engagement. Before I went into the shower I laid out my clean underclothes, shirt, and socks on the bed. By the time I came out of the shower, all those things were already in the dryer. But Nannie and I got along fine because, as Anne always has said, "Nannie took Paul's side." Nannie was wonderful with Steve and Kathie.

But since we had to search for a place to live, we decided to ask Anne's

We celebrate the eighty-fifth birthday of our beloved Nannie, Anne's mother.

brother, Tom, if Nannie could temporarily live with his family in Washington, D.C. Well, Nannie didn't particularly want to go, but we told her it was only for a while. She was about ninety years old, but she was very strong for her age, and her mind was clear as a bell. So she reluctantly went to live with Tom and Lil Wilson in their small house, but she was not a happy camper. We moved into a rented apartment in Lexington and converted one of the rooms into a storage area where we put extra furniture from our previous home. We had a lot of friends in Lexington, so it was great to be back.

But Washington was a complete change for Nannie, and she was out of sorts. After only two weeks, she had a heart attack and was hospitalized. Anne and I went to Washington to see her. She said that she had lived too long and she refused to eat. On a very sad day we had to say good-bye to our beloved and irreplaceable Nannie. We never had a chance to move her back to live with us, which I deeply regret. Tom still resides in Washington with his daughter Susan. His other daughter, Barbara, has a son and a daughter. Barbara and her husband, Bill Woodward, reside in nearby Maryland. Tom's health has been failing and his wife, Lil, recently passed away after a long illness.

In Lexington, I found a space in a new building for the conference office, which turned out to be very nice. I hired Ralph Stout, who had been an official for many years, to serve as conference director of officials. Laura Hardesty became my office manager. One of the member schools, Morehead State, had a very fine industrial arts department. I asked their staff to create a map of Kentucky and Tennessee with the words *Ohio Valley Conference* as its title. This became our conference logo. Next, I designed a brochure that listed facts and figures describing

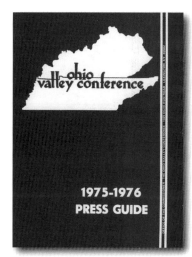

The annual Ohio Valley Conference press guide, featuring the new logo

Dr. Adron Doran, the colorful president of Morehead State University

all of the schools and included a history of the Ohio Valley Conference. I chose green and white for the conference colors because no school in the conference used green.

Anne and I scheduled a visit to each school in the conference. At each, I interviewed the president, the vice president, the faculty chairman, the athletics director, the coach and assistant coaches of every sport, and a cross section of the athletes. That gave me a good insight into what each school was all about. We were warmly welcomed at every institution, and I honestly don't believe I had ever met a finer group of people. On each campus, we were treated as distinguished guests and were put up in their finest quarters; in some cases we stayed in the president's home. I have said many times, and it's true, that that year was one of the happiest of our lives.

At each school, I got to know the president better than anyone else. I thought that the president of East Tennessee State, Dr. Delos Culp, was one of the brightest people I had ever met. The one I got the biggest kick out of was the president at Morehead State. His name was Dr. Adron Doran, and his wife was a very lovely lady named Mignon. Dr. Doran was somewhat of a character and a great horseman. He had a Tennessee Walker and at the football games would lead the band onto the field on his horse. He had been known to leave the stands and go out and accost officials with whom he disagreed. People warned me that I would have problems with Dr. Doran. It turned out that I had lots of conversations with him but I had no trouble. After about their second or third game, I received a letter from Dr. Doran, who totally disagreed with some calls the officials had made. In fact there were quite a few calls that he thought were incorrect, and he proceeded to tell me about each incident in detail. So Ralph Stout and I got the game film and studied it play by play, which was nothing new to me, since I'd been going through film all my life. We examined each incident that he felt had not been called properly and ascertained that the officials had been right. In my response to Dr. Doran, I told him exactly what I thought. I wrote, "We'll never completely agree on this, I expect, but you know you did hire me to run the conference and I did hire Ralph to serve as Director of Officials. He is very competent and able to manage the officials, and as long as I am the Commissioner, this is how I feel." I signed it, "Very sincerely." I got a letter right back that read:

Dear Coach Dietzel,

I have received your letter and, although I do not completely agree with your analysis of the game, I do agree that you are the Commissioner and it is your call to make. Therefore, I accept your letter and thank you.

On the bottom, he had scrawled in his handwriting, "And the same to you, fellow." I thought that was one of the funniest messages I had ever received, and we became very good friends—in fact I didn't have a better friend in the conference.

Dr. Doran and Mignon were wonderful to Anne and me. About this time, he had a very fine, modern dormitory constructed on campus. The dormitory was faced with large, five- by six-foot white marble slabs. Dr. Doran was not pleased with how the slabs were attached to the building, so he had them removed and demanded that the work be redone to his satisfaction. He ended up with a lot of spare marble. Dr. Doran gave me one of those slabs, which I kept and eventually used to very good advantage. Incidentally, that dormitory was named "Mignon Hall" in honor of his wife and her contributions to the university and the people of the region. Dr. Doran had the dormitory capped with a neon sign that blazed "Mignon Hall."

I visited Tennessee Tech, another very beautiful school, and met the president, Dr. Arliss Roaden. Dr. Roaden was a rock hound, a collector and polisher of rocks, and a very interesting person.

One of the real stars of the Ohio Valley Conference was the football coach at Eastern Kentucky, Roy Kidd. Roy was one of the most successful coaches in NCAA history, a wonderful fellow, and an outstanding person. He was a legend at Eastern Kentucky. But of all the people in the conference, there was none that I enjoyed and respected more than Dr. Dero Downing. What a wonderful man!

Little did I know that my time as commissioner of the Ohio Valley Conference was soon to come to an end. Anne and I were about to move once again.

Dr. Dero Downing, president of Western Kentucky University, a truly outstanding leader

## Athletics Director at Indiana

I'd been commissioner of the Ohio Valley Conference for about a year when Anne and I decided to go and see a Cincinnati Reds baseball game. This chance outing turned out to be a life-changing event. While we were waiting to pick up our tickets, guess who we ran into: Bobby Knight, my old friend and the former basketball coach at West Point. Bobby proceeded to tell me that Indiana University's athletics director, Bill Orwig, had retired and that I should apply for the job. I told Bobby that I didn't know anyone at Indiana. He said, "Well you know Bobby Knight, and through me, you know Doc Counsilman. That's all you need to know." Doc Counsilman was the legendary swimming coach at Indiana, the most famous swimming coach in the United States at the time. Indiana had won many swimming titles under his tutelage.

I asked him, "Didn't they end the interviews?"

"Yeah," he said, "but we'll open them up again, so bring your resume to me, and I'll see to it that you get invited to interview." Bobby swung a pretty heavy stick at Indiana.

Dr. Tony Mobley, dean of Health, Physical Education, and Recreation at Indiana University, with his son, Derek, and wife, Betty—our neighbors and great friends.

I decided to apply for the job. Art Goldner, an old neighbor and dear friend, drove with me to Bloomington. I had not been there before and was very impressed by the town and the beauty of the university. We arrived during basketball practice and went into the Assembly Hall, but the basketball manager immediately came over and said he was sorry but the practice was closed. I said, "I'm not here to watch the practice. I just came here to hand this to Coach Knight. He asked me to bring it to him." I was referring to my resume, of course. About then, Bobby saw us and motioned for us to come on in. We went in, I handed him the resume, and he said, "Wait until practice is over and I'll talk to you." We watched Bobby's team practice, and when it was over, he came and told me that he would deliver the resume to the search committee.

Soon after, I received a call from the committee chair, who invited me to interview. I was offered the position as athletics director and I accepted. I had served as commissioner of the Ohio Valley Conference for only one year and had been very happy in that position, but I felt I could not refuse Indiana's offer.

I invited Ralph Floyd, my former assistant at South Carolina, to join me at Indiana as assistant athletics director. He agreed and temporarily moved in with Anne and me in our small apartment. Ralph was not hard to please when it came to food; his menu consisted mainly of steak and fries. I think that combination did him in later, because both he and his wife passed away much too early.

I took over the reins at IU. We made two wonderful friends there, Tony and Betty Mobley. Tony was the dean of the School of Health, Physical Education, and Recreation. The Mobleys lived right across the street from us and have remained good friends even though they have become world travelers now that Tony is retired. They have a fine son, Derek, who became prominent in the television business. Derek used to mow our grass until he ran the mower over our electric cord and cut it. Each time I look at that cord, which I still have, I think of Derek Mobley. It was wonderful to have someone in the physical education department who was friendly to intercollegiate sports. In many schools, physical education and varsity sports are on a collision course all of the time, but at Indiana with Tony heading up PE, it was a pleasant relationship.

Tony and I jointly purchased a snowplow, which as it turned out, we would sorely need. When I took the job at Indiana, I asked Tony how the winters were there. He responded, "Oh, no problem at all; if we have snow, it's gone the next day." Famous last words! My second year at IU was the year of the big blizzard. It became impossible to clear the streets or for coal to be delivered, so there was no electricity and no heat. The entire campus of thirty thousand students was closed. There we were in the little house we had built, and we couldn't get out of the driveway. We stayed indoors for three weeks surrounded by four feet of snow. We'd turn on the television and all we would see would be the four-wheel drives and tractors sliding around in Indianapolis. Those were about the only vehicles that could operate in the deep snow that covered the streets. Fortunately, we had plenty of food in our freezer but had to find creative ways to get to the store to buy milk. It was the darndest experience. We had built an atrium in the middle of our house, about six by ten feet, and it was open to the sky. It filled with snow, and Anne got so tired of looking at it that I finally got the hose out and sprayed that snow until it all melted. This episode turned out to be one of our more interesting experiences in Bloomington, where the snow never lasts overnight. Right.

Our twenty-five-foot Helms sailboat, a pure delight

Anne had bought me a ship modeling kit for Christmas. When I was a young boy, I liked to build models of ships. I would buy one of the *Bounty* for a dollar and then sell it for a small profit after I had built it. Since I didn't have much else to do while we were snowed in, I worked on the model Anne had given me for hours on end. It was a model of the *Cutty Sark*, and it had three masts. It turned out pretty nice, and we still have it. Anne put it in a glass case, about five feet long and about three feet high. Each time we moved, it went with us.

While in Bloomington, I met a fellow named Jack Helms, who had designed and developed the Helms 25, a marvelous twenty-five-foot-long sailboat. For several years, it held the record as the fastest sailboat in its class in America. Jack invited Anne and me to join him for a sail. We had never been in a sailboat in our lives, so we decided to go. We drove out to Lake Monroe, a beautiful big lake just outside of Bloomington. As we sailed around, Jack said, "Take over." I told him I didn't know how to sail. He said, "That's OK, there's nothing to it." I took over the helm, and it was lots of fun. Jack told me that I was a born sailor and that he had never seen anyone learn so fast. Maybe that was just part of Jack's sales pitch, but the next thing we knew, we had bought a Helms 25, and it turned out to be one of the best purchases we had ever made. We went sailing as often as we could. I would phone Anne and say, "Why don't you make some sandwiches and we'll go sailing?" She would make some tasty sandwiches, put some Cokes in the cooler, and sailing we would go.

We would sail out as far as we could on the lake, and then we'd turn around and sail right into the sunset. I can't imagine anything more beautiful than sailing into the sunset—very romantic. We'd have our sandwiches and Cokes and sail back to the dock. Of course if the wind was down, the boat was equipped with a little twenty-five-horsepower motor, and we could motor back. Jack told us that a boat never depreciates. More famous last words. When we were preparing to leave Indiana and return to LSU, we had to decide what to do with the boat. We really didn't want

The athletics directors of the Big Ten Conference

to sell it because there's a lot of water in Louisiana, so we contacted Jack, who had talked us into buying that boat in the first place. He and his wife agreed that, for a small amount, they would haul the boat down to Louisiana for us. Then they could visit New Orleans, which would be a nice vacation for them. Well, they brought it down, we put it in the water, and then we advertised it and tried to sell it. Though we very much enjoyed having the boat in Indiana, we took a real financial loss on it. It's simply not true that a boat does not depreciate in value. Another lesson learned.

A good thing about the Big Ten was the monthly athletics directors meetings at O'Hare Airport in Chicago, where we discussed all the things that were going on in the conference and anything that was a problem. We would discuss mutual problems and try to find solutions. These meetings also helped a person like me who was new in the job become acquainted with the other athletics directors. The Big Ten Conference had some outstanding athletics directors. Among them were Hugh Hindman of Ohio State and Johnny Pont of Northwestern, both Miami University of Ohio alums. Cecil Coleman of Illinois and Don Canham of Michigan also became close friends of mine.

Don was a real character and an extremely talented fellow. While I was at South Carolina, he visited us to learn about our efforts in the area of sports merchandising and spent several days with our staff. Later, when I became Indiana's athletics director, I visited Michigan for the same purpose. Don had taken our achievements at South Carolina and improved upon them. Now I learned from him.

Two other Big Ten athletics directors at that time were Paul Geil of Minnesota and Elroy "Crazy Legs" Hirsch of Wisconsin. Every year the Big Ten held a meeting attended by the athletics directors, the faculty athletic chairmen, and all of their wives. It was a very fine affair. We would sing the fight songs of all the schools and swap stories. Since the wives were there, the stories were a lot cleaner than they might have been otherwise. One of the funniest I remember from these meetings was one told by Elroy about the time they were getting ready to go to a hockey match. Hockey is extremely popular in Minnesota and Wisconsin. Elroy's wife was trying to speed up Elroy, and she said, "Elroy, you'd better hurry or we're going to miss 'puck-off.'" I thought that was one of the funniest things I had ever heard. I enjoyed my association with the Big Ten very much, and I also enjoyed being the athletics director at Indiana.

I started a sports committee at IU whose members would meet and greet incoming teams and present their head coaches with courtesy cars. The players were given IU pen sets as mementoes. Crimson sports coats with cream-colored IU logos were designed for the members of the committee to wear when meeting the visiting teams. The sports committee grew by leaps and bounds. It certainly helped make players, coaches, and fans from other schools feel welcome and appreciated.

Bobby Knight had played a key role in bringing me to IU, and we got along very well. You have to understand Bobby, as he has a tendency to be volatile. For example, I heard that Bobby was not going to attend the Tip-Off Breakfast, an annual function for the Hoosier basketball faithful. Knight, naturally, was the star of the show. For some reason, he had become upset with some of the members of the Tip-Off Club. When I learned that he was not going to the breakfast, I called him into my office and said, "Bobby, I hear you're not going to the Tip-Off Club breakfast."

He snarled, "No, those no good ——s!"

"Bobby," I calmly replied, "these are your biggest backers. These are the people that are always willing to go to war for you every time you show your backside, which you have a tendency to do rather often. They always stick up for you. You have no better backers. When you say you are not going to that breakfast, that's like kicking your faithful supporters in the stomach. You're just telling them, 'To heck with you, I don't need you.' But everyone needs others, and so do you. By the way, Bobby, when you go out to practice in the Assembly Hall, I think you'll notice that there are some national champion banners that predate your time here. You know, Indiana had great basketball before you arrived. Honestly, I don't care whether you want to go or not. You've got to go!"

In the Oval Office being congratulated by President Gerald Ford on Indiana's winning the national basketball championship under the direction of Bobby Knight.

He stared at me for a minute or so in silence, and then said, "Well, I'll go for you, but I'm not going for those ——s." Bobby went to the Tip-Off Club breakfast and absolutely charmed everyone there in his usual way, telling them how stupid they were, that they didn't know anything about basketball, and then proceeding to absolutely mesmerize them.

In the two years that I was at IU, Coach Knight's basketball team won the Big Ten championship and the NCAA championship. In soccer, Indiana placed second in the NCAA, and in 1978, Doc Counsilman once again won the Big Ten championship in swimming. During my tenure as Indiana's athletics director, the Varsity Club increased its annual donations from three hundred thousand dollars to more than eight hundred thousand dollars—quite an improvement.

Little did I realize that very soon I was about to hear once again from LSU.

# VIII
## Once Again, LSU

In early 1978, I received a call from Paul Murrill, the chancellor of LSU, who said, "Paul, I know you probably know that we're hunting for an athletics director since Carl Maddox has retired, and we wondered if you would be interested."

I said, "Chancellor Murrill, this comes out of the blue, but I did read where Carl Maddox had retired, and I'm really not sure what to say."

"Well," he said, "we would like to have you come down here to be interviewed by the Board of Supervisors."

I told him, "Dr. Murrill, I'm really sorry, but I can't do that. In the first place, if Indiana found out that I was looking at another job, they would probably fire me. Very honestly, the board of supervisors at LSU already knows me; I don't think they need to interview me. They know everything about me, I believe. I just cannot come down there for an interview."

The chancellor replied that he'd get back in touch with me. He called back and said, "Paul, several of the supervisors would like to fly to Bloomington in our private airplane and interview you."

I said, "Chancellor Murrill, if they do, it would have to be strictly on the q.t. They can land at the small airport here, and I'll meet the airplane. I just don't want anyone to know they are coming. Furthermore, if they're coming here to interview me about coming to LSU as the athletics director, I just can't do that because I haven't said anything to Dr. Ryan, our president, and I don't believe you have either. If they want to talk to me about what I think they should be looking for in an athletics director, I'll be glad to talk with them. But if they want to try to interest me in coming to LSU, I don't think that's a good idea."

Several members of the board of supervisors flew up, along with John Ferguson, the announcer for the Tiger radio network. I very quietly picked them up at the airport and took them to my home, where I cooked steaks for them. We chatted for a spell, and finally they got around to the point and asked, "Are you sure you're not interested in coming back to LSU?"

My daughter, Kathie, who was a Wilhelmina model in New York City at the time, was home visiting. She joined in, "Mother has always gone wherever you wanted to go, and she would like to go back to Louisiana.

She has lots of friends there, and she's had more than enough of this weather."

When they returned to Louisiana, I got a call from Chancellor Murrill, who said, "Paul, we're very interested in you as athletics director, and we'd like to know if you are interested in the job."

"Dr. Murrill," I responded, "I cannot go any further until I know whether or not you are offering me the job."

He said, "I'm in a position to say yes. We would like to hire you."

I said, "All right, then, I'll have to go see Dr. Ryan."

When I visited the president, he said to me, "Paul, I understand the situation because of your past experience at LSU. It would be like going back home, and I would not blame you. I had much the same thing happen to me once. If you would like to leave, then I would certainly wish you well."

Shortly thereafter it was time to go to a national athletics directors' meeting in Las Vegas. One morning as we were walking across the lobby, Anne and I ran into Carl and Clare Maddox. By this time, Anne and I had quite thoroughly discussed the possibility of moving back to Louisiana. I had made up my mind that I wasn't going to take the job at LSU. Carl said to me, "I sure would like to talk with you."

Kathie as a Wilhelmina model

"Carl," I said, "I was just getting ready to call LSU and tell them I wasn't interested in the job."

"Oh, don't do that," he said. "Come on up to my room."

So Anne and I went to Carl's room, and he said, "Paul, you know the situation down there, and I don't know anyone else but you who can handle it."

"You know I do spend a lot of money, Carl," I said.

"I know you do," he said, "but you also generate a lot of money. I really wish you'd take the job."

His comments made me think again about the offer. It was a difficult decision to reach because I had a very good job at Indiana, and I had some misgivings about going back to Baton Rouge, but I decided to accept the offer. I realized that there were probably some people who were still mad at me for leaving when I did. This proved to be all too true.

When we returned to IU from Las Vegas, I told Dr. Ryan of my decision, and the same morning, I called Dr. Murrill and informed him that I would take the job at LSU. He said, "Great! When can you start?"

When you know you're going to leave a place, you can leave pretty quickly. We had designed and built a comfortable house in a fine subdivision. It was not a big house, but it was one of my favorite houses of the twenty-eight that we have lived in since we have been married. It was announced on television that night that I was going to leave Indiana and return to LSU. How the news spread so rapidly I do not know, but my neighbor immediately came over and offered to buy our house. We put a reasonable price on it, which was a bit more than it had cost us to build. While he was there, I got a call from another neighbor who wanted the house, too. Actually, there were three people competing for that house, and we hadn't even put it on the market. The one who bought it was a professor at Indiana, who initially offered us about five thousand dollars less than we had asked. I told him we couldn't take that because we had another offer for the asking price. He said, "OK, I'll take it," and wrote out a check right then and there.

It wasn't long before we moved to Baton Rouge and I began my tenure as LSU's director of athletics. I couldn't have had a finer boss than Chancellor Murrill. He and his wife, Nancy, became good and true friends. Paul did me a real honor because every Monday morning, he had a meeting of all the vice chancellors at LSU and always included me. That was very nice.

Charlie Mac and his wife, Dorothy Faye, were always very kind to me and the family. When we first arrived, Dorothy Faye brought a wonderful dinner to welcome us home. Almost every coach on Charlie Mac's staff was someone that I had coached here at LSU: Lynn LeBlanc, Dave McCarty, Scooter Purvis, and Jerry Stovall. They were fine coaches and a great group of people. Dale Brown was the basketball coach, and he and I hit it off immediately. Dale has always remained a very close friend, and I admire him greatly. He has a tendency from time to time to say a little bit more than he means to say, but you always know exactly where you stand with Dale. I really liked him, and I still like him very much.

Shortly after arriving at LSU, I instituted a varsity club similar to the ones that had been so successful at Indiana and South Carolina. Because of these organizations, the athletics departments at both universities were running in the black. The Varsity Club at LSU began with nothing and within three and a half years generated an income in excess of one million dollars annually. In later years, the Varsity Club was renamed the Tiger Athletic Foundation, or TAF. This fine organization kept the athletics department in the black.

At South Carolina, the Gamecock Club kept the athletics department in the black and still does. All of the excellent new facilities such as those for outdoor track, the spring sports center, improved locker and weight rooms, and more could not have been built without the voluntary donations of many friends of the university. In exchange, donors were given the privilege of purchasing preferred seating and parking privileges. I brought the varsity club idea with me when I became athletics director at LSU. The Tiger Athletic Foundation is now marvelously run by General Ron Richard and his staff and continues to provide the same privileges to loyal Tiger friends and fans. The seat tax inaugurated by

TAF in recent years is exactly what I suggested to the chancellor back in 1981–1982.

Before taking the job as athletics director at LSU, I had been assured by members of the board of supervisors that I would not have to deal with the problem of firing my longtime friend, Charlie McClendon. I had been told that the problem had already been taken care of, but it had not. Alumni and fans were howling for Charlie's head. Signs like "Help Mac Pack!" abounded. It's very unfortunate that even when a person has done a wonderful job, some people are never satisfied. As Dorothy Faye was quoted as saying in the local newspaper, "The LSU fans will not be satisfied unless you win every game by at least thirty points."

At this time, Coach McClendon was serving as first vice president of the American Football Coaches Association, and he was next in line to become president. But to hold that office, a person must be actively coaching. It was very important to me that Charlie McClendon be allowed to become president of the AFCA. I talked with Dr. Murrill about a plan I had, and he thought it was a fine idea. So I called Mac and Dorothy Faye into my office, and the conversation went like this.

I started by saying, "Mac, you and I worked together here at LSU for seven years when I was head coach and you were my first assistant. We also served together on Coach Bryant's staff back in Kentucky. During all that time, have you and I ever had an argument? Maybe we might have differed on how we should line up our defense, who we might start at cornerback, or something like that, but did we ever have a real argument?"

He said, "No."

I said, "Have we ever, ever had any trouble getting along together?"

He said, "Absolutely not."

"Was it a problem to you when I was the head coach and you were my first assistant here at LSU?" I asked.

He said, "No."

I said, "Is there any reason why we can't continue working together?"

He said, "Well what do you have in mind?"

I replied, "Mac, both of us know that it is important to you and Dorothy Faye that you become the president of the American Football Coaches Association. Isn't that right?"

He said, "Yes, it is."

I said, "You've waited a long time. I know how long I had to wait before I got the job, and I know you've been waiting and thinking about it, and I want you to have that job."

Then Mac said to me, "I want that, too."

"Mac," I said, "everyone has to retire at some time or another. The best time to retire is when you've had a good year. The problem is that many coaches decide that they're going to retire after they've had a good year, like the great year I had at South Carolina, but everyone around says, 'You think you want to retire? Why do you want to retire? You've got a

great team coming back!' And you say, 'Well, we had a great year, and that wasn't so hard. Why leave now?' And a year or so later, these same people want you fired. We both know there are only two kinds of coaches, those who have been fired and those who are going to be fired. I don't want you to have ever face that second option. What would you think about becoming my first assistant after you retire?"

I said, "Mac, you're going to have a winning season this year, you have a good team returning. It would be a great year for you to go out on top. Every coach has got to find a time to retire, and frankly, we both know that it gets tough when people turn on you. It is especially hard on your wife and family. I know because I've been there. What would you think about announcing now, before the season starts, that you're going to re- tire at the end of the year and that you will stay on as first assistant direc- tor of athletics? We would be in the same situation that we were in when I was the head coach and you were the first assistant. Would you have any problem with that?"

He said, "Well, what would I do?"

"Mac, there are tons of things that you could do. You have a vast fam- ily of friends and would be tremendous at organizing events like golf out- ings and get-togethers where you can build strong relationships with peo- ple who are in a position to help the university. You could be a lot more than just a fund-raiser. You would be very valuable to LSU, as you always have been. You could coach one more year. Then the pressure will be off, and you can look forward to having a job for the rest of your life. Your salary will remain unchanged. What do you think about that, Mac? What do you think about it, Dorothy Faye?"

Her response was spontaneous: "Praise the Lord," she said. "I'll be so glad to get this off our backs!"

Mac said, "Yes, I think that would be good, I think that would be fine."

I said, "Well, if its all right with you, then, we'll go ahead and announce that you have decided to retire at the end of this year, that this will be your last year of coaching, and that you are going to move into the athletics department as my first assistant at the same salary you are now making. How does that sound to you?"

Mac said, "Sounds good. I think that's fine." When they left my office, they were as happy as I've ever seen them. If I could read anyone, they were relieved.

Well, the news came out and everything seemed fine. I had also told Mac that if he announced that he was retiring now, before the season, his assistant coaches would have time to decide what they were going to do in the future. Everyone seemed contented; there wasn't any backlash or any problems that I saw until a headline in the *Alexandria Town Talk* proclaimed, "Dietzel Fires Old Buddy." That was far from the truth. I tried to protect Mac as best I could and to enable him to end his football career with some dignity. Sadly, from that time on, our relationship deteriorated. We were still friends, but this unfortunate episode had come between us.

By this time football season was in progress, and the team was doing very well. I went to work to search for a replacement for Mac. I had a short list of coaches I thought might be a good match for LSU. Basically, I wanted someone who was a fine football coach with a winning record and the charisma necessary to be successful at LSU. That short list was headed by Bobby Bowden of Florida State, who was a very close friend of mine, and Lou Holtz of Arkansas, who had been on my staff at South Carolina. A third prospect was Bo Rein of North Carolina State, who Woody Hayes (whom I had known when he was coach at Miami of Ohio) said was the finest young coach he had ever had on his staff. Importantly, Bo had been highly successful at North Carolina State. Also on the list was George Welsh, who was coaching at Virginia. He was an excellent coach and had a fine record wherever he had been. I wanted to make sure that the new coach, whoever he might be, would abide by the rules of the NCAA. I didn't want to worry about rules violations or NCAA investigations and sanctions.

The first prospective coach I talked with was Bobby Bowden. Since we were in football season, I had to be a little careful. Bobby told me that he would be very interested in the job.

In the meantime, I met with all the others. I spoke with Lou Holtz and he said, "Coach, I'd be real interested. I would like to work for you."

"Well," I explained, "you know, you wouldn't be working *for* me, you'd be working *with* me because this is something that takes everybody's efforts."

He said, "I know that, and I'd be real interested."

I talked with Bo Rein, who was very interested in coming to LSU. After a couple of conversations with George Welsh, he told me he appreciated the offer but was just not interested.

I wanted to hire Bobby Bowden, who was my first choice. We were both very involved in the Fellowship of Christian Athletes, and that's how I had gotten to know Bobby. Bobby is a great fellow and a fine coach. He is also a great recruiter. But about the fourth time I called Bobby, he said, "Paul, I would really like to work with you—it would be an honor and I know we would get along beautifully—but I just signed a ten-year contract, and I can't leave. I really think LSU is a great spot, but I can't leave Florida State." I was disappointed but told him I understood.

Next, I focused on Lou Holtz. When I called him, he said, "I'm busy getting ready for the game coming up this week, but I'm still very interested. Please don't forget me. Give me a call next week." So I called him back the next week. This was about the third or fourth time I called Lou, and he said, "You know, I've been thinking about it, and I know the pressure that's on down at LSU. Frankly, I think I'm better off here at Arkansas. I don't think I want to leave Arkansas for LSU."

I said, "I'm sorry to hear that, but if that's your decision, that's your decision."

He said, "Well, that's what I've decided to do."

"OK, Coach," I said. "Good luck with your game on Saturday."

Though I had been turned down by three of the four, never had Bo Rein been on the back burner. When I had spoken to Woody Hayes about Bo Rein, Woody had said, "Paul, I'll tell you one thing, there are some fellows that you know are going to be highly successful. Bo Rein is such a fine young man. Bo has been All–Big Ten in both football and in baseball. He is a fine recruiter, because he can really get close to people. I have never had a better assistant coach on my staff, nor have I ever coached a finer young man. You can't possibly miss with Bo Rein."

I again contacted Bo, who was doing extremely well at North Carolina State. Although he hadn't been there very long, he had a solid record and was well liked. Negotiations progressed, and eventually I hired him. I think some people were a bit disappointed because they had never heard of him.

"Who is Bo Rein?" people asked. Unfortunately, they would never know. Bo set out immediately recruiting for LSU and made a tremendous impression on the recruiting trail. He was recruiting in Shreveport and had been loaned a private company's new jet for the trip. He and the pilot were the only two on board this pressurized jet. The pilot had hundreds and hundreds of hours of experience.

They took off from Shreveport on the same night that I was in New Orleans at a coaches' meeting. When I returned home, Anne said, "Call up the coaching staff, they can't find Bo." I phoned the coaches who had gathered at the football office. Paul Manasseh, the sports information director, was there with the staff and said, "Coach, we can't find Rein." As the story goes, he had taken off from Shreveport, and when the plane was at about twenty thousand feet, the pilot had radioed and reported turbulence and requested permission to go to a higher altitude. Ground control cleared them to go higher.

"Roger," the pilot radioed back, and that was the last thing that was ever heard from that airplane. Then it was reported that Bo's airplane had been flying out over the ocean. When I heard that, I said, "You mean over the Gulf, from Shreveport to Baton Rouge, you know." But, no, the plane had been spotted over the Atlantic Ocean. That airplane just kept climbing and climbing and flew right over Raleigh, where North Carolina State is located, and right over Bo's home, where his wife and family were in bed asleep. The airplane continued on a straight path, and when it didn't report in, the FAA sent up two military jets, which flew right beside the aircraft that Bo and the pilot were in. The windows were frosted. No one could be seen in the cockpit or cabin, and the airplane was flying straight and steady in a very slow climb. It climbed to over forty-one thousand feet (its ceiling was thirty-four thousand feet), and continued out over the Atlantic Ocean. The F-4s flew right beside it trying to raise someone, but they were unsuccessful. They flew right beside Bo's plane until it ran out of fuel and plunged into the Atlantic Ocean. That tragic crash into the ocean ended the lives of Bo Rein and his pilot. What might have been a brilliant career was cut short.

Meanwhile, Mac's last team at LSU had worked hard, played extremely well, and received an invitation to play in the Tangerine Bowl. We accepted the bid, and the Tigers played a fine game and won it going away. Mac, as he always did, made a great impression on the people who ran that bowl. They later hired him as director of the bowl. Mac really did a fine job for them, raised a lot of money, and sold a lot of tickets. They thought the world of him, as they should have, because Mac did a great job.

When we learned what had happened to Bo, we were all in a state of shock. Bo had already brought his entire North Carolina State staff to LSU. I had told Charlie McClendon's staff that we would keep them on the payroll for another year, and so we had Bo Rein's staff and Charlie McClendon's old staff at LSU at the same time. When Bo came, I said, "Bo, most of Charlie McClendon's staff are young men that I coached. You could not possibly find a greater group of coaches than they are. They are all very young, they're all LSU through and through, and they're just a great bunch." I discussed each of Mac's assistant coaches in detail. I said, "I would appreciate it greatly, and it would do you a real service, if you would keep as many of them as you possibly can."

The situation was different when I came to LSU in 1955 because I took over the entire staff of Gaynell Tinsley. But Bo wanted to bring his own staff. Bo did call each one of the former staff and talked with each man. He did the right thing about that, and he told Scooter Purvis that he would like to have him stay. Scooter asked if he was keeping any other members of the staff. Bo said, "No, I've got my own staff."

Scooter, being the kind of a man he is, said, "If you aren't going to hire any of the others, I can't do that. I wouldn't feel right about that at all."

But, as I said, we kept Charlie Mac's assistants on staff for what would have been Bo's first season, so after the tragic accident, we had two full coaching staffs and no head coach. Paul Manasseh, who was really a pretty bright fellow, said, "Paul, you've got to take over as head coach."

"Oh, no, no, no," I said. "There is no way I would do that because someone might think that I was just waiting for the chance to become the head coach again. I don't want to be a head coach ever again. We have to hire someone to run these staffs."

So I thought about it a great deal and went over to see Chancellor Murrill. I explained the dilemma of having two full coaching staffs, and I said, "We've got to hire someone from these staffs to serve as head coach. I do not know Bo's staff at all. They seem like nice people and are proven coaches, but I don't know them. I know one man on Coach Mac's staff who I think would do a fine job as a head coach, and that's Jerry Stovall. Jerry was a fantastic athlete at LSU and very narrowly missed winning the Heisman Trophy. He's been on my staff, and I know what a good job he did recruiting for me at South Carolina. My suggestion is that we appoint Jerry Stovall as the new head coach. I would like to have your advice."

Well, Paul Murrill knew Jerry Stovall, too, as Jerry was held in high regard among the LSU faithful. He was a star player at LSU and was well known throughout the state. I thought Jerry was a perfect selection. Given our circumstances, he was by far the best choice we had. So Jerry Stovall became LSU's new head coach.

Jerry studied the two staffs and kept a combination of coaches. Jerry did a remarkable job. It was unfortunate that he was not allowed enough time to have the success that he would have had, but, again, LSU fans have a tendency to be a little short-sighted, and they can be very impatient.

It had become apparent that expenditures were outrunning revenue in the athletics department, and we were obviously going to have to do something to increase revenue even though the Varsity Club was now bringing in around a million dollars annually. With this in mind, I had written a long treatise on three different options we could use to increase income. One of them was to inaugurate a seat tax almost exactly like the one Skip Bertman and TAF are now using. Another was to raise the price of tickets to the games, and I very carefully explored this possibility in my treatise. The third possibility was one that I really did not want to entertain at all, but it was an option, and that was to increase the price of student tickets. When I was at South Carolina and at Indiana, student ticket fees were never raised. I firmly believed that the students are what the university is all about and to try and get more money from them really was far from my mind.

Each year in June and July, about one million dollars was transferred from the Varsity Club to the athletics department account. However, when the financial report was presented at the board of supervisors meeting in Alexandria in the spring of 1982, no mention was made of that fact. Without that one-million-dollar boost, naturally the financial report showed that we were on shaky ground. With the addition of that million dollars, the department's finances were in very good shape. At the time, I didn't know how to defend myself because I had no idea this was going to come up. I was told to leave the meeting room. A little later, Tommy Neck, one of my former players who was on the board at that time, left the meeting to tell me what was going on. Tommy said, "The board is going to move you into the position of special assistant to the president of the university." I was really crushed. It was hard for me to believe that after all the years that I had spent in athletics, my career was going to end like this.

So I became the special assistant to President Martin Woodin, who was very gracious to me. He was as helpful and as sympathetic as anyone could possibly have been. But I was not very happy. In fact, I was not happy at all. Once again, I had some thinking to do. The very next morning, there was a knock at our front door. I opened the door and there stood Jimmy and Laura Field. They had baked a coffee cake and had come by to offer their support. They assured us that they loved us and thought what had happened was terrible. That had to be one of the finest gestures of friendship that Anne and I had ever experienced. We will never ever forget Jimmy and Laura. They are magnificent people, and we will always love them.

With Jimmy and Laura Field, two of the finest friends we have ever had—always there in a clutch!

# IX
## Golden Years

### Retired to North Carolina

I felt very uncomfortable in my new job at LSU. Anne and I discussed our situation at great length and decided to move back to Beech Mountain, where we owned a nice little house. I guess you could say that I more or less escaped to North Carolina. It was far away from LSU, and we had some very good friends there. Our home was only five minutes from the ski slopes, and I love to ski.

Very early on at Beech Mountain, when my grandson Paul II was only four months old, Steve, Judy, and Paul visited us. Young Paul was fussing, so I held him and gave him his bottle. After the feeding (and burping), I sat in our rocking chair and sang to him the same Indian lullaby that I was taught by Kittu Parker years before in Green Springs, Ohio. In the lullaby, "baba" is repeated over and over. Months later, strange as it seems, Paul II called me "Baba." To this day, I am Baba to my family.

Feeding our first grandson, Paul Dietzel II

Those years in the mountains of North Carolina turned out to be some of the most memorable years I ever spent with my family. During that time, I really got connected with my two grandsons, Paul II and David, as they grew older. They became adept skiers, and Anne and I enjoyed being with them. Many battles were fought in their "fort," which David's father, Dale, and I built in the wooded area beside our home on Beech Mountain. We even had some art lessons, which were fun but didn't really "take." We gave rewards for achievement in skiing and artwork or for very special valor in defense of the fort. Sometimes these rewards were my special blueberry pancakes shaped like rabbits, with hot maple syrup. This was a favorite of everyone, including me.

After settling down, I completed the hours of class required to become a real estate salesman and eventually passed the state exam and obtained a license as a real estate broker. From time to time, I sold a lot here and a lot there, and once in a while, a house. To be honest, I never really got excited about the real estate business. I had spent my entire professional life working on weekends. In the real estate business, you work on weekends. That's when most people have time to shop around for a new house. I felt that Anne and I deserved weekends to ourselves. So much for a career in real estate!

Anne and I kept driving by one place that was for sale, right in one of the hairpin curves coming up the mountain. It was a magnificent spot with a fantastic view, a big house made of stone and cedar with a huge fireplace large enough for me to lie down in. There were stone steps going down into a sunken living room and stone steps going to rooms upstairs. Next to it was a barn. It was an odd barn because the fellow that built this place, whose name was Albert, was a little bit unusual. At the very least, he was eccentric. It was supposed to be rectangular, but the rectangle wouldn't fit on the part of the land that Albert wanted to put it on, so the walls ended up not being at right angles, and the building was actually pointed at both ends. Albert had installed an old-fashioned grease pit in the barn for lubricating motor vehicles, and he used some of the space in the structure to house a small nursery business that he ran.

Inside view of our home at Beech Mountain

The house itself was wonderful but quite unusual. One year, after some very heavy rains, the sunken living room had flooded with about a foot of water. To cope with the situation, Albert gathered all the shrubbery from the nursery in the barn and placed it in the sunken living room so the plants could soak up the water. The house and the owner were both unusual.

Each time we went down the mountain, we had to drive by that house. I told Anne that I didn't want to go see it because if I did, I'd probably want to buy it. Eventually, we looked at it and asked Albert how much he wanted for it. Basically, he was just trying to get out from under the payments. We got a heck of a bargain. We sold our little house and bought this property. We thought a lot about the use we could make of the barn, which just happened to have a good-sized driveway and a fairly spacious parking lot.

When we lived in Indiana, we liked to visit a little town in Brown

County where the townspeople had transformed old buildings into attractive shops and restaurants. They would section off a large building to create five or six smaller spaces, which would then be converted into various kinds of retail shops. Anne and I thought that this concept might work very well for us, so we went to work on our barn.

We filled the grease pit and put some indoor-outdoor carpeting down and then divided up this strangely shaped barn into about five or six little shops. I built the partitions to separate the shops with green isinglass going about half-way up and then white latticework rising up to about eight feet. This allowed you to stand in any of the shops and see what was going on in the others. Then either Anne or I, or both of us, could run all of the shops at the same time, as long as we didn't have an overflow of customers. We had to find a name for this place, and once again, I got an idea from an earlier experience. When we were at West Point, I used to ski at Hunter Mountain. After skiing one afternoon, on the way home I stopped for a hamburger at a place called the Wobbley Barn. Several young entrepreneurs had taken an old barn, converted the stalls into booths, and created a small café where they sold hamburgers, hotdogs, sandwiches, Cokes, and beer. It was cleverly done. At the time, I thought that was one of the neatest things I'd ever seen. When we were trying to name the place we had just opened, I immediately thought of the Wobbley Barn. To make sure that I didn't step on anyone's toes, I called Rutland, Vermont, which was in the vicinity of Hunter Mountain, and asked for the telephone number of the Wobbley Barn. The operator asked which one; it seems that there were two of them. I said, "Oh, give me the number of the number-one Wobbley Barn. By the way, I want to make sure you have the right place. How do you spell it?"

"W-O-B-B-L-E-Y," she said.

So, I asked Anne, "How about naming this place the Wobbley Barn?" She thought that was a great idea, but finally we settled on "Wobbly Square." Our new property had a huge stone-faced sign at the entrance to the driveway. The sign was at least twelve feet long and eight feet tall. I cut out some letters and shaped them to look like they were wobbling, and the barn was christened "Wobbly Square."

We put in a little sports shop, managed by Orvis Sigler, an old friend of mine. Anne is very handy with crafts and has had several craft shops during our marriage, so she opened a shop we called Crafty Anne's. Another lady opened a knitting shop. We opened a bookstore, which offered a great variety of children's books. We also had a homemade ice cream shop, which was furnished with little round tables and wire-backed chairs. Then we bought a freezer cabinet to display the ice cream. We had a pretty nice operation. To get ice cream, we drove to Johnson City, Tennessee, which was about an hour away. We found a place that made fantastic homemade ice cream in a wide variety of flavors. In the middle of summer, we would drive our van with the air-conditioning full tilt, the win-

Our big sign advertising Wobbly Square

dows up, and our ski jackets on. We did our best to prevent the five-gallon cartons of ice cream we had just purchased from melting. We'd haul them back to Beech Mountain and Wobbly Square as fast as we could.

We were doing all right with our little shops. Business wasn't great, but it was good enough. Anne and I decided to travel to Texas to visit the Dallas Market Center, which houses hundreds of wholesalers. After two days of shopping, we had walked our legs off and had made up our minds to return home the next day.

It was then that I stumbled across this fudge machine. I am a choco-holic and make no bones about it. I love chocolate! I couldn't resist sampling the fudge from the machine, and I'd never tasted fudge any better. It was moist and delicious and rich. It was as good as the fudge I used to make when I was a boy back in Green Springs, Ohio. The salesman sensed that I was hooked and asked, "Would you be interested in becoming one of our outlets? We've got a market special. For $3,500, you can buy this thirty-six quart stainless-steel mixing vat plus one year's supply of chocolate mix and one year's supply of powdered cream. You get all the pans and all the mixing utensils and all the flavors that you need. All of this for just $3,500."

This sounded like a great deal to me, so I found Anne and told her about the fudge kettle. Her first reaction was less than enthusiastic: "I don't think so!" she said.

But I persisted, saying, "Honey, we've got to have this. I mean, we've got to have this!"

To make a long story short, I won Anne over, and we bought the fudge

The Dietzel clan in July 1993: Paul II and David DuTremble in front; Steve Dietzel standing behind wife Judy, who is standing beside Anne, Kathie and husband Dale DuTremble, and myself.

kettle and headed for home. The salesman represented the Calico Cottage Candy Company of New Jersey. Within a few weeks, he delivered the kettle to us and taught us how to operate it.

Anne and I redesigned one of the rooms in Wobbly Square to accommodate the fudge kettle, and I found the perfect use for that huge slab of marble which had been given to us by Dr. Adron Doran of Morehead State when I served as commissioner of the Ohio Valley Conference. I took that slab of marble and used it as the top shelf in the fudge case. I bought a big piece of glass for the front, built a wooden frame around it, and then installed glass trays that would slide in and out. We had the best-looking fudge case I've ever seen. So I started making fudge, and life was never the same again. Some of our best customers were some folks who lived in Florida. They would call and order several pounds of fudge at a time. So I bought these neat boxes with Wobbly Square logos so we could mail fudge to them.

I had at least twenty-five different flavors of fudge in the case. I could make about thirty-five pounds in a batch. Since I didn't want to clean the kettle after each batch, I would make one batch after another, and after the third batch I would clean the kettle. The kettle had fingers that rotated and kept stirring the fudge to make it really smooth. With my squeegee, I could get most of it out, but a point was reached where I couldn't get all the fudge from between those fingers. The only way I could remove it was to use my own finger. Since I couldn't sell those bits of fudge, I would eat them. I figured out that there would usually be about two pounds of fudge that I could not get out of the kettle with my squeegee. I always ate the two pounds and never got sick. The recipe for the fudge included two bags of chocolate mix, two quarts of pure cream, and two pounds of butter. That fudge was incredibly rich and delicious. In those days, people weren't so concerned about cholesterol the way they are today.

From that time on, I wished that we hadn't opened those other little shops, because I would have preferred having nothing but the fudge shop. We sold so much fudge that I had to make it twice a week. We were selling 250 pounds of fudge a week, and that's a lot of fudge for a one-man operation. The fudge shop was doing extremely well, and every time someone would drive up, I'd count how many people were in the car. As soon as they came to the door, I would cut little slivers of fudge for each of them and served them the fudge on little pieces of waxed paper. "So you won't have a chocolate fit, I want you to taste this." Invariably, they would come back and look at that delicious fudge. The fudge was always fresh be-

With grandson David at Wobbly Square

cause at the beginning of each day, I would take a tiny slice off the edge of the pieces of fudge that were in the case. I'd refrigerate these until it was time to make another batch and then add the slivers to the fudge in process.

We never had any fudge that got stale, and it always stayed really moist, thanks to all that rich butter and cream. Folks would look at that fudge in the case and say they wanted a piece of this or that. "How big a piece?" I'd say. I knew by feel about how much a pound was, and I'd usually hit it very close. I had rocky road, chocolate cherry, maple, maple chocolate swirl, and pecan fudge—every imaginable flavor. Some of the flavors were extra rich. Sometimes I crunched up Heath bars and mixed them in with fudge. With so many tempting varieties, I would end up selling three or four pounds of fudge to visitors who hadn't planned on buying any. The fudge operation was fantastic, and we really came to enjoy running it.

At that time Mack Brown (currently head coach at the University of Texas) was head football coach at Appalachian State. He had been an assistant coach at LSU when I was the athletics director there. Mack and his athletics director came over to visit with me and asked if I would do the color commentary for their radio broadcasts. That sounded like an interesting possibility, so I agreed. I visited the campus early in the preseason to get acquainted with the players, and then later, I'd go over on Tuesday and Thursday afternoons to interview several of the players. On Friday, if the team played out of town, I would make the trip with them. Anne finally said, "You might as well go back to coaching—you're gone as much as you were when you were coaching." So we hired two young ladies to help us at Wobbly Square so Anne and I could attend away games together. When we returned home after one trip, our helpers pleaded, "Don't ever leave us alone again! We have been so busy!" We really were doing extremely well. The next year I did the color for the Southern Conference television package, and that was really fun.

Finally, Anne and I realized that we were working harder than we ever had and decided to sell Wobbly Square. It was late in November, football season was over, and we put the place up for sale. We were told that you can't sell anything in the winter at Beech Mountain. Wrong! About two weeks later, this fellow came in and made us an acceptable offer. The man who bought it was the president of Days Inn of America, and he had a daughter who married a young man from Montana. He wanted to buy our place for his daughter and her husband so that they might move to Beech Mountain. Our home along with the fudge shop and Wobbly Square was purchased in mid-December. So much for thinking a place can't be sold in the wintertime.

Just about this time, one of my old friends from Hunter Mountain was hired to run the ski school at Beech Mountain. His name was Carl Plattner, and he had been the Austrian downhill racing champion. He skied like a demon. He and his wife, Margo, also Austrian, came down, and we

Broadcasting on the Appalachian State University Network

invited them to dinner at our home. We still had Wobbly Square at the time. Carl said, "Oh, you've got to be one of my ski instructors."

"Carl, you don't need a sixty year old ski instructor," I said.

He said, "Oh, I have them older than that at Hunter Mountain."

So I agreed. That winter, I was a full-time ski instructor, and I assure you that I learned more about skiing than I ever taught. Naturally, these young instructors, referred to as flat-bellies, would get all the cute young girls, and I would end up with the older ladies. Many of them were not in very good shape—it seemed like a lot of heavy women wanted to learn to ski! I spent so much time picking them up off the snow that I began to think that's where the saying "I've fallen and I can't get up" originated. I literally got a hernia from picking my students up off the snow and had to have an operation. I decided the business of being a ski instructor was not all it was cracked up to be, and you don't really make much money for all the wear and tear. But I did learn a lot about skiing, and that was a great experience.

We bought a condominium and redid it and then decided to build a house in Fox Run, a nice area in the town of Beech Mountain. I drew up the plans for our house and found a contractor, who was a fine young man. He was also a pilot who had his own airplanes. He had hired a group of carpenters from Tennessee to work for him, and I'll never forget them. Their leader was Teddy Joe Green, and he had four helpers. He was extremely talented, and I was very impressed with Teddy Joe and his men. In all of the months they worked on our house, I never heard a swear word or a bad or angry word. They were gentlemen craftsmen.

Paul II and David going skiing with Baba

I had gone to a lumber yard that stocked rare woods to select the wood for the house. There were about fifteen different varieties on display. One kind caught my eye. It had many different shades of purple and brown in it and was very hard. I thought I had surely picked out the most expensive one, but the salesman said it was actually one of the cheapest. As the house was being built, Teddy Joe would always pick out wood with real character to use for framing doors and windows. The house turned out beautifully. The builder, whose name was Bob Birk, became a good friend. One day, Bob told me, "You know we are building on a really steep lot." I told him I wanted to be able to walk right into the main part of the house without any steps. He said, "We're going to have at least one step, unless we decide to put another course of concrete blocks around the house on the foundation."

I said, "Well, you're going to have to do that because I don't want steps going up or down into the house." As a result that house had almost a thousand concrete blocks in the foundation. It was a house that got a little larger than we meant it to. It also had a two-car garage under it.

It wasn't very beautiful on the outside, but it was a fantastic house on the inside, with a huge living area and a loft upstairs with a TV room. As the house was nearing completion, Bob said, "You know, as you walk out on the deck in the rear of the house, which is the view side, there is a forty-two foot drop to the ground. Since the lot is so steep, we can very easily and with very little extra cost build you a floor underneath this."

"OK," I agreed, and then said, "I'd also like to rough in a bathroom down there."

So Bob roughed in the bathroom, and then he said, "For a little more, we could actually finish this bathroom, and for a just a very little more, we could actually finish those bedrooms, too." Once again, I agreed. Then, after he did all of that, he suggested, "You know, Paul, we actually have another floor underneath this where you could make a fine dark room or

David (left) and Paul II having their rabbit blueberry butter-milk pancake reward

The boys getting an art lesson

wine cellar, whatever you want." But by then I had finally realized that the house was large enough with four bathrooms and six bedrooms and a total living area of just under six thousand square feet. That was wonderful, but our children had their own lives to live and did not visit much anymore. We found that we had far too much space in that house, so we put it on the market.

We made a list of the things we were going to take with us, and the realtor, who was actually the developer of Fox Run, brought a couple to see it. The young lady looked very sharp in a leather skirt and leather boots, and she wore her hair in nice bouffant. Her husband was Richard Dickinson, a vice president for Carnival Cruise Lines at the time. He eventually became the president of that company and then its CEO before recently retiring. The couple bought the house and the vacant lots on both sides to keep anyone from building near their property. As it turned out, the Dickinsons used the house sparingly, living in it only a few weeks each year.

Before we sold the house, I had learned that if you're the only one who lives in a place like Fox Run year-round, you end up being president of the property owners association. I decided that we needed to pave Fox Run, and I finally got everyone to put up his share of the required money in advance. That is, everyone except the developer. He balked and promised to pay his share after the paving was finished. I said, "No, we won't do it that way. If you don't put up your money, I'm going to return everyone else's and tell them the reason we can't pave Fox Run is because you will not put up your share." We had the money the next day. Fox Run is now completely paved and is quite a beautiful subdivision.

To celebrate our fiftieth wedding anniversary, Kathie and Steve took us to Red Lodge, Montana. It was a beautiful place, but it was late in the year and skiing was not very good. Although the snow was slushy, we still had a good time. Our flight home landed at Johnson City, and upon our arrival, we learned that Beech Mountain had four feet of snow on the ground as a result of one heck of a blizzard.

We drove from the airport into Johnson City and luckily got the very last room available at the town's largest hotel. The Southern Conference was having its women's basketball tournament in Johnson City that weekend, and the hotel was packed. After checking in, we went to eat at the buffet, but there wasn't any food left; it had all been gobbled up. The snow was deep and treacherous, and the hotel clerk gave us our room at half price because of the bad weather. The next day, we called friends at Beech Mountain who said, "We've gotten lucky. They brought a backhoe in here and made one swath down through Fox Run." As we drove back, there were just two open lanes on the highway, and ruts had been created in each lane by the heavy traffic. The snow was so deep you didn't dare get out of those ruts. When we finally reached home, our neighbors informed us that there was no way to get down the driveway to Bill and Jean Schooly's house, where we were temporarily staying. They said a backhoe was on its way. By the time we got up the mountain, the backhoe had arrived and had made a single path that enabled us to drive right in. We had to stop up above the house because the snow was nearly five feet deep. That's the most snow I've ever seen in one place. As I was getting our bags down off the top of the car, along came the man with the backhoe and asked, "Would you like to have me plow you out?" He made one swipe coming down, turned around, and was getting ready to go out. I asked him how much I owed him and he said forty dollars. That was the fastest forty dollars I've ever spent. He took his backhoe and left, and we could get in and out of the drive. I'd bet that backhoe man sure did a land-office business that day!

## Vice President at Samford

In the spring of 1983, I received a phone call from Dr. Tom Corts, president of Samford University in Birmingham, Alabama. He asked if he might come over and visit with me. President Corts arrived and proceeded to tell me that he wanted me to come to Samford to create an athletics department there. At first, I wasn't sure I was interested, but he made it sound awfully good. After a while, I agreed to join his staff at Samford for a term of two years with the title of vice president for athletics.

I meet the press at Samford
University.

*Lew Arnold, Samford University*

I hired Bill McClure to run the track and cross-country program. He
was my old friend from LSU days, a talented and famous track man. We
had a good basketball coach, and I felt we had a fine football coach, too,
but Dr. Corts was not satisfied with his football coach, and he wanted to
hire Terry Bowden. I was at Beech Mountain preparing to fly to California for the national coaches meeting, but Dr. Corts wanted me to come
to Samford to interview Terry Bowden. I said, "Well, you've already decided to hire him, haven't you?"

"Yes," he said, "but I want you to be here to hire him."

I said, "Tom, if you've already hired him, there's no sense in me coming there. I've already got my ticket out of here and I'd have to change it, which wouldn't be cheap. You've already decided to hire him anyway."

He said, "No, I want you to come here and interview him."

So I told President Corts, "You may not always be right, but you are always the boss." So I returned to Birmingham, interviewed Terry Bowden, and Dr. Corts hired him. Terry came and brought his own quarterback and proceeded to coach some fine teams at Samford.

After I had been at Samford for about a month, I realized that being vice president for athletics just wasn't any fun. I had promised to remain at Samford for two years, and I was determined to honor that promise. I'd stay for two years, but at the end of those two years, I'd leave. And that's exactly what I did.

The time at Samford was rewarding in one par-

Anne playing golf with Samford trustees. Left to right: Olivia Byrd, Helen Macon, Anne, and Marlene Dean.

The "Sam Pros." Left to right: Austin Dean, myself, Joe Macon, and Bill Byrd.

ticular respect. Anne and I met and became close friends with three couples: Joe Macon, a retired judge, and his wife, Helen; Bill Byrd, also a retired judge, and his wife, Olivia; and Austin Dean, a businessman from Cullman, Alabama, and his wife, Marlene. The three gentlemen were all members of Samford's board of trustees. All three of the men and their wives played golf, and every time there was any kind of a function involving the board, there would always be a golf outing, which Anne and I would attend. I must confess, though, that they were all better golfers than I. In due course, we played on quite a few of the Robert Trent Jones golf courses that dot the entire state of Alabama. Those courses are absolutely gorgeous. Each course provides attractive housing that can be rented for golf getaways.

Once when Anne and I were at Beech Mountain, the three golfing couples came to visit us. I made a banner out of a large piece of butcher's paper and wrote on it in big letters, "WELCOME SAM PROS," which was the name I had given our little group. One of the blessings of taking the job at Samford was getting to know these wonderful people. Unfortunately, Bill Byrd and Austin Dean have passed away, so Joe Macon, who is pushing ninety, and I are the only men left from that foursome. Happily, Helen and Joe Macon, Marlene Dean, and Olivia Byrd are still among our closest friends, but we have all slowed down a great deal.

## Retired Again

After we returned from Alabama to our place in Beech Mountain, we moved from a very large house of fifty-six hundred square feet with six bedrooms to a smaller house of about four thousand square feet, which was a beautiful Lindal Cedar Home. Then finally, we moved into a Southland Log Home that might have been one of the nicest houses we've ever had. It had an area of twenty-two hundred square feet, with eight-inch-thick walls, and was the snuggest house we've ever owned.

We lived only five minutes from the ski slope, and I would buy a season ski pass. Early in the morning, when the ski lift opened, I was generally the first person in line. If it was a pretty day, I would ski for hours. If it was foggy or icy, I would return home after one run.

Our summers were filled with visits and get-togethers with friends who were summer residents at the mountain. In the winter, we had fewer visits and get-togethers, but I enjoyed lots of skiing. It snowed heavily at Beech Mountain, and the ski slope remained open until sometime in March, depending on the weather.

One morning there was lots of snow. I had a snowplow and always cleared our driveway, which inclined slightly towards the main gate. A few days later, as I was attempting to drive to the ski lift, I could not get up the incline, so I backed up to get a running start. There was so much snow that I couldn't distinguish the road itself, and I managed to back our trusty Subaru into a ditch and got it stuck. That didn't bother me; I went in and got the snow shovel and proceeded to dig the car out.

Once again, I was set to go skiing. Before I left the house, all of a sudden I began having severe chest pains. I was sure it was my hiatal hernia. When Anne saw me, she said, "We're going to the hospital." Since I was in quite a lot of pain, I agreed. We went out and got into the Subaru. As Anne was backing out, she ran into the ditch. She could have panicked but calmly went into the house and called 911. I got into the driver's seat and started rocking the car back and forth and got us out of the ditch. When Anne came back out, she told me she had already called 911. We began to drive out of the subdivision, and when we got to the main road, Beech Mountain Parkway, a police car was there. The police officers were also EMS personnel. We were now in a blizzard. They put me in the backseat of the car and attached all the wires and things. Both doors of the car were open, and I almost froze to death right on the spot. Before they had hooked me up to all the equipment, the ambulance arrived to take me to the hospital in Johnson City, about an hour away.

One of many great moments shared by Anne and me

The ambulance had to be the hardest-riding vehicle I've ever been in. The roads were covered with snow and ice, and the chains on the tires caused the vehicle to ride like a truck. We finally arrived at the hospital. In the meantime, Anne had gone back home to get pajamas, toothbrushes, and other personal items I would need. However, as she attempted to get out of the driveway, she again became stuck. By now, a heavy blizzard raged, and Anne was in a panic. She got out of the car and trudged toward the front gate, which was quite a distance away. As she neared the gate, she saw a police car and waved her arms and shouted. The policeman finally saw her and took her back to our house and helped her get our car to the subdivision entrance. Finally, she was on her way to the hospital. It turned out to be a more traumatic experience for Anne than it was for me.

There were some wonderful doctors in the Johnson City hospital. After much testing, they could find nothing wrong with me except that my potassium level was very low. After several days, the doctors released me, and Anne and I returned home. That's when Anne announced that she was not spending another winter on Beech Mountain. She had had enough, and I could understand her feelings. When she said she was not spending another winter on Beech Mountain, I said, "If you're not, I'm not either." So the question was, where would we go now?

Some time back Anne and I had briefly lived in Charleston, South Carolina, which was about a six hour drive from Beech Mountain, so we decided to move there. After about a year, though, we found out that when you're older, it's difficult to reestablish your residence in a place where you really don't know anyone. Our daughter, Kathie, and her husband, Dale, lived there, but we didn't really know anyone else except Kitsy and General Westmoreland, but unfortunately they spent very little time in Charleston and traveled in different circles. So we sold the little house we had purchased, and returned to the mountain. But not for long!

## A Wonderful Family

Anne and I have been truly blessed with a wonderful family. Our daughter, Kathie, is an accomplished artist and is married to Dale DuTremble, a very active criminal lawyer in Charleston, South Carolina. We have had many wonderful times with them when they were able to visit the mountain.

Kathie and Dale have one son, David, who has developed into an exceptionally fine musician. Since he was seven years old, he has played the guitar and has shown a real affinity for the instrument. David reads music extremely well and writes his own music. He was recently awarded a full four-year music scholarship to LSU, where he is majoring in organ

My mother, Catherine, and her husband, Don Courtier, 1981

A family trip to Hawaii when I coached the Hula Bowl. We won!

and piano performance. Anne and I are delighted to have our grandson so close by.

Kathie's husband, Dale, volunteered for two tours of duty in Vietnam as a U.S. Marine. His son, Michael, followed his father's path into the Marine Corps and, after qualifying, served as a marine security guard at the U.S. embassies in Chengdu, China; Vienna, Austria; and Minsk, Belarus. Michael has since fulfilled his duty as a marine and is now working as a security officer for a private company that provides security for U.S. embassies worldwide.

Our son, Steve, has enjoyed a successful career in business. At the age of thirty-five, he felt called by the Lord to become an evangelist. Steve and his wife, Judy, packed up and moved to Fort Worth, where Steve en-

Three generations: my son Steve, grandson Paul II, and myself

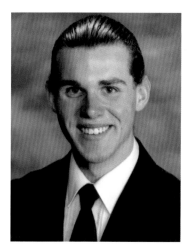

Grandson David DuTremble

rolled in the Southwestern Baptist Theological Seminary. Soon after, Judy gave birth to our grandson Paul Dietzel II. Steve has continued his full-time financial business dealing with senior adults. He speaks at churches and in other settings on a regular basis.

Judy has been a real blessing to Anne and me. She comes from a very large family and was raised in the town of Livingston, Louisiana, near Baton Rouge. When her family gets together with her parents, Allie and Olga DuBois, nearly forty relatives can be counted. Judy has become involved as a partner with Steve in his business, and together, they make a fantastic team.

Their son, Paul II, is a very talented young man. Through junior and senior high school he maintained a nearly straight-A average. He is active in Campus Crusade for Christ and the rowing team and serves as president of the College Republicans at LSU. Paul recently became the first student to be named Outstanding Sophomore, Outstanding Junior, and Outstanding Senior in the Manship School of Mass Communication in successive years at the LSU Chancellor's Honors Convocation.

Anne and I are very proud of our family. Naturally, being grandparents, we are extremely proud of our two grandsons, David and Paul II. They have always been fine young men and have never given their parents any cause for concern. Considering the behavior of many of today's youth, that is especially rewarding.

# Home to Baton Rouge

After our short stay in Charleston, we moved back to Baton Rouge, where Anne and I had lots of friends. Frankly, I had mixed feelings about returning to Baton Rouge because of my painful experience at LSU in 1982. However, mothers like to be close to their sons, and Steve and his family lived in Baton Rouge. We rented an apartment here, which was fine for a while. Soon we bought a condominium, which was very nice but also very small. Eventually we found a house in a beautiful subdivision. The house is lovely and comfortable.

Once we were settled, some old friends invited us to attend a Sunday service at the First United Methodist Church. The pastor, Chris Andrews, is one of the most charismatic and dedicated ministers that Anne and I have ever known. I feel fortunate to count Chris as a friend. Several friends were involved in a Sunday school class called Rings and Ivy and invited us to join. We attended one of their parties and were quickly assimilated into the group. If I had any misgivings about going back to Baton Rouge, they were gradually and definitely eliminated.

LSU had a great football season that same year, 2003. Coach Nick Saban's Tigers won the national championship, and Anne and I were invited to join the official party for the championship game in the Superdome in New Orleans. Before the kickoff, I was invited to go on the field with some LSU notables. In working our way back up to the press box, we were still underneath the stadium when LSU made a great run, which we completely missed. We sat in Coach Saban's box and greatly enjoyed LSU's victory over Oklahoma.

I enjoy working on my painting while vacationing in the mountains.

The year 2003 produced LSU's second national championship. Coach Saban and his staff did a remarkable job. The Tigers were a very fine football team, especially the defensive unit. In the championship game with Oklahoma, LSU just out-toughed the Sooners. Oklahoma came into the game with tremendous hoopla, but after it was all over, there was no doubt who had won the national championship. Since the Sugar Bowl was the game sanctioned by the Football Coaches Association as the championship game, LSU was proclaimed the national champions. On the west coast, however, the University of Southern California also claimed the championship, hanging on to their number-one ranking in the Associated Press poll with a win in the Rose Bowl. That didn't sit well with the LSU fans, just as being left out of the BCS championship game had not sat well with the Southern California fans.

It had taken LSU forty-five years to win its second national football championship. But the next year, Tiger fans learned the same hard lesson that we had learned back in 1959: it is very difficult to repeat as national champions! We had a fine year in 1959 and at the end of the season were ranked number four nationally. In 2004, LSU once again had a fine year but, as in 1959, did not repeat as number one. Just three years later, though, Coach Les Miles did a marvelous job leading the Tigers to their third national championship by soundly beating a fine Ohio State Buckeye team coached by Jim Tressel—again, in the Superdome.

After LSU's 2003 national championship, many fans wanted Nick Sabin to sign headgear, footballs, jerseys, programs, and other memorabilia. They seemed to think it would be even better if I would also sign those same items. They would then have the signatures of the only two LSU coaches who had ever produced national championship football teams. After the 2003 season, I signed my name more times on football-related items than I had signed in all the previous thirty years put together. It seemed to me that fans were in a frenzy to get the signatures of the two national champion coaches. Finally, I learned that Nick had stopped signing memorabilia when he discovered that people were selling the signed items on E-Bay. Thereafter, whenever anyone wanted an item signed, I made sure they told me exactly what they were going to do with it. I refused to sign anything that was going to be sold on E-Bay.

Prior to the Sugar Bowl game with Oklahoma, Anne and I were invited to Atlanta to attend the Southeastern Conference championship game. Each year, representatives from each conference school are invited along with their wives on an all-expense paid trip. They are designated "Legends" of their respective schools. Although it is embarrassing to be selected as a "Legend," deep in my heart I really did appreciate the gesture. It's always nice to be remembered.

Shortly after, Louisiana Public Broadcasting selected me and a few others—Kix Brooks of Brooks and Dunn, former ambassador to the United Nations Andrew Young, and Lady Tigers basketball coach Sue Gunter—

as "Louisiana Legends." An event commemorating the honor was held at the Shaw Center in Baton Rouge, a local focal point for the arts and cultural activities.

More recently, I received a call from Joseph Maselli, founder of the American Italian Renaissance Foundation of New Orleans, notifying me that I had been selected as the national honoree for the Foundation's Sports Hall of Fame. Even though I informed Mr. Maselli that I was not Italian, he said that nevertheless, I was to receive the honor as had such previous winners as Tommy Lasorda, Joe Torre, Vince Ferragamo, and many other notables. The affair was a wonderful black-tie banquet at the New Orleans Hilton with over five hundred guests in attendance. In honor of this award, I received a beautiful marble statue depicting an American eagle in flight. I am greatly appreciative of this honor.

It was after we moved back to Baton Rouge that my painting of watercolors took off. This hobby originated at Beech Mountain years before when I had undergone a heart bypass in the late 1980s. After the bypass, it became obvious that I needed to find something to do as a hobby other

In 2005 I was honored as a Louisiana Legend by Friends of LPB.

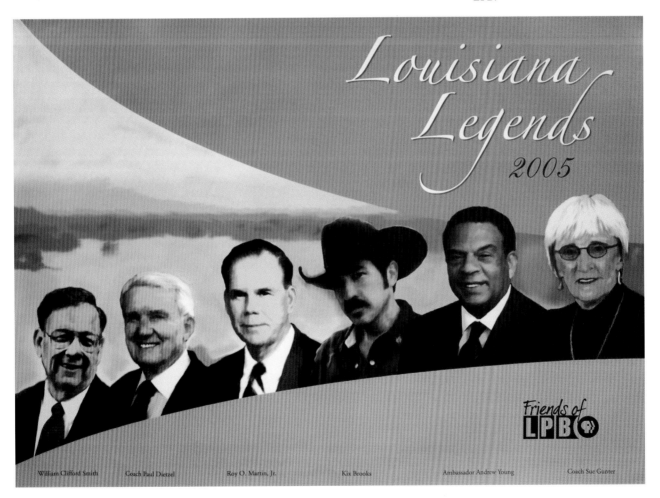

Louisiana Legends 2005

Friends of LPB

William Clifford Smith    Coach Paul Dietzel    Roy O. Martin, Jr.    Kix Brooks    Ambassador Andrew Young    Coach Sue Gunter

Fred Pfohl, a good friend and the owner of Fred's Mercantile

than skiing, so I decided to start painting. During all the years I coached, I constantly drew cartoons of and for my players. Somewhere along the line, someone asked me if I would sell them one of my paintings. It had never occurred to me that one day I might sell one. I said, "Do you mean to tell me that you would like to buy one of my paintings?" And whoever it was said, "Yes, how much do you want for it?" I said, "Want for it? I don't know, what would you like to pay for it?" In the end, I naïvely offered to sell it to him for thirty-five dollars.

At the end of every summer, Fred and Marge Pfohl sponsored a crafts exposition in Beech Mountain called "Art in the Park" in a little grassy area adjacent to their store, Fred's Mercantile. The sign at Fred's read, "If we don't have it, you don't need it." Fred and Marge were gracious enough to allow me to display my paintings in the Mercantile's coffee shop. When it came time for Art in the Park, I'd erect my small tent and offer my paintings for sale. Each year, I would sell a few more paintings and seemed to sell many to people who had previously purchased my paintings. It was a great deal of fun, but it was a lot of hard work, too. I got up very early in the morning to set up and then remained near my tent until the show closed at 5:00 in the afternoon. Our daughter, Kathie, would drive up from Charleston and set up right beside me in the meadow. Kathie's paintings were large and extremely well done. One year, our grandson David brought up some of his paintings, which were very abstract, and I think he outsold both Kathie and me. Of course, his paintings were a little cheaper than ours.

When Anne and I returned to Baton Rouge, word got out that I painted. The *Baton Rouge Advocate* sent reporter Ed Cullen to our home, where he took pictures of some of my pieces. He then wrote an excellent article about Anne and me and my paintings. His article stirred a great deal of interest in my watercolors.

In the late 1990s, Dr. Jack Andonie, an LSU alumnus and a marvelous New Orleans physician, donated thousands of sports-related memorabilia items to LSU. To house these artifacts, the LSU Alumni Association decided to build and operate the Jack and Priscilla Andonie Museum. LSU hired a tremendously talented person, Tom Continé, to serve as the museum's founding director. Tom had been a band director and professor at several universities, including the University of Nebraska and the University of Michigan. He is a graduate of LSU and the University of Michigan and is one of the most talented people I have ever met. He has so many good ideas and so much energy that he absolutely bubbles over. He developed the wonderful Andonie Museum on the LSU campus to honor and memorialize all of LSU's athletes, coaches, and teams. Included is a display honoring the unbelievably successful LSU baseball coach Skip Bertman and the exploits of Dale Brown and his unmatched career as basketball coach at LSU. There is a special tribute to Charlie McClendon and his successful tenure as head football coach. Tom also designed a colorful display featuring the 1958 national championship team, the coaching staff, and me.

Anne and Kathie at the outdoor art show at Fred's in 1991

In September 2004, Anne and I decided to hold our sixtieth wedding anniversary celebration the next year at the Andonie Museum. We had problems getting our invitations out because of Hurricane Katrina and the water damage it caused in New Orleans, so we had to call people on the phone to tell them they were going to get an invitation. The reception was absolutely splendid.

While designing the Andonie Museum's opening exhibition, Tom Continé visited with many other museum directors around the country. Among those was a gentleman by the name of Forrest Dunn, who is the Administrator of the Louisiana State Exhibit Museum in Shreveport. It is an outstanding museum built as a WPA project and is located adjacent to the fairgrounds in Shreveport. Forrest is an extremely talented person and a successful businessman who has served in the Louisiana legislature. In one particular conversation between Tom and Forrest, Tom suggested that Forrest's museum might host and sponsor a reunion of the 1958 national championship team. I thought it was a splendid idea; I'm always delighted to have a reunion of any sort with my old players, many of whom live in the Baton Rouge area. It is always rewarding when they inform me that they're teaching their sons and grandsons the same things I taught them when they were my players. It was decided that we would have a reunion at the Louisiana State Exhibit Museum in August 2005 to kick off the Andonie Museum LSU sports exhibit, which was scheduled to open there in September.

In preparing for the reunion, Forrest asked me to have a showing of

In 2005 I got to visit with many of my old players at a reunion of the 1958 national championship team.

my artwork at his museum. I thought that would be very exciting, so we arranged to have a show in April 2005, preceding the reunion to be held in August. I completed thirty-four watercolors for the exhibition and also brought along prints of a painting of the LSU stadium that I had done several years previously. I titled this piece *The Way We Were* because it depicts Tiger Stadium as it existed back in 1958.

The watercolor exhibition was a resounding success because of the efforts of Forrest Dunn and his staff. Forrest developed television commercials, newspaper articles, and radio spots to promote the show, and by the time it opened, it had been very widely advertised. I did my part by preparing a taped sound bite for the radio and by speaking to the downtown Rotary Club and to elementary, junior, and high school students, who were bused in to the museum's auditorium.

Flanked by two true friends, Joe Dean and Dale Brown

The museum is home to several dioramas, the likes of which I had never seen before. These dioramas are huge and beautiful and depict the various industries in the state of Louisiana. All the miniature figures in the dioramas are carved out of beeswax and are amazingly true to life. One of my favorites is a scene of perfectly carved barnyard animals. Each of these extremely valuable dioramas is insured for a million dollars.

My exhibition opened at 2:00 P.M. on a Sunday with a fabulous reception planned by Forrest. Refreshments included, among other treats, punch and three extremely large cakes, each one lettered, "WELCOME, COACH DIETZEL." I especially liked the chocolate one!

Because of the tremendous amount of publicity Forrest had arranged, a huge crowd showed up. In the first hour and a half, twenty-nine of my thirty-four paintings were sold. Never before and probably never again will I sell that many paintings in such a brief period of time. After the reception and the opening of the exhibition, Forrest arranged a dinner for forty of the museum's supporters. Anne and I, along with Forrest and his lovely wife, Donna, joined these fine folks at a popular restaurant in Shreveport. The high point of the evening for me was when Forrest said to the guests, "I know that Paul Dietzel has more plaques and awards than he needs, so I decided to give something to Anne." I thought that was absolutely marvelous! Anne was presented with a beautiful Waterford glass bowl, which is one of her most prized possessions. I was so grateful to them for recognizing Anne.

After the showing in Shreveport, Tom Continé told me that it was possible for artists to exhibit their artwork in some of the local libraries in Baton Rouge. That led to a watercolor showing, preceded by a reception, at the Bluebonnet Library, which is located near our home. The

Left: Dr. Jack Andonie (left) and Forrest Dunn (right). Below: Anne receives a Waterford crystal from Forrest Dunn and Friends of the Louisiana State Exhibit Museum.

Two of my latest paintings, *The Chickadee* and *Down to the Sea*

Manager of the Bluebonnet Library is a very charming lady, Gay Yerger, who could not have been nicer or more pleasant. Soon after, there was another month-long exhibit at the Greenwell Springs Library, and I found the manager there, Lucy Parham, to be equally helpful. I have found the East Baton Rouge Parish libraries to be beautifully equipped and extremely well maintained.

Next, Tom arranged for me to have an exhibition of my watercolors at the West Baton Rouge Parish Museum, just across the Mississippi River in Port Allen. The curator there is Loren Davis, an extremely talented young lady and an LSU alumnus. By coincidence, she completed her graduate work at the University of South Carolina. The museum hosted a well-attended reception, and my paintings were displayed there for three months. Forrest Dunn has already scheduled a return visit for me to the Louisiana State Exhibit Museum in the fall of 2008. This exhibit will be a Father-Daughter show, featuring works by Kathie and yours truly. Forrest teased me a bit, saying, "That's fine as long as it doesn't bother you that Kathie is a better artist than you." I said, "I've known that for years!"

It's now obvious to me that my misgivings about returning to Baton Rouge were unfounded. As I look back, I am convinced that my painful departure from LSU in 1982 was in reality a blessing in disguise. Even though it was a very hurtful experience, I think that the chancellor did me a favor. I left athletics at a time when my career had been extremely successful, and I was forced to find other things to do. As I have always said, I have been very, very lucky. I feel that the Lord has blessed me greatly. I have been blessed with an absolutely wonderful wife, who has always been my guardian, best friend, and sweetheart. I love her more right now than ever.

Anne and I have fond memories of our time at Beech Mountain, but Beech Mountain has changed tremendously since we first lived there in

Watercolorist Paul F. Dietzel,
2007
*Photo by Jeffrey D. Myers*

My first painting of a tiger

Grandsons David (left) and
Paul II (right)

the late 1960s. We have owned, built, and lived in six houses at Beech
Mountain and still have many close friends there. Although we have
sold our home and no longer own property there, we rent a house on the
mountain each summer.

Our return to Baton Rouge coincided with Nick Saban and the LSU
Tigers winning the national championship. It brought back fond memories of the national championship the Tigers had won in 1958. Nick returned to the pros, where he had previously coached, but this time as the head coach of the Miami Dolphins. Some LSU fans were disgruntled when he left after such a wonderful run at LSU. Quite a few members of the media and many friends asked me what I thought about Nick's leaving. That he left LSU when he was very successful was indeed a parallel to my situation in 1962. I said, "I think one of the real tests has to be whether or not he left LSU better than he found it." In other words, had he put LSU football on a higher plane than it had been when he arrived? I believe the answer is obviously yes, and I felt the same way about

Anne and her brother Tom

All in the family. Top row: Paul II, David, Judy, and Steve. Front row: Dale, Kathie, myself, and Anne.

the state of the program when I left LSU for the head coaching job at West Point.

Had I remained at LSU, Anne and I would never have had the wonderful experiences we went on to enjoy in different places and at different schools. We wouldn't have met the wonderful people that we have met in every section of the country. When I have been asked which place we enjoyed the most, I honestly have to say that we have never been anywhere we didn't thoroughly enjoy. In addition, we left some awfully good friends at almost every stop. We have been very, very lucky.

In preparing this book, I have thought about many of the things that have taken place along the way. It has caused me to look back on some wonderful moments and a few heartaches. As to whether I regret not having tried to become a doctor as I once planned to do, I have to say that I think I would have enjoyed being a doctor very much, but I wouldn't trade my chosen profession for any other possible occupation. Having been a coach is the most rewarding job I could ever have had.

Before undertaking this autobiography, I browsed through some of my old photos and clippings and scrapbooks to refresh my memory. I found that they had faded, turned yellow, and were crumbling. The awards and the plaudits are now long forgotten. Only three true rewards still remain, and will remain with me until my time on this earth is over:

1: *The joy of good and loyal friends who know my faults and still love me—friends like Pat Dale, June Goldner, Scooter Purvis, Jimmy Field, Tom Continé, Jerry Stovall, and Jake Netterville.*

2: *My family: a great son, Steve; his loving wife, Judy; and my grandson Paul II; and a wonderful daughter, Kathie; her fine husband, Dale; and my grandsons David and Michael.*

   *The love of my life, Anne, who is my best friend, and who has been my strength for more than sixty years.*

3: *And finally, my personal relationship with our Lord and Savior Jesus Christ, who forgives us of our sins and will be with us until the end of time.*

My life has truly been blessed.

# Football Lettermen Coached by Paul F. Dietzel

**Louisiana State University**

Alexander, Arnold: 1955
Amadee, Lynn: 1960–61
Anzalone, Fanancy: 1955
Ascani, Peter: 1960
Aucoin, Alvin: 1955–56–57

Baldwin, Bob: 1955
Bergeron, Carroll: 1957–58–59
Blankenship, Fred: 1957–58–59
Bond, Jimmy: 1959
Booth, Billy: 1959–60–61
Bourgeois, Andy: 1958–59–60
Bourque, Hart: 1958–59–60
Branch, Mel: 1957–58–59
Brodnax, J. W.: 1956–57–58
Brown, Harley: 1957
Brown, Henry: 1960
Burns, Matthew: 1955–56

Campbell, Bo: 1961
Campbell, Edward: 1960
Cannon, Billy: 1957–58–59
Carroll, Ronnie: 1956
Cassidy, Ed: 1955–56–57
Chaney, Walker: 1961
Chantrey, Alan: 1960
Chappius, Richard: 1960
Coley, Don: 1955
Cranford, Charles: 1960–61

Dampier, Al: 1957–58–59
Davidson, Freddie: 1958
Davis, Tommy: 1958
Daye, Donnie: 1958–59–60
DeCrosta, Robert: 1955–56–57
Delaney, Joe: 1955
Denstorff, Jerry: 1956
Derbonne, Jimmy: 1957–58
Dosher, Joe: 1958
Dumas, Jerry: 1956
Dunham, John: 1957–58

Estes, Don: 1960–61

Faulk, Jimmy: 1955
Ferguson, O. K.: 1955
Field, Jimmy: 1959–60–61
Fisher, George: 1955, 1957
Flurry, Bobby: 1960–61
Fogg, Ed: 1955

Fort, John: 1956
Fournet, Emile: 1957–58–59
Frayer, Jack: 1957–58–59
Frey, Gerald: 1958
Fugler, Max: 1957–58–59
Fuller, Johnny: 1955

Gardner, James: 1955–56
Gary, Dexter: 1960–61
Gates, Jack: 1960–61
Gaubatz, Dennis: 1960–61
Givens, Jimmy: 1958–59
Gonzales, Vince: 1955
Graf, Bob: 1955
Graham, Durwood: 1955–56
Granier, Richard: 1961
Graves, White: 1961
Greely, Jimmy: 1958
Greenwood, Bobby: 1958–59
Griswold, Jack: 1956
Gros, Earl: 1959–60–61
Guillot, Monk: 1961
Guillot, Rodney: 1959–60–61

Habert, Eddie: 1960–61
Hamic, Buddy: 1961
Hanley, Jim: 1957
Hardin, Jimmy: 1957–58
Hargett, Dan: 1960–61
Harrell, Gene: 1960
Harrington, Horace: 1960–61
Harris, Wendell: 1959–60–61
Haynes, John: 1956
Hendrix, Billy: 1956–57–58
Hodges, Harry: 1955
Horne, Jackie: 1957, 1959
Hucklebridge, Robbie: 1961

Jenkins, Darryl: 1958–59–60
Johns, Chuck: 1955
Johnston, Jerry: 1956–57
Johnston, Ronnie: 1956–57
Juul, John: 1961

Kahlden, Larry: 1956–57–58
Kinchen, Gary: 1960–61
Kinchen, Gaynell: 1958–59–60
King, Larry: 1955
King, Lindley: 1959
Kozan, Don: 1956–57–58
Kozan, Wayne: 1958

Lacassagne, Herb: 1958
Laiche, Jimmy: 1955
Langan, John: 1957–58–59
Langley, Willis: 1960–61
Lavin, Jim: 1956–57
LeBlanc, Lynn: 1957–58–59
Leggett, Earl: 1955–56
Leopard, Duane: 1957–58–59
Lester, Darrell: 1960
Lott, Bobby: 1956–57
Lott, Tommy: 1957–58–59

Mangham, Mickey: 1958–59–60
Matherne, Durel: 1957–58–59
May, Joe: 1955–56
May, Robert: 1960
McCarty, Dave: 1957–58–59
McCaskill, Ronnie: 1955, 1957
McClain, Scotty: 1957–58–59
McCollister, Don: 1960–61
McCreedy, Ed: 1958–59–60
McDonald, Robert: 1960
McMichael, Ken: 1958
Mercer, John: 1960–61
Miller, Fred: 1960–61
Mitchell, Jim: 1956
Mitts, Lester: 1959–60
Morgan, Mike: 1961

Neck, Tommy: 1959–60–61
Nelson, Manson: 1957–58–59
Neumann, Danny: 1960–61
Norwood, Don: 1957–58–59
Nunley, Lynn: 1957
Nunnery, R. B.: 1955

Odom, Sammy: 1960–61
Ott, Al: 1958–59

Pannebaker, Frank: 1958
Paris, Ted: 1955–56
Parish, David: 1961
Parker, Enos: 1955–56
Pavel, Wayne: 1957
Pere, Ralph: 1961
Pere, Ronald: 1960–61
Pringle, Bob: 1956
Purvis, Don: 1957–58–59

Rabb, Warren: 1957–58–59
Randolph, Ted: 1961
Rebsamen, Paul: 1955–56

Renfroe, Olin: 1956
Reynolds, M. C.: 1955–56–57
Rice, Bobby: 1960–61
Richards, Bobby: 1959–60–61
Riess, Gus: 1958
Riley, Perry: 1961
Roberts, Henry Lee: 1958
Robinson, Dwight: 1960–61
Robinson, Johnnie: 1957–58–59
Rodrigue, Ruffin: 1961

Sanders, Joe: 1961
Schexnaildre, Merl: 1957–58–59
Schwalb, Gerald: 1955–56–57
Scully, Don: 1955–56
Shaw, Fletcher: 1958
Sheehy, Bill: 1956
Simmons, Charles: 1961
Skinner, Doug: 1957
Slack, Bain: 1961
Smith, Bill: 1955–56–57
Smith, Jim: 1956–57
Soefker, Buddy: 1961
Spence, Hartie: 1960
Spence, Ray: 1956–57
Stinson, Don: 1955
Stone, David: 1957
Stovall, Jerry: 1960–61
Strange, Charles "Bo": 1958–59–60
Stupka, Mike: 1957–58–59
Swope, Don: 1956–57
Sykes, Gene: 1960–61

Taylor, Jimmy: 1956–57
Thomas, Durwood: 1961
Thomas, Lynn: 1957
Thompson, Steve: 1955–56–57
Thompson, Tommy: 1960
Trosclair, Milton: 1961
Truax, Billy: 1961
Tuminello, Joe: 1955
Turner, Jim: 1961
Turner, Win: 1956–57

Upshaw, Elton: 1958–59

Ward, Dallas: 1958
Ward, Steve: 1960–61
Wenner, Andy: 1956
West, Keith: 1956

Westerman, Bob: 1956–57
White, Al: 1957
White, Gordie: 1957
Whittington, Royce: 1957
Whittman, Ken: 1958
Wilkins, Ray: 1960–61
Winston, Roy: 1959–60–61
Wood, John: 1955–56
Wyble, Fred: 1956

Young, Jerry: 1961

Ziegler, Bob: 1955–56

**United States Military Academy**

Barofsky, Frederick J.: 1964–65
Bartholomew, Samuel W.: 1964–65
Bedel, Robert L.: 1962
Beierschmitt, James J.: 1961, 1963
Berdy, Michael E.: 1964
Blackgrove, Joseph F.: 1961–62
Braun, Peter E.: 1963–64–65
Butterfield, R. Ronald: 1961–62

Carber, John B.: 1963–64–65
Casillo, Vincent L.: 1964–65
Champi, Samuel F.: 1963–64–65
Chescavage, William A.: 1962–63
Clark, Townsend S.: 1964–65–66
Clark, William N.: 1962
Cook, S. Curtis: 1965
Cosentino, Frank C.: 1965
Cunningham, Thomas N.: 1962–63

Dietz, Donald W.: 1964–65–66
Dusel, Thomas B.: 1965

Eckert, Richard E.: 1960–61
Ellerson, John C.: 1960–61–62

Grasfeder, Lee R.: 1962–63
Hamilton, Mark R.: 1964–65–66
Hansen, Dean D.: 1966

Hawkins, Raymond J.: 1963
Hawkins, William C.:
  1961–62
Heim, Bruce K.: 1960–61–62
Hennen, James M.: 1962
Herman, Claude P.: 1966
Heydt, Richard H.:
  1961–62–63

Johnson, John T.: 1962, 1964

Kempinski, Chester F.:
  1961–62–63
Kerns, Thomas C.:
  1961–62–63
Koster, James L.: 1962

LaRochelle, David F.: 1964
Lewis, Arthur C.: 1962
Lindler, Curtiss M.: 1963

McMillan, Harry A.: 1961–62
Meyer, Clarles R.: 1965
Miller, Michael D.: 1961–62
Montanaro, John D.: 1965–66

Neuman, Michael J.: 1965–66
Nickerson, Barry E.: 1964
Noble, W. Edward: 1964–65
Nowak, Richard A.:
  1961–62–63

O'Grady, Michael J.: 1964

Pappas, George: 1960, 1962
Parcello, Donald C.:
  1962–63–64
Paske, Raymond J.:
  1961–62–63
Peterson, Richard E.:
  1961–62–63
Pyrz, Anthony P.: 1963–64

Ray, J. David: 1964–65
Rivers, David P.: 1964–65–66
Ryan, Martin F.: 1962

Sarn, James E.: 1961–62
Schillo, Edward C.:
  1961–62–63
Schwartz, Thomas A.:
  1964–65–66
Scott, Alan H.: 1961
Seymour, John B.: 1962–63–64
Sherrell, William W.:
  1962–63–64
Sipos, William G.: 1962
Stanley, Paul D.: 1960, 1962
Stichweh, Carl R.:
  1962–63–64
Stowers, Charles T.:
  1963–64–65

Uberecken, Henry M.: 1966
Unruh, Edward P.: 1964

Vaughan, Curry N.: 1962
Vaughan, H. Gwynn:
  1961–62–63

Waldrop, Kenneth M.:
  1961–62–63
Woodbury, Kent S.: 1962

Zadel, C. William:
  1962–63–64

## University of South Carolina

Abraczinskas, Don: 1973–74
Adamski, Jacyn:
  1973–74–75–76
Amrein, Tom: 1972, 1974–75
Andrews, Lee: 1971
Anthony, Rick: 1971–72–73
Austin, Darrell: 1971–72–73

Bailey, Don: 1968–69–70
Bailey, Leroy: 1965–66
Bank, Chris: 1968–69–70
Barber, Charlie: 1974, 1976
Bass, Ron: 1973–74, 1976–77
Baxley, Mel: 1972–73
Beard, Jim: 1971–72–73
Beasley, Chan: 1971–72
Bell, Hugh, Jr.: 1974, 1976
Bell, Tommy: 1970–71–72
Berry, David: 1964–65–66
Bice, Tim: 1966–67–68
Black, Greg: 1971–72
Blackmon, Steve: 1973–74
Bolton, Eddie: 1968
Boyd, Candler: 1967, 1969–70
Boyte, Billy: 1969–70–71
Brant, Don: 1970
Brown, Allen: 1968
Brown, Jackie: 1970–71–72
Brown, Rick: 1970–71–72
Bryant, Bobby: 1964–65–66
Buckner, Don: 1967–68–69
Bunch, Ron: 1967–68

Carpenter, Al: 1973–74
Carpenter, Dana: 1971–72–73
Carter, Casper: 1973,
  1975–76–77
Cash, Dave, Jr.: 1971–72–73
Chastain, Randy: 1973–74–75
Chavous, Andy: 1967, 1969
Cline, Mike: 1972–73
Cole, Bob: 1965–66–67
Coleman, John: 1968
Colson, Keith: 1973–74, 1976
Courson, Steve:
  1973–74–75–76
Crabb, Greg: 1969–70–71
Cregar, Bill: 1972–73–74
Currier, Bill: 1974–75–76
DeCamilla, Dave: 1968–69–70

DePasquale, Kerry:
  1974–75–76
Dickens, Bill: 1964–65–66
Dobson, Alex: 1972
Dubac, John: 1971–72
Duncan, Dale: 1972–73
Duncan, Hayden: 1974
DuPre, Billy: 1968–69–70
Dyches, Danny: 1968–69–70

Efird, Dwight: 1973–74–75

Fair, Mike: 1965–66–67
Farrell, Mike: 1972–73–74
Files, Neville: 1970–71–72
Ford, Dennis: 1970–71
Freeman, Billy: 1969–70–71
Fusaro, Tony: 1967–68–69

Galloway, Benny: 1965–66,
  1968
Ganas, Rusty: 1968–69–70
Garnto, Ben: 1965–66–67
Genoble, Richard: 1968
Gibson, Gordon: 1967
Gobble, Jimmy: 1965–66–67
Grant, Dave: 1966–67–68
Grantz, Jeff: 1973–74–75
Gregory, Johnny: 1966–67–68
Gribble, Steve: 1972–73
Grossman, Dobby: 1972
Grotheer, Bill: 1974

Haggard, Mike: 1970–71–72
Hall, Deane: 1970–71
Hamrick, Doug: 1968–69–70
Harbour, Randy: 1964–65–66
Harris, Bob: 1965–66
Harris, Dick: 1969–70–71
Hellams, Tyler: 1968, 1970–71
Hipkins, Rick: 1969–70
Hodge, Lynn: 1968, 1968–69
Hodgin, Jay Lynn: 1972–73–74
Holloman, Rudy: 1967–68–69

James, Jack: 1967
Jetton, Charlie: 1971
Jones, Carroll: 1970–71
Jones, Howard "Butch": 1971
Jowers, Jeff: 1963, 1966
Juk, Stan: 1964–65–66
Killen, Jimmy: 1965–66
Kline, Brad: 1973–74–75
Kohout, Pat: 1969–70–71
Komoroski, Joe: 1964,
  1966–67
Krokos, Paul: 1974, 1976
Kuritz, Russ: 1970

Laws, Henry: 1973–74
LeHeup, Andy: 1973–74
LeHeup, John: 1970–71–72
Leslie, Tommy: 1972

Leventis, Andy: 1972–73
Logan, Philip: 1974–75–76–77
Long, Kevin: 1974–75–76
Lucas, Dave: 1967–68–69

Manzari, Russ: 1974–75–76
Marino, Bobby: 1973–74–75
Matthews, Monty: 1971, 1973
Mauro, Bob: 1967–68
McCabe, Mike: 1973–74–75
McCarthy, George: 1969
McCord, Toy: 1966–67
McLauren, Gary: 1972–73–74
McMillan, Van: 1972
Meadow, Dave: 1966
Medlin, Wally: 1967–68
Middlebrook, Tommy: 1971
Mimms, Chuck: 1970–71
Miranda, Bob: 1970
Mitchell, Jim: 1969–70–71
Mooney, Kevin: 1970
Morris, Bob: 1967–68
Morris, Bob: 1971
Morris, Glen: 1971
Mott, Garry: 1973–74–75
Moye, Richie: 1969–70–71
Muir, Warren: 1967–68–69
Muldrow, Eddie: 1972–73–74
Mulvihill, Jim: 1965–66–67

Nash, Jimmy: 1969–70–71
Nelson, Andy: 1973–74–75
Nelson, Billy: 1964–65–66

Orrel, Wally: 1966–67–68

Padgett, Benny: 1968–69–70
Parker, Bill: 1968–69–70
Parson, Ron: 1972
Payne, Johnny: 1972
Payne, Ricky: 1974–75, 1977
Pepper, Tony: 1972–73–74
Phillips, Grahl: 1973–74
Phillips, Paul: 1964–65–66
Pierce, Hyrum: 1966–67
Poole, Jimmy: 1965–66–67
Pope, Jimmy: 1968–69
Poston, Jimmy: 1968–69–70
Privette, Jimmy: 1971–72–73
Provence, Jerome:
  1974–75–76–77

Ragin, Mike: 1964–65–66
Reeves, Roy Don "Butch":
  1965–67–68
Regalis, Joe: 1969–70–71
Reynolds, Robby: 1971–72–73
Rhodes, Tommy: 1971
Rice, Billy Ray: 1969–70–71
Roe, Bob: 1971–72–73
Rose, Donnie: 1966
Ross, Ken: 1968
Rowe, Thad: 1971–72–73

Runager, Max: 1974,
  1976–77–78
Rushing, Lyn: 1971

Saldi, Jay: 1973, 1975
Schwarting, Gene:
  1966–67–68
Shue, Zeb: 1973–74–75
Shugart, Bubba: 1974–75–76
Simmons, Tommy:
  1969–70–71
Sistare, Byron: 1969–70
Smith, E. Z.: 1973–74–75
Soles, Jerry: 1963–64, 1966
Somma, Don: 1965–66–67
Spinks, Randy: 1973
Stewart, Don: 1974, 1976–77
Stirline, Mike: 1971
Stone, Mack: 1970–71
Suggs, Tommy: 1968–69–70

Tharpe, Mack Lee:
  1968–69–70
Thomas, Scott: 1973–74–75
Thompson, Buck: 1972–73–74
Tope, Jeff: 1970
Townsend, Scott: 1965, 1967
Toy, Roger: 1971–72–73
Trevillian, Tom: 1969–70
Troup, Bill: 1972

Usher, Al: 1968, 1970–71

Wade, Steve: 1971–72
Walkup, Ken: 1968–69–70
Wallace, Phil: 1971–72–73
Watson, Pat: 1967–68–69
Wehmeyer, Bob: 1966
Wheat, Ken: 1969–70–71
Williams, Clarence:
  1974–75–76
Williams, Curtis "Cooter":
  1965–66–67
Williams, Randy: 1970
Wilson, C. A.: 1972–73–74
Wingard, Joe: 1968–69–70
Wingard, Ted: 1965–66
Wingard, Tom: 1966–67
Witherspoon, Jerry:
  1972–73–74
Witt, Gerald: 1972, 1974
Wood, Robert: 1972
Woolbright, Marty:
  1971–72–73
Woolbright, Roger: 1974,
  1977–78
Wright, Jake: 1969

Yoakum, Randy: 1968–69
Young, Jackie: 1970–71
Young, Steve: 1973–74–75

Zeigler, Fred: 1967–68–69
Zipperly, Tom: 1972–73–74

"THE WAY WE WERE"